THE BRI AND THE INDO-PACIFIC

REINVENTING TRADITIONS

一带一路与印太

天下大势

THE BRI AND THE INDO-PACIFIC

REINVENTING TRADITIONS

一带一路与印太

天下大势

Edited by

BHAVNA SINGH

宝伟娜 邢

KW Publishers Pvt Ltd
New Delhi

ISBN 978-81-986658-5-0 Hardback

Published in India by Kalpana Shukla

KW Publishers Pvt Ltd
4676/21, First Floor, Ansari Road
Daryaganj, New Delhi 110 002
Phone: +91 11 43528107
Marketing: kw@kwpub.in
Editorial: production@kwpub.in
Website: www.kwpub.in

Printed and bound in India
Quiinkit Infotech Pvt. Ltd., Gurugram

To

an Odyssey

of Chinese Scholars

Contents

Preface ix

Figures xi

Abbreviations xiii

1 The BRI and the Indo-Pacific: Reinventing Traditions over a Turbulent Decade 1
Bhavna Singh

2 The BRI and China's Charm Offensive in the Maldives 34
Eshita Rudra

3 China's BRI and Responses from Provinces: The Case of Fujian Province 60
Md. Yasin

4 China's BRI: Revisiting the Labyrinth Post a Decade 76
Gunjan Singh

5 Geopolitical Contestation in the Indo-Pacific and the Belt and Road Initiative: An Evolving Great Game in the Maritime World 92
Vishal Rajput

6 The Zheng He Voyages: China's Encounters with the Sea-Faring Nations of the East and the Maritime Legacy 117
Anuraag Khaund

7 US-China Geopolitical Competition: A Showdown between the Indo-Pacific and the BRI 132
Raymond Kwun-Sun Lau

8 BRI: The Dragon's Great Eurasian Sphere of Influence 179
Jayadev Parida

9 The BRI and South Asia: Tracing the Variations in Chinese Engagements 199
Cyriac S. Pampackal

10 Mahan's Theory of Sea Power and Chinese Politics in the Indo-Pacific 216
Anuraag Khaund

Editor and Contributors 231

Index 237

Preface

This volume by a select group of Chinese scholars is an attempt to understand the transformation of the emerging world order over the last decade, especially one which is propounded by China and India and the vagaries of their growth. Ever since the fall of the US and the rise of China began to be anticipated, other great powers also started asserting their primacy on the world stage and endorsed that now the majority of trade, manufacturing, and production is in the emerging parts of the world—a fundamental seismic change. Subsequently, China's extolling of the BRI and India's resurgence of the Indo-Pacific construct have paved the way for other traditional powers to reassess their motives and agendas and contribute to this great momentum.

Like it is often said, "*no one can stop an idea whose time has come*", so one can procrastinate whether it really is indeed China's century or does India have an equal stake in the growth of humanity? This volume makes an attempt to understand in the historical as well as contemporary sense the factors that propelled the growth of these two Asian tigers and led to the recalibration of trajectories—as Adam Smith would have liked to describe as "a further rearrangement of the wealth of nations" and a simultaneous ascendance of political power. The catalyst for such a huge change perhaps lies deep in the structural division of power among nations with big pockets (resources) and even bigger manpower. The Silk Road Project is an embodiment of an interconnected world—a world that needs reformed global institutions, from an updated World Bank and IMF to an expanded G20—to cope with the rise of China and Asia. China's ability to achieve things within a short span of time is no longer unbeknownst to others, yet its sense of credibility and social responsibility is undermined by the self-image created by unscrupulous dealings and arm-twisting of smaller powers.

This volume is largely a comparative endeavour that aims to understand the evolution of these two concepts, which at the first appear antithetical to each other but when delved into carefully appear to be complementing each other in a world where there is enough sky for two suns. Without getting into a country-wise analysis of the BRI, while some case studies have been mentioned, the book aims to provide a general outlook on how fragile or sturdy is the growth promised under these two different yet complementing paraphernalia.

The editor is sincerely grateful to the contributors and the publisher along with the team for making this volume possible. On a personal note, I would like to dedicate this volume to all the contributors; my parents, Richhpal Singh and Rajbala Singh; my husband, Jeganaathan; my sons, Vihaan Naathan and Takshaan Naathan; my friends; the fraternity of Indian scholars who are engaged in the study of China; and to those lovely souls who are lost to us due to the COVID-19 pandemic.

New Delhi, January 2025 **Dr Bhavna Singh**

Figures

1.1 Gross Domestic Product (GDP) at Current Prices in China from 1985 to 2023 with Forecasts until 2029 4
1.2 Key BRI projects in ASEAN 17

2.1 The Maldives Exclusive Economic Zone 41
2.2 China-India Trade in South Asia 50

5.1 Map of the Indian Ocean Region illustrating the Maritime Silk Road Security Implications and Investments 101
5.2 Map showing China's strategy of 'String of Pearls' 104

8.1 Map of Europe 190

Abbreviations

AAGC	Asia-Africa Growth Corridor
AIIB	Asian Investment Infrastructure Bank
APEC	Asia Pacific Economic Cooperation
ASEAN	Association for Southeast Asian Nations
B3W	Build Back Better World
BBIN	Bangladesh-Bhutan-India-Nepal
BCIMEC	Bangladesh-China-India-Myanmar Economic Corridor
BRF	Belt and Road Forum for International Cooperation
BRI	Belt and Road Initiative
BRICS	Bank-Brazil Russia India China South Africa Bank
CAD Bank	China Africa Development Bank
CCAWEC	China-Central Asia-West Asia Economic Corridor
CCECC	China Civil Engineering Construction Corporation
CCG	Chinese Coast Guard
CCWAEC	China-Central Asia- West Asia Economic Corridor
CDB	China Development Bank
CEE	Central and Eastern European Countries
CICPEC	The China-Indochina Peninsula Economic Corridor
CIPS	China's Cross-border Interbank Payment System

CISPDR	Changjiang Survey, Planning, Design and Research Co., Ltd
CMEC	China-Myanmar Economic Corridor
CMREC	China-Mongolia-Russia Economic Corridor
COIDIC	China Overseas Infrastructure Development and Investment Corporation
CPC	Chinese Communist Party
CPEC	China Pakistan Economic Corridor
DoD	Department of Defense
DSR	China's Digital Silk Road
EEC	European Economic Committee
EMALS	Electro Magnetic Launch System
EU	European Union
FDI	Foreign Direct Investment
FTA	Free Trade Agreement
FTAAP	Free Trade Area of the Asia-Pacific
FYP	Five Year Plan
GCI	Global Civilization Initiative
GDI	Global Development Initiative
GDP	Gross Domestic Product
GFC	global financial crisis
GMCP	Greater Male Connectivity Project
GSI	Global Security Initiative
IMF	International Monetary Fund
INSTC	International North-South Transport Corridor
IONS	Indian Naval symposium
IOR	Indian Ocean Region
IPRD	Indo-Pacific Regional Dialogue
ISFTA	Indo-Sri Lanka Free Trade Agreement
ISL	International Shipping Lanes
MCC	Millennium Challenge Corporation
MDP	Maldivian Democratic Party
MOFCOM	Ministry of Finance and Commerce
MoU	Memorandum of Understanding
MSRI	Maritime Silk Road Initiative

NDRC	National Development and Reform Commission
NDS	National Defense Strategy
NELB	New Eurasian Land bridge Corridor
NMF	National Maritime Foundation
NPC	National People's Congress
NSS	National Security Strategy
OBOR	One Belt One Road Initiative
PAFMM	People's Armed Forces Maritime Militia
PLA	People's Liberation Army
PLAN	People's Liberation Army Navy
PoK	Pakistan-occupied Kashmir
PRC	People's Republic of China
QUAD	Quadrilateral Security Dialogue
RMB	Renminbi
SACPTA	South Asian Association Regional Cooperation Preferential Free Trade Agreement
SAFTA	South Asian Free Trade Agreement
SAGAR	Security and Growth for all in the region
SCS	South China Sea
SLOC	Sea Lanes of Communication
SOE	State-owned enterprise
SREB	Silk Road Economic Belt
TCM	Traditional Chinese medicine
TEN-T	Trans-European Transport Network
TPP	Trans-Pacific Partnership
UNCLOS	United Nation Convention on Laws of Seas
USD	United States Dollar
USINDOPACOM	US Indo-Pacific Command
WIO	Western Indian Ocean

1

The BRI and the Indo-Pacific: Reinventing Traditions over a Turbulent Decade

Bhavna Singh

The relative loosening of the US' grip over world affairs has engendered a flux in the current world order, which has led to political realignments and given rise to myriad possibilities for multilateral engagement. As the US attempts to reinvent itself, so as not to lose its hegemony, with aspirations of the Build Back Better World (B3W) along with the G7 countries, a more profound change has been on the horizon since Xi Jinping announced his signature project the 'the Silk Road Economic Belt and the 21st century Maritime Silk Road' or commonly known as the 'One Belt One Road' (一带一路)/BRI in 2013, calling it the 'Project of the century', crowning himself constitutionally as an 'Emperor for Life'. Born in an unprecedented pursuit and simultaneous assertion of power that was meant to resurrect its traditional grandeur—from the ancient town of Xi'an to its influence in the far-off regions of the world, the OBOR/BRI initiative has left the other Asian powers somewhat simultaneously opposing as well as conceding it,[1] and sometimes even contending for spheres of influence in a game of nations that sought a counter-play to the BRI. As a brave new world order takes shape, resurgence of Asia is now a near reality that few can deny; India also clearly doesn't want to be seen lagging behind in this scramble for power.

This realignment of interests however is not unprecedented, though the scale might be so. A deeper understanding of this great change validates the traditional argument put forward by Samuel Huntington in his book 'The Clash of Civilisations and the Remaking of the World Order', where he argues that people's cultural and religious identities will remain the primary source of conflict in the post-cold War world. He describes how in the past, world history was mainly about the struggles between monarchs, nations and ideologies, such as that seen within Western civilization. However, today global politics has moved into a new phase, in which non-western civilizations will no longer be exploited recipients of Western civilizations but will become additional important actors, joining the west to shape and move world history. Today, history has come full circle to represent this clash in identities and ideologies, with modern day democrats behaving like emperors and changing norms at will and the idea of a post-west led world gaining further acceptance amongst all the nations across the world.[2]

It is evident that for China, manufacturing consensus has been a difficult ordeal even amongst the beneficiaries, as some of the countries felt politically undermined and questioned the thrust and intent behind China's self-aggrandizement. In 2017, the initiative was incorporated into the constitution of the Chinese communist party. It has been a decade since China, under Xi Jinping launched this extremely ambitious and labyrinthine project that aimed to connect various parts of the world and was implemented with tremendous rigour, high-octane propaganda and massive political will. Sometimes also referred to as the new Silk Road, it is a global infrastructure development strategy adopted by the Chinese government to invest in more than 150 countries and international organisations. The project is aimed at building onto the old trade routes that once connected China to the west, Marco Polo and Ibn Batuta's routes in the north and the maritime expedition routes of the Ming dynasty Admiral Zheng He, in the south and *reinvent* these traditional trade routes along the six new routes proposed under the BRI framework. However, due to the COVID-19 pandemic, not much has been achieved substantively when one carefully looks at Xi Jinping's interaction with the several countries that are a part of this initiative.

Despite the Chinese belief of its supremacy among all under heaven (Tianxia/天下), other traditional powers have returned to reassert their claims to build an alternative world order. India, a primary contender and opponent of the BRI (due to the CPEC), has chosen to adhere to its traditional affinity to the Indo-Pacific construct. Considering both these Asian tigers scramble for the same pie of influence in Asia, the smaller Asian countries try to balance their influence and gain as much as possible from both these countries. This is also reflected in China and India's attitudes while dealing with other countries across the world. The BRI helped to develop new markets for Chinese firms, channel excess industrial capacity overseas, and strengthen China's ties with partner countries. Simultaneously India also has ambitions to be able to play a leading role through its prowess in science and technology and help other countries find their niche in space and solar technology and in the field of education, as it moves to resurrect its traditional role of being a 'Vishwa Guru'.

BRI and a Tumultuous Decade of 'Xiconomics'

The launch of the BRI on September 7, 2013, at Nazarbayev University in Astana, Kazakhstan,[3] and further, in a speech delivered by Xi Jinping in Indonesia in October 2013, not only introduced a new face of China that was primarily driven by a self-seeking agenda of making others kowtow to China by giving access to wealth to smaller players but also introduced a fundamental change in the economic system that the emerging/third world were engaged with. This came to be termed by scholars as his new 'Xiconomics'. It is difficult to fathom what the tenets of this Xiconomics are, given how opaque China's data is, but it is clear is that matters of ideology and security have become deeply entwined in China's economic and business environment.[4] Not only is it a centerpiece of Xi Jinping's foreign policy but also forms a central component of Xi's "Major country diplomacy", which calls for China to assume greater leadership commensurate to its rise and global status. Moreover, China has been willing to invest without much consideration for returns given its deep pockets and is willing to wait for a longer duration to reap the benefits that endue. Till 2018, it was estimated that trade between China and other Belt and Road countries exceeded USD 6 tn, and China's investment in BRI countries surpassed USD 50 bn dollars. Chinese companies have set up 56 economic cooperation zones in over 20 countries, generating some USD 2.4 bn dollars of tax revenue and 270,000 jobs for them.[5] This investment was facilitated by China's domestic growth over the last two decades—in 2023 the GDP growth of China amounted to USD 17.8 tn. The stagnation of China's GDP in US dollar terms in 2022 and 2023 was mainly due to the appreciation of the US dollars. China's real GDP growth was 3 per cent in 2022 and 5.2 per cent in 2023. In 2023, per capita GDP in China reached around USD 12,600.[6] As of early 2024, 140 countries were part of the BRI. For more information, see the figure below:

Figure 1.1: Gross Domestic Product (GDP) at Current Prices in China from 1985 to 2023 with Forecasts until 2029

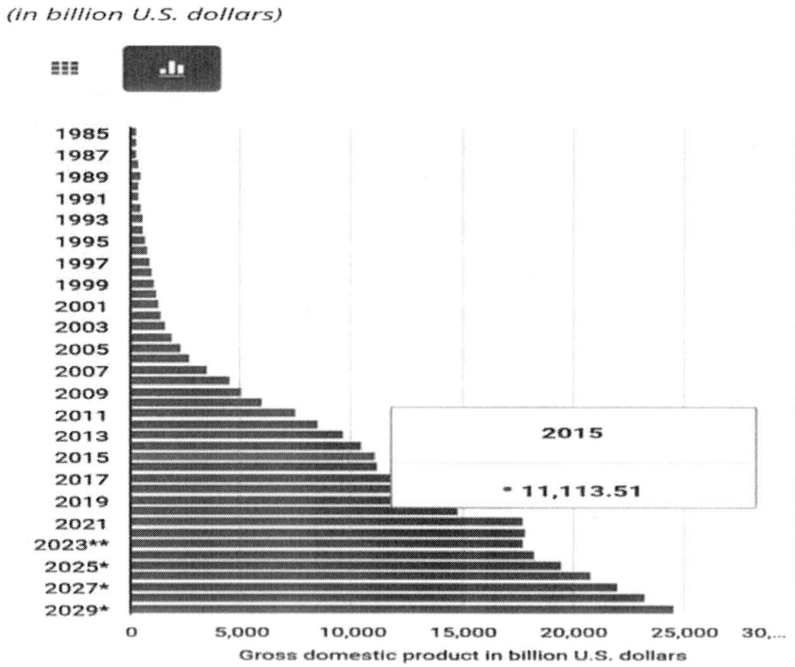

Source: Statistica—GDP Growth of China in USD.

This expansion of interest was facilitated through several institutions like the Asian Investment Infrastructure Bank (AIIB), BRICS-bank, China Investment Corporation, policy banks and Silk Road Fund as well as state-owned banks such as the China Development Bank, Export-Import Bank of China.[7] As of 2015, China announced that over USD 160 bn of infrastructure related projects were in planning or construction. The BRI had several political implications which gave rise to a new crop of young Turks in the parliament. Politically, the Steering committee responsible for dealing with the BRI reports directly to the State Council of China and comprises several political leaders. Initially Vice-premier Zhang Gaoli, who was also a member of the 7-man CCP politburo Standing Committee was the head, with Wang Huning, Wang Yang, Yang Jing, and Yang Jiechi as deputy leaders.

According to London-based consultants Centre for Economics and Business Research, the BRI is likely to increase the world GDP by USD 7.1 tn per annum by 2040.[8] Other than China, which by 2040 will be by far the world's largest economy, the biggest single potential beneficiary is likely to be the US, even though it isn't directly participating in the project. This will be due to the sheer size of the US economy, despite the fact that the boost to US' GDP is only 1.4 per cent. The findings of this survey may be drafted in accordance to China's strategy of assuaging US' concerns on China's rise, yet there is a certain truth to the predictions made. According to this report, the next largest impact is on Russia, followed by Japan, Indonesia, Korea, UK, India and the Netherlands. However the region most likely to be transformed is Central Asia where GDP in 2040 will be 18 per cent higher. GDP is also likely to be boosted in Central Europe (6 per cent) and western Europe (5 per cent) and East Asia (5 per cent). This study however made a caveat that in case the BRI is delayed for any reason such as the world economic slowdown due to COVID, global GDP will be reduced by USD 0.9 tn or 0.5 per cent. The region most affected will be Central Asia where GDP would be reduced by 5.9 per cent.[9]

Consistent growth domestically does not imply that the BRI had a smooth trajectory over its first decade; largely due to reservations from Chinese people and the general public disapproval of Xi Jinping's extravaganza abroad, the money flow into BRI was halted and diverted to domestic issues. A survey conducted in 2024 of Chinese attitudes towards the economy found the people were growing pessimistic and disillusioned about their prospects, which gave rise to violent incidents driven by economic grievances. These also stemmed from the COVID-19 pandemic, which halted the growth of several decades. China witnessed several issues like crisis in the real estate, steep public debt and rising unemployment, which was quite sobering for the

CCP, as it could no longer offer stable prosperity as a rationale for legitimacy and its grip on the society.[10] Post-Covid, the above-stated estimates became self-evident, as economic slowdown forced a slower pace of growth in these regions.

China and Asia

China's interaction with South Asian countries has been largely drawn across the contours of its competition with India. So far China has signed memorandums with most of the South Asian countries but only few projects have fructified on the ground. In case of Bhutan,[11] while the 2017 Doklam crisis had led to a tapering away of relations, China still managed to build the highest Buddha statue in Thimphu which costed USD 20 mn and has finished several other projects in expediting Bhutan's modernization process via exporting, farming and in telecommunications equipment.[12] And while China invited Bhutan to participate in the 2nd Belt and Road Forum for International cooperation (BRF) held in Beijing in April 2019. According to a report China's export to Bhutan has increased at an annualized rate of 18.3 per cent from n 1995 to USD 13.4 mn in 2020, whereas Bhutan's export to China has increased at an annualized rate of 18.3percent. While several analysts have pointed out China's surreptitious strategic depth in Bhutan by building 22 villages and settlements in and around Doklam,[13] yet bilateral relations remain unhampered as China continues to build roads and connectivity in the region. Similarly, in Nepal, though it agreed to 35 projects at the first, only 9 have materialized since 2017. Several issues on funding, operability and division of labour have stalled these projects. For instance, a strategic cooperation framework agreement was signed recently between China's Yunnan province and the Nepal-China Executives Council to strengthen the trade and investment relations between the two sides, but not much has been achieved after that. The development of the Madan Bhandari University agreement was renewed between Nepal and China for the second time in 2019, but was not implemented. In 2022, a six-point agreement was signed by both countries to increase Nepal's engagement and exchange information on governance, legislature and supervisory practices. There was also a controversy around the inauguration of the Pokhara International Airport which was a 'flagship project' of China-Nepal BRI cooperation.

While China wants to showcase increased visibility and influence in the region, Nepal is cautious and still suspects China's intentions.[14]

Launched in 2013, the China Pakistan Economic Corridor (CPEC), a flagship project of the China-proposed BRI, spanned a corridor that linked the Gwadar Port in Pakistan with Kashgar in northwest China's Xinjiang Uygur Autonomous Region covering 3000 km, which aimed at cooperation in the energy, transport, and industrial sector in the first phase, while expanding to the fields of agriculture and livelihood in the new phase. It was launched at a critical time when Pakistan faced challenges like internal security crises due to increased terrorist attacks and economic issues such as declining foreign investments, macroeconomic instability and electricity shortages. It gained further momentum in 2015 when Xi Jinping visited Pakistan. However, since 2018 progress on the CPEC has slowed down due to militant attacks prompting Chinese leaders to call for better security measures for their citizens in Pakistan. So far around USD 25.4 bn has been invested in various CPEC projects, including coal and hydel power projects, the orange line and road infrastructure. Islamabad continues to be economically unstable and a report published by the Associated Press in May 2023 revealed that approximately 50 per cent of Islamabad's foreign loans come from China which leave a legacy of debts due to high interest rates ranging from 4.5 to 6 per cent. Lately, a total of 43 exceptional Pakistani staff members from various CPEC projects were recently honoured for their outstanding contributions for their dedication to strengthening the friendship between China and Pakistan as a symbolic gesture to enhance trust among both sides.

In May 2023, the extension of the Belt and Road Initiative to Afghanistan raised suspicions about China's intentions in tapping the nation's abundant resources, especially considering Afghanistan's war-torn but resource-rich status. China agreed to extend the USD 62 bn CPEC to Kabul after the Taliban's agreement to join.

As far as Sri Lanka is concerned China has been following a policy of deep engagement under the strategic guidance of the heads of state of the two countries, to push forward their "strategic cooperative partnership featuring sincere mutual assistance and a lasting friendship." This has been reflected in their investments in several ports like the Hambantota. While Sri Lanka itself proposed the Hambantota Port project in cooperation with a profit seeking

Chinese SOE, it became more of a geo-strategic venture than a commercial one. The port invariably became a white elephant like several others promoted by Mahinda Rajapaksa as a part of corrupt and unsustainable development programme which led many to criticise China.[15] Some scholars have made a case that Sri Lanka's debt distress was unconnected to Chinese lending and instead arose from excessive borrowing on western-dominated capital markets and from structural problems within the Sri Lankan economy but India has been closely watching this relationship and believes that China is using BRI to pursue 'strategic ambitions' in South Asia creating a 'Chinese naval outpost' as a part of a 'salami-slicing approach'.[16]

Under the BRI Bangladesh is set to receive USD 26 bn and USD 14 bn for joint venture projects, totalling a USD 40 bn package. Bangladesh has primarily seen BRI projects in the energy and transportation sectors, with infrastructure investment needs projected to reach 1.5 per cent of GDP by 2040. Padma Bridge, Metromail, Karnaphuli Tunnel have been the key feathers in China-Bangladesh bilateral engagement's success caps. In the last 10 years, China has released USD 4. 45 bn for 35 projects under the BRI and the total investment from China in Bangladesh is USD 7.07 bn. Chinese companies have invested USD 22.94 bn in different sectors.[17]

When it comes to Myanmar, China has been the sole individual nation investing in Myanmar since 1988, and has significant interests in Myanmar due to cost-effective transport of oil through its territory. Myanmar signed the memorandum of understanding on BRI in 2018 and the China-Myanmar Economic Corridor (CMEC) became a flagship project under the BRI framework. The BRI projects in Myanmar aim to connect Kunming, the capital of Yunan, China, to Mandalay and then onwards to Yangon and Kyaukphyu, where a number of projects that had been paused were revived and new projects were conceptualised. These include projects such as the Letpadaung Copper mine project (USD 1.065 bn), the railway linking Kunming to Kyaukphyu (USD 8.9 bn), the New Yangon City project (USD 1.5bn), as well as other economic zones. The February 2021 coup slowed the progress on these projects as Myanmar was marred by political instability. 32 Chinese backed factories were wrecked as anti-Chinese sentiments grew amongst the masses. China revamped the BRI post-coup, showing its commitment to do business with the military regime despite losing people's goodwill. It reorganised several working committees and quickly implemented CMEC projects and allowed the Myanmar regime to open a consulate in Chongqing. Moreover, a 650 mn RMB grant is also being provided to Myanmar. A new LNG plant financed by China has been approved by the military regime.[18]

China and Central Asia

The Central Asian states hold a significant place in the BRI framework being a gateway for China's increasingly diversified land routes to other markets located to the west of China.[19] A cumulative set of figures presented by the Aiddata estimated that Chinese aid to Kazakhstan stood at a staggering USD 6756.2 mn, while that of Uzbekistan was USD 1998.2 mn, Kyrgyzstan got an aid of USD 2,143.6, while Tajikistan received an aid of USD 717.2 mn between 2010-2014. It has only increased over the years.[20] Politically also Xi Jinping attached great importance to this region as witnessed in his 2024 mini-tour to Central Asia; it was his fifth visit to Kazakhstan and Tajikistan. But along with investment, China's generous loans have given rise to a serious debt spiral in Central Asia - about 40 per cent (or USD 1.5 bn) of Kyrgyzstan's public debt and 50 per cent (or USD 1.1 bn) of Tajikistan's, is owed to Chinese institutions. The most emblematic of the BRI projects in Central Asia is the Khorgos dry port, on the border of China and Kazakhstan. This project connects Kazakhstan and Eurasia with China via an ultra-modern logistical hub of railroads and roads, a free economic zone and trade pavilions. New cities and industries are quickly growing around Khorgos as well as other smaller logistical hubs and free economic zones are being established in the region. The new Kazakh city of Nurkent, close to the Khorgos dry port on the border with China, arose from nothing to meet BRI development needs. The current population of about 3000 is expected to grow to 100000 in the coming 20-30 years. More cities of this type are likely to appear as new logistical and other needs arise.[21]

Central Asia currently imports from China mostly electronics, clothing and construction materials and exports primarily energy and minerals, especially from the Dordoi and Kara-Suu markets. Yet in the context of China's total trade, Central Asia is a small partner. The reason why China is still interested in this region is due to its geographical proximity to the Europe and the prospects for developing an important transit route; China's exports do not add much to local employment. Now, growing and importing food from Central Asia is gaining interest from China.

Meanwhile there are several constraints like underdeveloped road connections, cumbersome customs and limited export promotion efforts, plus technical challenges related to cold storage, inefficient irrigation and productivity. Central Asian countries are also seeking the development of rail systems both for transport independence and for international trade which stands to benefit from China's presence. At present only Kazakhstan has rail connections to China and is working to expand the transit capacities across the Caspian Sea. The cost of a railroad from China through Kyrgyzstan to the Ferghana Valley in Uzbekistan—between 270 and 300 kms in length—is estimated at USD 3 bn. Despite China's willingness to offer long-term leases and low-interest rates, the Central Asian states continue to grapple with a problematic business environment, endemic corruption, and brain drain that threatens their human capital. Yet, China's growing involvement in Central Asia is a long-term phenomenon and a turning-point in Central Asia's post-Soviet history and economic development. A special element as far as Central Asia is concerned is the greening of cities both ancient and new which entails a number of complementary strategies like designing energy efficiency into buildings and transportation systems. Building ring roads and regulating traffic to avoid congestion, smart planning hubs. Central Asia has an opportunity to incorporate China's advanced electric and mobility technologies into a range of applications. The Chinese success in improving air quality in urban areas provides a model for cities in the region.[22]

China and West Asia

The China-Central Asia-West Asia Economic Corridor (CCAWEC) is an add-on corridor that takes off from Central Asia. A report by the OECD in 2018 classifies the following countries as a part of the corridor: Albania, Armenia, Azerbaijan, Bosnia, Bulgaria, Georgia, Iran, Iraq, Israel, Jordan, Kyrgyzstan, Lebanon, Macedonia, Moldova, Montenegro, the Palestinian Authority, Romania, Serbia, Syria, Tajikistan, Turkey, Turkmenistan, and Uzbekistan. The China Railway Express, the first freight train to travel along the corridor, made its maiden trip in November 2016 from China

(Xi'an) to Europe (Prague) in 18 days. The corridor overlaps with several other regional transportation initiatives. The Baku-Tbilisi-Kars railway going through Azerbaijan, Georgia and Turkey is nicknamed the "Iron Silk Road". The railway line and the Port of Baku rail head are both included in the list of BRI corridors and projects. The most significant aspect of this corridor is that CCAWEC provides an alternative land route between China and Europe which avoids Russian territory.[23] Xi Jinping recently visited Kuwait and signed several agreements with the Kuwaiti Foreign Minister Abdullah Ali Al-Yahya, which include six major projects[24] that are being currently implemented in coordination with the Chinese side, yet not much progress has been made on the BRI front.[25] Their cooperation is borne from their similar position on the Palestine issue.

China and Europe

China's extension of BRI to Europe to facilitate connectivity has seen a bumpy road. Italy's official exit from the BRI at the end of 2023 has been a blow to Chinese President Xi Jinping's signature foreign policy project. Yet the BRI in Europe is being reconfigured rather than being terminated. Earlier on there was considerable enthusiasm for this project as the Mediterranean Sea, previously neglected by Chinese strategic thinkers, would emerge as an increasingly important area connecting the Indian Ocean and Europe via the Red Sea. Early implementation of the BRI in Europe focused on financing infrastructure projects, in particular railways in Southeast Europe and ports in the Mediterranean. This was accompanied by a surge of Chinese green-field investments, complemented by monetary linkages between the People's Bank Of China and European central banks through the establishment of the currency swap agreements and yuan or renminbi (RMB) bank clearing whose aim was to lower transaction costs of Chinese investments.[26]

However later, many projects were downsized as Germany and France had become increasingly wary of China's predatory investments, while some of them continue in Central and Eastern European (CEE) countries. The flagship infrastructural project has been the land-sea express route which directly links the port of Piraeus—one of the largest container ports in Europe—with Central and Eastern European countries, thus turning the

Piraeus into a Chinese hub for trade with Europe with involvement of several companies like the COSCO. They also have a heavy presence in Italian ports of Naples and Genoa. In fact Italy had been the biggest recipient of calibrated investments by the People's Bank of China which acquired 2 per cent of several strategically important companies, including energy giant Eni, electricity producer Enel, carmaker Fiat-Chrysler (now part of the Stellantis group), telecommunication company Telecom Italia, insurer Generali, and investment bank Mediobanca. Along with this some companies in Germany were also acquired like the acquisition of Kuka but these later ran into trouble with imbalances between China and Europe. Yet they had common motives for enhancing non-dollar trade as they were concerned about US's tendency to weaponise the dollar, which has already impacted the functioning of several European banks including French bank BNP Paribas.

Several European countries have established RMB bank clearings, also called offshore hubs, where the Chinese currency can be traded For instance, in Budapest, Frankfurt, Luxembourg, Madrid, Milan, Paris and Prague. China has also opened itself to countries participating in the BRI. This was evident in the case of Portugal where Macao has emerged as a focal point for contact; uniquely having both Chinese and Portuguese as official languages. The city hosts the Forum for Economic and Trade Cooperation between China and Portuguese-speaking Countries, also known as Forum Macao, China's only multilateral platform leveraging linguistic ties. Since its establishment, trade between China and these nations has grown by about 20-fold. In 2021, the Macao SAR government formed a committee to deepen integration into national development, with eyes on initiatives like the Belt and Road and the Greater Bay Area plan. That same year, the Guangdong-Macao In-Depth Cooperation Zone was launched on the neighboring Hengqin island, marking a milestone in regional collaboration. The zone, which has expanded Macao's development space by over 100 square kilometers, now serves as a critical platform for over 6,500 Macao-funded enterprises, making it the most concentrated area for Macao-funded enterprises in the Chinese mainland.[27] According to the Swift-produced RMB tracker, Europe is second only to Hong-Kong when it comes to global cross-border renminbi transactions. The use by European actors of China's Cross-border Interbank Payment System (CIPS), an alternative to the western-dominated Swift, is expected to grow. BRI continues to have an enduring influence over the European market.

China and Africa

As far as China's relations with Africa are concerned, China has entered into agreements with the AU as well as independent countries and BRI has gained traction in Africa since its launch in 2013. In 2023, African countries received USD 21.7 bn in BRI deals, including investments in ports, railways and renewable energy. at this time Xi Jinping extolled during the 3rd Belt and Road Forum (BRF) a strategic shift to towards more sustainable, community-focused projects. The 'small and beautiful' BRI model focused on less financially risky projects for Beijing and 'smaller, greener, less financially risky' projects for host countries but the shift from the Dakar Action Plan (2022-2024) to a new framework has already sparked debate about its potential impact on Africa. China has already lent loans exceeding USD 170 bn to 49 African countries and regional institutions from 2000-22. In case of Egypt, China agreed to give full play to the role of the intergovernmental cooperation committee mechanism, promote high-quality Belt and Road cooperation, and create new growth poles of cooperation in new energy, aerospace, electric vehicles, 5G construction, agricultural technology, artificial intelligence, digital economy and other emerging fields.[28]

However not all BRI projects are well conceived or strategically chosen, leading to outcomes that fail to deliver desired economic impact.[29] Kenya's standard Gauge Railway for example has been criticised for not being economically viable or benefitting local communities. Also, while BRI projects have contributed to debt distress in some host countries, experts argue that this isn't a deliberate strategy by Beijing. The 'debt-trap diplomacy' narrative has been challenged, with an emphasis on Chinese banks' need to recover their investments. For instance, Ethiopia renegotiated its USD 4 bn railway project loan, extending the repayment period without losing control over the infrastructure. However, the impact of commercial loans for BRI projects still comes under scrutiny.

Earlier in 2017, the China Overseas Infrastructure Development and Investment Corporation (COIDIC) had inaugurated its African headquarters in Johannesburg, being China's first overseas platform for the early stage development of infrastructure projects. COIDIC's founding shareholders include: the China-Africa Development Fund (CADFund), a subsidiary of China Development Bank (CDB); China Gezhouba Group Overseas Investments Co. Ltd; China Civil Engineering Construction Corporation(CCECC); China Telecom Global Limited; Changjiang Survey, Planning, Design and Research Co., Ltd (CISPDR); China ENFI Engineering Corporation; and HCIG Energy Investment Co., Ltd. With its designed capital USD500 million, COIDIC is the world's largest fund ever targeted for project preparation in emerging market countries.[30]

Terminal 3 of Abeid Amani Karume International Airport of one of the most-visited Unguja island, has been constructed and built by a Chinese company, which now serves as the main gateway for international passengers. Meanwhile, Nyerere Road, the artery linking the airport to Stone Town, has also been freshly renovated with the help of Chinese builders. The project of upgrading 100-km routes in the core city area and constructing two flyovers is also nearing completion. The locals believe that "without the support of the Chinese government and the Chinese constructors, it would have taken many years (15-20) to complete these projects." Recently Aboud Suleiman Jumbe, principal secretary for Zanzibar's Ministry of Tourism and Heritage, said China's support to Zanzibar under the BRI has facilitated infrastructure construction, thereby improving the living conditions of local people.[31]

However, of late, it was discovered that China was no longer in a position to provide advantageous loans to its BRI partners. Some African governments have also been under scrutiny for signing loan agreements with China that included non-disclosure of loan terms. The Africa Report acknowledged that the level of indebtedness of some African governments to China was worrying—the case of Angola (USD 25 bn), Ethiopia (USD 13.5 bn), Zambia (USD 7.4 bn), Republic of Congo (USD 7.3 bn) and Sudan (USD 6.4 bn). Much of it is obviously propaganda.

China and Latin America

Since 2017, 22 countries in Latin America and the Caribbean have formally joined the BRI, prominent ones being Argentina and Mexico. China is now Latin America's second-largest trading partner, only after the US. Though in 2000, the Chinese market accounted for less than 2 per cent of Latin America's exports, over the next few years, trade grew at an average annual rate of 31 percent. By 2021, trade exceeded a record USD 450 bn, and some economists predict it could exceed USD 700 bn by 2035. However, Brazil's unwillingness to sign an official pact with China on BRI reflects a cautious approach and pursuit of strategic autonomy. Brazil's selective engagement has led China to showcase greater flexibility, adapting BRI principles to meet Brazil's strategic autonomy, expanding infrastructure, connectivity, and trade.[32] A host of projects jointly built under the BRI, include the Belo Monte Hydropower Plant ultra-high-voltage transmission line in Brazil, Argentina's Belgrano Cargas railway and the Jamaica North-South Highway. With Chinese investments and technological assistance, Argentina built one of Latin America's largest solar energy plants, Cauchari Solar Park, in Jujuy. After officially launching commercial operations, the world's highest altitude facility provided power to 160,000 families. It turned into a poverty alleviation and social welfare effort when it hired locals after giving them technical training. The plant was also projected to generate USD 400 million in net profits for the province.[33]

In 2022, Argentina and Nicaragua joined the China-proposed BRI while Cuba and China signed a cooperation plan to promote the BRI in December the same year. Worth mentioning is the case of Peru. In November 2024, Xi Jinping alongside Peruvian President Dina Boluarte officially inaugurated the deep-water megaport, marking the launch of a new Asia-Latin America land-sea corridor. With the arrival of the 'Xin Shanghai' a vessel operated by the China COSCO Shipping Corporation Limited, at Shanghai's Yangshan Port from Peru's Pacific coast, China marked a completely unbelievable chapter in the growth of BRI as this ship not only carried goods but carried the promise of a new maritime corridor bridging South America and Asia. It also marked a new step toward deeper trade ties and turned their vision of shared development into reality by cutting shipping time to China to just 23 days from 33 days and slashing logistics costs by at least 20 percent.[34] Before Chancay, South American goods bound for China were shipped through North America but now Chancay is strengthening Peru's strategic role as a vital gateway, linking land and sea routes while serving as a bridge between China and Latin America. It is believed that Chancay Port could generate up to USD 4.5 billion in annual revenue for Peru and create over 8,000 direct jobs.[35] Latin American exports to China are mainly soybeans and other vegetables, animal products, copper, petroleum, oil, and other raw materials that the country needs to drive industrial development.

Beijing has invested heavily in Latin America's space sector and has strengthened its military ties with several countries, particularly Venezuela.[36] Meanwhile there have been reports about how the US is interfering with Chinese interests in this region and the China-US competition is intensifying in Latin America. With regards to this aspect, Chinese spokesperson Guo said that China had never engaged in geopolitical competition or spheres of influence when conducting economic, trade and investment cooperation in Latin America and there was always a scope for cooperation based on extensive consultation, joint contribution and shared benefits.[37] Besides, Chinese state-owned firms are heavily involved in energy development; Power China has more than fifty ongoing projects across fifteen Latin American countries as of late 2022. The China development Bank has funded major solar and wind projects, such as Latin America's largest solar plant in Jujuy, Argentina, and the Punta Sierra wind farm in Coquimbo, Chile.[38] Overall, China and Latin American countries have highly complementary economic advantages and their cooperation has shown great resilience and potential, especially in the field of infrastructure and agricultural industry, and technological cooperation, including new energy, artificial intelligence and electric vehicles. Most importantly, Argentina, Brazil, Chile, Ecuador, Peru, and Uruguay are members of the Asian Infrastructure Investment Bank, where they have some voting power.

China and ASEAN

Thailand was among the primary supporters of BRI, when Xi Jinping introduced the BRI a decade ago. This resulted in the notable Thai-Chinese high-speed railway project as well as several other infrastructure development projects, special economic zones, and promoting cultural activities. However, due to debt-concerns, Thailand decided to finance the rail with domestic funds and allowed China a concession to construct the tracks and operate the train. Initially during the presidency of Benigno Aquino III, the government did not pursue any major BRI projects but under Rodrigo Duterte, large-scale projects were agreed upon and implemented, for instance, the Chico River Pump Irrigation Project and the new Centennial Dam, as well as state-facilitated direct investments such as the Ant Financial's joint venture with Globe telecom to form Mynt, and the Mindanao Islamic Telephone company partnership with China telecommunications to launch Dito Telecommunity. Chinese medium-sized enterprises in services, which have indirectly benefitted from the BRI, have become joint-venture partners to Philippine businesses.[39] However their mutual relations are marred by illicit Chinese capital in the Philippines, online gambling investments, money laundering, sex trade and violence.

Figure 1.2: Key BRI projects in ASEAN

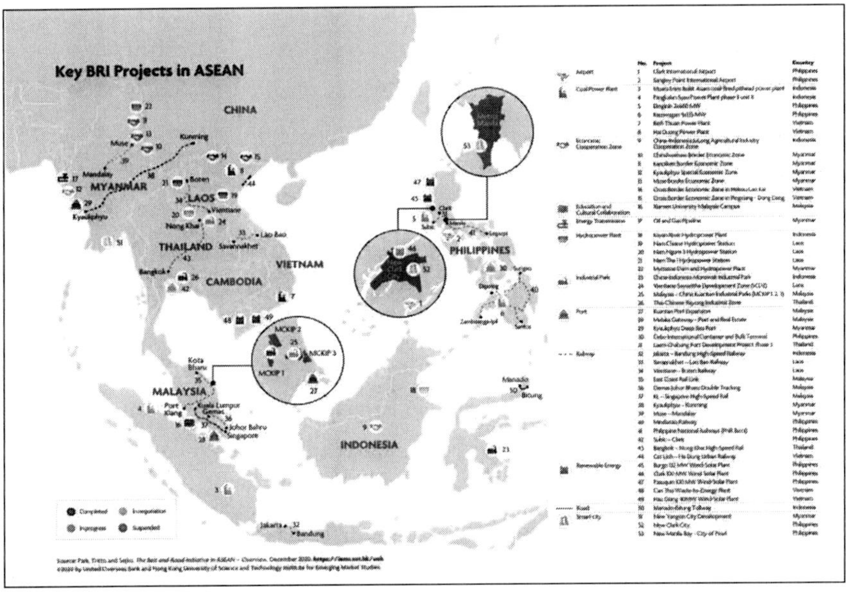

Source: Park, Trtko and Seqto, The Belt and Road Initiative in ASEAN – Overview, December 2020. HKUST IEMS

When looking at the cases of Chinese cooperation with Indonesia and Malaysia, it becomes apparent that these states channeled new capital and technologies towards national strategic economic outcomes. This was especially evident in the electric vehicle GVCs; in Indonesia President Widodo's state Capitalism efforts employed Chinese investments to bring new smelting and refining technologies to restructure and industrialize the country's mineral sector. As a result, Indonesia became a leading nickel-processing destination for stainless steel production and, more recently, for electric vehicle batteries.[40] The Indonesian government's priority is connecting Java Island to the eastern regions, along the lines of the Jakarta-Bandung high-speed Railway. Presently, there are seventy-one BRI projects with a total valuation of USD 20.3 bn. Here also, social issues act as an impediment to China-Indonesia cooperation. The Morowali Industrial Park (IMIP) in Central Sulawesi raises concern about worker safety. Currently, the Indonesian government is anticipating further Chinese investment in the new Indonesian capital city, named Nusantra (IKN), with a USD 32 bn contract, as well as the Rempang Island eco-city project valued at USD 11.5 bn. Yet more reliance could mean more dependency and backlash from locals in the future.

Meanwhile the Malaysian government has directed investments toward green energy and smart manufacturing, which resulted in the brokerage of a pivotal car manufacturing joint venture. Both countries employed a mix of statism and state activism to partake in the emerging GVCs connected to the electric vehicle sector, with Indonesia preferring the former by primarily employing industrial policy interventions to prioritise private sector investments, while Malaysia predilected hybrid forms of state and private sector coordination.[41] Cambodia has also benefitted from BRI projects focused on all types of infrastructure. One of the notable ones being Phnom Penh-Sihanouknille Expressway. BRI has also promoted the transnational transfer of money between China and Cambodia with the use of QR code technology. The China-Laos Railway, which connects Vientiane with Kunming is another notable example promoting regional connectivity and trade.

Regarding Vietnam, Vietnamese President Vo Van Thoung attended the 3rd Belt and Road Forum (BRF) in October 2023, and underscored cooperation with BRI projects. However, Chinese-funded projects in Vietnam included mostly coal-power plants, railway system improvements and a metro-line in Hanoi. In fact, Chinese investments in Laos and Cambodia surpassed those in Vietnam in terms of the number of projects and disbursed finances between 2015-2021.[42] More so due to past controversies with Chinese-funded projects, such as the cat Linh-Ha Dong metro-line, the Thai Nguyen steel plant, and bauxite mining in the Central Highlands, have contributed to scepticism. Teo projects in particular have undermined Vietnam's central role as a transit country in ASEAN. First, the 414-km Boten-Vientiane railway linking

China's Kunming province with Laos' capital city and the proposed Funan Techno Canal in Cambodia which could have significant repercussions on Vietnam's economic and ecological well-being. Nevertheless, during Chinese president Xi Jinping's recent visit to Hanoi, both sides signed a number of connectivity-related agreements, focusing on cross-border rail and road transport indicating Vietnam's receptiveness to establish connectivity with China. In future a key indicator of their cooperation could be the extent of China's involvement in building Vietnam's ambitious North-South high-speed train where China faces competition from Japanese firms.

China's Maritime Silk Road

The maritime Silk Road runs with its connections for the Chinese coast to the south, linking Hanoi, Kuala Lumpur, Singapore and Jakarta then westward linking the Sri Lankan capital city of Colombo and Male in the Maldives and onward to East Africa and the city of the Mombasa in Kenya; moving towards Djibouti, through the red sea and the Suez canal to the Mediterranean, thereby linking Haifa, Istanbul and the Athens, to the upper Adriatic region to the northern Italian hub of Trieste, with its international free port and its rail connections with Central Europe and the North Sea. The Baltic States, Northern Europe and Central Europe are also connected to the maritime silk road and logistically linked to East Africa, India and China via the Adriatic port sand Piraeus.[43]

China Ice Silk Road

Alternatively known as the Polar Silk Road has also been proposed along the Northern Sea Route in the Arctic, along the Northern Sea Route in the Arctic, along a maritime route within the Russian territorial waters. China COSCO shipping Corp. is involved in the Arctic shipping routes and Chinese and Russian companies are cooperating on oil and gas exploration in the area and to advance comprehensive collaboration on infrastructure construction, tourism and scientific expeditions.

Digital Silk Road

China is also trying to network worldwide research activities under its "Digital Silk Road Initiative". China's Digital Silk Road (DSR) falls under its objective of 'facilitating connectivity' and was launched in 2015, through a white paper on 'Information Silk Road'; it is also facilitated under the 2016 National Informatisation Plan. The DSR is, however, is a more future-oriented component of the BRI. The DSR's geopolitical, economic and security consequences are substantially more pressing than typical BRI rail, road and port projects. In Europe Chinese 5G technology, electronic payment systems and collaborations between Chinese and European entities on research and development (R&D) have made headway despite concerns by some European stakeholders over their security implications. By 2018, BRI and DSR related investments already stood at estimated USD 79 bn in digital infrastructure projects overseas and were engaged in 80 telecom projects around the world.[44] The DSR also provides support to Chinese exporters, including many well-known Chinese technology companies, such as Huawei.

In 2018, Nepal operationalised a joint fibre-optic link with China, providing the landlocked country alternative internet access routes to those via India. The same year a cross-border Pakistan Economic Corridor (CPEC) and the Pakistani military began replacing its use of GPS with Beidou in 2020. DSR projects are also active in other countries like Indonesia, Myanmar and Thailand.[45] A 2016 study on Chinese engagement in media sectors in Africa found that Beijing's inroads through content supply and content delivery technology have resulted in the growth of "more favourable public opinion."

It basically aims to develop six ultra-high voltage electrical grids across China, Northeast Asia, Southeast Asia, South Asia, Central Asia and West Asia. It would largely encompass wind power generation. There have been other additionally proposed corridors for instance the Bangladesh-China-India-Myanmar Economic Corridor which was proposed to run from Southern China to Myanmar and was initially officially classified as "closely related to the Belt and Road Initiative."

Impact of COVID-19 and the Health Silk Road

China's BRI dreams were temporarily but severely dampened by the COVID-19 pandemic that swept away a large chunk of liquidity and human resources off the list of China's boon. Disruptions to supply chains around the world, lockdowns and travel restrictions on foreign workers were some of the reasons for project suspensions and slowdowns. Yet China took up this opportunity and moulded its policies introducing the "Health Silk Road" to provide assistance for the international community in handling the pandemic. A report published by the Chinese Academy of International Trade and Economic Cooperation under China's Ministry of Commerce acknowledged that China aimed to inject new momentum into the BRI in 2020 while it was in its eighth year despite the global economy being devastated by the COVID-19 pandemic. China reassured its partners that the Belt and Road Initiative may experience short-term delays from the COVID-19 pandemic, but its long-term momentum will be sustained and even strengthened.

The biggest cause of any setbacks in BRI projects were the travel restrictions and border control. For example, work on Sri Lanka's Port City Colombo project has slowed by travel restrictions as Chinese workers have not been able to return to work. Workers on the Jakarta-Bandung High-Speed Railway project were also unable to return to Indonesia after the Lunar New Year holiday. But China maintained that these restrictions were a small obstacle that could be easily overcome to sustain the momentum of the BRI and worked towards this direction.[46] In the Latin American continent China was accused of using COVID-19 diplomacy as an effort to curry favour with regional governments and use its vaccine leverage to push for the expansion of Huawei. Notwithstanding these accusations, China made an effort to improve its image by distributing medical equipment such as ventilators and diagnostic test kits, offering billions of dollars in loans for countries to purchase Chinese vaccines, and investing in local vaccine production facilities.

An overall assessment of the BRI over the last decade would imply that while domestically BRI was designed to provide an outlet for Chinese companies' excess capacity in infrastructure construction and promote the "Chinese dream" of becoming of prosperous nation with a global role, at the international level it was meant to serve as a solution to several dilemmas such the Malacca dilemma, and remove security dilemmas from piracy to potential naval blockade by the US or its allies in the Middle East. Through these alternative corridors, it meant to extend its political and economic as well as to some extent cultural influence and check its adversaries in its neighbouring region. China is also used the BRI to enhance its global leadership image.[47] China's Green credit Guidelines became sustainable and begun to be considered amongst the most progressive sustainable finance policies in the world. Over the years, China and its partner countries have established international groups of stakeholders committed to promoting green and sustainable investments as a part of the BRI. But critics of BRI have accused China of pursuing a policy of 'debt-trap diplomacy': luring poor, developing countries into agreeing unsustainable loans to pursue infrastructure projects so that, when they experience financial difficulty, so far as to blame Beijing for seizing assets thereby extending its strategic or military reach in these countries. So far three Belt and Road Forums (BRF) have been held, in 2013, 2017, 2021 respectively, much has been achieved and some things still throw up new challenges, but China has managed to keep its ambition steady and its work consistent. Given the wide spectrum of the policies in BRI, effective implementation remains a challenge.

India's bet on the Indo-Pacific

Just like the BRI, the Indo-Pacific[48] is expected to be another essential driver of the world's economy in the near future, as the multilateral relations of the Indo-Pacific region will help to determine much of the world's economic, logistical and infrastructure. By 2013 Australia formally adopted the geographic concept in its Defence White paper, the US joined in 2017, and the ten-nation ASEAN group followed up in 2019. Japan also assented to the concept of a 'Free and Open Indo-Pacific', safeguarding international sea lanes from the Indian Ocean to Western Pacific. Along with this the QUAD group has also helped to establish a non-China dominant group in the east. Encompassing 40 economies, over four billion people and USD 47.19 tn in economic activity, it is the world's fastest growing-region. Many believe it is an idea whose time has come, it has supplanted the term Asia-Pacific.'[49] Modern use of the term was coined by the then prime minister of Japan, Shinzo Abe, in a 2007 landmark speech titled "The Confluence of the Two seas", since then many countries have bandwagoned onto the ship of the Indo-Pacific.

In his speech at the Shangri La Dialogue in 2018, PM Narendra Modi mooted India's position on the idea of the Indo-Pacific defining its geographical reach from Africa to the Americas, which covers both the Indian and Pacific Oceans, in tandem with that of Japan. He emphasised that India's outlook on the region is that of "inclusiveness, openness, ASEAN centrality" and that the concept was not directed against any country. The focus is largely on connectivity, enhancing maritime security, counter-terrorism, non-proliferation and cyber issues. The government introduced the concept of SAGAR (security and growth for all in the region) to focus on the oceans that connect maritime nations like Indonesia, Singapore and Sri Lanka. In 2019, at the second round of the Indo-Pacific Regional Dialogue (IPRD) held in New Delhi, the countries discussed solutions for achieving cohesion in the region through maritime connectivity; a regional approach to the region's transition from the existing 'Brown' to a 'Blue economy'; what is the maritime impact of 'Industry 4.0' and India's 'SAGAR' and 'SAGARMALA' initiatives to reinforce the regional order. So by 2018, the Indo-Pacific had progressed from a recognised region to an official policy framework.

Yet, India has restrained from participating in several military and naval exercises keeping in mind its crucial and sensitive relationship with China. Despite a robust relationship with the US, New Delhi sought to maintain its strategic autonomy and avoid the perception of aligning lockstep with Washington's Asian policy. It also did not allow Australia to take part in the annual India-led multinational Exercise Malabar. This is rooted in some primary elements that India adheres to in its Indo-Pacific approach: First, it underlines the Indo-Pacific as an opportunity to expand its footprint across the region while facing significant capacity and capital constraints, second, it places partnerships at the core of India's Indo-Pacific interests. Finally, although the Indo-Pacific presents new opportunities to India's great power ambitions, India's priorities and significant investments will remain in the Indian Ocean.[50] India's own approach is shaped by a new strategic environment coinciding with the rise of China. Further India's prioritisation of the Indian Ocean, along with concerns about differing priorities among Indo-Pacific partners, led India to carefully navigate its role in the region.[51] India primarily hopes to avoid 'alliances of containment' and wants to collaborate with countries to address shared concerns with via issue-based partnerships, embrace evolution rather than revolution in regional order and also recognise regional institutions and groupings as an important underpinning of future order.

India's implementation of the strategy occurs through its interactions with key states in the region. For example, the Quad partnership with the US, Japan and Australia is a key vehicle for India's engagement with the Indo-pacific. QUAD countries cooperate on technological security and cyber security threats and also engages in economic collaboration. Joint military exercises among the quad members enhance their collective military capabilities. It also facilitates a positive agenda for the Indo-Pacific by providing a platform for multilateral initiatives like vaccine diplomacy, alternative debt financing, maritime security and humanitarian assistance. Besides Quad the ASEAN is another forum that is a cornerstone of India's Act East policy.[52] India aims to enhance economic integration and people-to-people ties through physical and digital connectivity. Along with this the focus is also on the Western Indian Ocean. According to the 2015 Maritime Security Strategy, the WIO and the Gulf are of greater priority for India than Southeast Asia. Under the 'mission based deployment' strategy, combat vessels of the Indian navy have been stationed in the WIO to carry out policing, disaster relief and other missions. Most importantly, its engagement with France has given India the required edge in various domains, including defence, maritime security and economic advancement and most notably, the Indo-Pacific Triangular Development Fund.

The Indo-Pacific region got huge support from the US as evident in the existing USD940 bn in foreign direct investment from the US.[53] Since the release of the Indo-pacific Strategy in February 2022 the US made historic progress in advancing the shared vision for an Indo-Pacific region that is free, open, connected, prosperous, secure and resilient.[54] In 2022, US trade with the Indo-Pacific exceeded USD 2 tn and it benefitted from USD 956 bn in foreign domestic investment from the Indo-Pacific. There remains, however, an implicit agenda that segregates BRI and intends to be covertly exclusionist, this is because of several reasons like China's increasing reluctance to comply with the mandates of UN institutions, such as its efforts to block action on the discrimination against the Uyghurs, and its actions in the South China Sea (SCS).[55] For the US, of utmost importance is the will to advance a free and open Indo-Pacific, including upholding international law and freedom of navigation in the South China Sea, maintaining peace and stability across the Taiwan Strait, and enhancing maritime and security cooperation in the Indo-Pacific. This is reflected across in its dealings with most countries across the rim as documented by the US Department of State.[56]

Beside the US, Canada is also an active member in the region; its Indo-Pacific strategy outlines five interconnected objectives: promoting peace, resilience and security; expanding trade, investment, and supply chain resilience; invest in and connect people; build a sustainable and green future; Canada as an active and engaged partner to the Indo-Pacific. Canada's Indo-Pacific strategy is informed by its clear-eyed understanding of a global China and Canada's approach is aligned with those of its partners in the region.[57] Korea's Indo-Pacific strategy also involves making policy initiatives for individual sub-regions such as the Korean-ASEAN solidarity Initiative and make efforts towards to help the consistency and predictability of ROK's foreign policy as well as expand the horizon of our partnerships.[58] Similarly, the EU for its part has also acquiesced to cooperate with Indo-Pacific partners upholding a rule-based international order, based on the UN charter and promote international cooperation to reinforce stability, security and shared prosperity in the region. The EU-Indo-Pacific strategy promotes effective rules-based multilateralism, an open and fair environment for trade and investment, while supporting connectivity with the EU.[59] The declaration of tilt to the Indo-Pacific in general and outreach to India in particular encapsulated in the 2021 Integrated Review has been clearly welcomed by India. These are few examples of policy commitments that countries have outlined as far as the Indo-Pacific Strategy is concerned but most countries have their own strategy and understanding on what they want to contribute and how they want to engage with the region. However, beside its five tenets of "free and open, connected, prosperous, secure and resilient", not much has been brainstormed about amongst the closed group of countries that are party to it, which makes the objectives of the group vague and sometimes, non-assertive on the global agenda. Meanwhile, India's approach to the Indo-Pacific offers opportunities for engagement. Counter-terrorism, anti-piracy operations, supply chain resilience, climate change and renewable energy are shared priorities for the UK and India. While more is likely to come around when the idea gathers steam in future, it remains highly nebulous and very little has come to fore so far.

Meanwhile the BRI initiative propounded by China continues to roll out at a much faster pace. The Chinese have not only revised the components and objectives of this initiative but have also enhanced it with more recent constructs like the Global Development Initiative (GDI), the Global Security Initiative (GSI) and the Global Civilization Initiative (GCI) towards its vision of "building a community with a shared future for mankind." While these initiatives are a repackaging of Beijing's foreign policy principles of state sovereignty and non-interference in the domestic affairs of others as well as buttress the primary importance of "peace through development" yet they strongly emphasise China's role as a rising norm entrepreneur and are driven by Beijing's desire to cultivate authority in the international system. These three initiatives hope to shape an external environment that not only ensures regime security but are also favourable to China's security interests both domestically and internationally; this, it aims to do by reshaping key norms of global governance towards a fundamentally illiberal direction.[60] China has, in fact, at times, strongly opposed the concept of the Indo-Pacific. In May 2022, Foreign Minister Wang Yi, in response to a question that the US was redoubling its efforts to peddle the so-called Indo-Pacific strategy aimed at containing China, Wang Yi said, "the US Indo-Pacific strategy is triggering more and more vigilance and concerns in the world, the strategy has given itself away - it aims to change China's surrounding environment and make Asia-Pacific countries 'pawns' of US hegemony…it's fair to cite a Chinese saying to describe the strategy; that is Sima Zhao's ill intent is known to all."[61] He further stated that "irrespective of how it is disguised, it is in essence a strategy that creates division, incites confrontation and undermines peace, it is bound to be a failed strategy." With such strong sentiments both the rising great powers are likely to continue to oppose and reluctantly accept each other's vision for the future development of humanity. While both these rising powers- India and China have presented their positions to answer the vacuum in a rapidly changing world order, which of these binaries presented would become acceptable to the people at large and which of these camps may gain ground would largely depend on how much they are able to benefit mankind at large. The world today is in a state of disorder, great power contestation is increasingly intensifying, key norms of international relations are weakening, and the UN-centred institutional architecture is facing deep challenges from within and without;[62] in such a state both these groups have high chances of succeeding in holding the ground to their own beliefs and systems.

In this volume, many of these facets have been dealt with at length. While the first few chapters deal solely with how the BRI has impacted China's relations with other countries like the Maldives, or the Eurasian region and how it has been grounded in it's own provinces, the latter part deals with how the NRI has shaped its response to the simultaneous rise of the Indo-Pacific. In chapter 2, the Eshita Rudra identifies how the Maldives has become an anchor for China in South Asia since 2014 and has been involved with developing projects with local support. The infrastructure projects funded by China are mostly in Malé and the adjacent town of Hulhumalé for instance China built the Velana International Airport on Malé and also constructed the Sinamalé bridge connecting it to Hulhumalé; the Maldivian government has allocated a large amount of money in developing the area alongside China.[63] Such initiatives have given rise to a bonhomie between the two sides, though minor issues regarding fund-sharing arrangements remain. It can be observed that whilst the central authority formulates the top-down policy for BRI, there is a scope for local authorities to influence/reinterpret the same during bottom-up implementation. In chapter 3, Md Yasin argues that the notion of the Chinese central government's sole ability to design BRI as a grand strategy is a misnomer. Rather, BRI is ingrained in its sub-national practices and bears huge implications on its provinces.

In chapter 4, Gunjan Singh looks at what the Chinese government's response towards the BRI has been over the last decade in light of the mounting challenges it faced from the COVID-19 pandemic. In chapter 5, Vishal Rajput looks at China's attempts to further its own motives under the BRI paraphernalia while extolling how the Indo-Pacific construct is a propaganda tool of the US to isolate China in the region and aims to consolidate US' allies in the region to restore its influence in this region. In chapter 6, Anuraag Khuand takes a close look at the Ming era adventures led by Zheng He and the land-based expansion into neighbouring Southeast Asian polities of the Yunnan province and Annam (present-day Vietnam) which give a completely different picture of the China's maritime odysseys, as diplomatic-military campaigns were often disguised under the garb of 'benign trade furthering missions.

In chapter 7, Raymond Kwun-Sun Lau throws light on Trump's vision of 'Indo-Pacific' and how it stands in sharp contrast to the Chinese President Xi Jinping's advocacy of 'Asia-Pacific Century', and whether or not there can be any congruence between these two divergent constructs. In chapter 8, Jayadeva Parida makes a detailed study of China's BRI in the Eurasian region and compares it with the Marshall plan making a case for enhanced cooperation benefitting both sides equally. In chapter Cyriac looks at the progress of BRI projects in South Asia and how the Chinese have funded infrastructure dėvelopment projects which otherwise would have never materialised with the own resources of the geographically smaller South Asia. Yet these projects are often accused of being uneconomical and lack efficacy in generating monetary returns, making them huge liabilities to the host countries. In chapter 10, the last one, Anuraag Khaund looks at the scope of China's naval expansion and enhancing its presence and capabilities in the Indo-Pacific in order to secure its interests as well as counter the traditional presence of the US.

Notes

1. While China largely sought to make believe that the BRI strategy was initiated to lessen the effect of choke points such as the Malacca Straits, a 2023 study of Aiddata of the college of William & Mary determined that overseas port locations subject to significant BRI investment raise questions of dual military and civilian use and may be favourable for future naval bases.
2. Samuel P Huntington, The Clash of Civilizations, Foreign Affairs,1993, 72(3):22-49, doi:10.2037/20045621, ISSN0015-7120.
3. Xi Jinping in Kazakhstan described the BRI and "a road for peace, prosperity, opening-up, and innovation, connecting different civilizations" that will "build a broad community of shared interests." He has also framed it as "a new option for other countries and nations who want to speed up their development while preserving their independence."
4. Xiconomics—What China's Dual Circulation Strategy Means for Global Business, Columbia University Press, 2023, p. 1.
5. https://mtoutiao.xdf.cn/cet4-6/202404/13702732.html
6. Gross Domestic product (GDP) at current prices in China from 1985 to 2023 with forecasts until 2029, www.statista.com/statistics263770/gross-domestic-product-gdp-of-china/
7. The B3W plans to use bilateral and multilateral loans and private sector capital to mobilise capital such as the Development Finance corporation, USAID, EXIM, the Millenium Challenge Cooperation and the US trade and Development Agency.
8. Benjamin Mwadi Makengo, Joseph Mimbale Molanga, et al., Understanding the Strategic Opposition between the Build Back Better World (B3W) and Belt and Road Initiative, Academia Letters, Article 5202, https://doi.org/10.20935/AL5202. April 2022. The authors believe that the B3Wand

the BRI are, strictly speaking strategies of influence and incentivisation in order to gain an increasingly unavoidable importance in the management of international affairs.

9. Belt and Road Initiative to boost world GDP by over USD 7 ton per anumm by 2040, 27 May 2019, https://web.archive.org/web/20220925074129/https://cebr.com/reports/belt-androadinitiativetoboostworldgdpbyover7trillionperannumby20240
10. https://www.bbc.com/news/articles/c3e95lny0x9o.amp
11. Although China and Bhutan have not formally established diplomatic relations, China has expressed its willingness to expand practical cooperation to achieve common development based on mutual respect and shared benefits.
12. Belt and Road Initiative in Bhutan, BRI Watch, Volume 5, May 2022.
13. Doklam witnessed a 73-day standoff between Indian and Chinese troops in 2017. New Delhi had lodged a strong protest against the latter's attempt to build a road there, which could have added to the strategic vulnerability of the Siliguri Corridor, a narrow land passage between India's mainland and the northeastern states.
14. Chandan Prakash, 10 years of China's Belt and Road project: South Asia barring India and Bhutan, in a bind over Beijing's predatory tactics, 25 July 2023, https://firstpost.com
15. There were some covert aspects that made believe people the Chinese were using influence over the local bureaucrats. Colombo's application for Chinese funding was strongly encouraged by China Harbour Engineering Group (CHEG), which had been implementing Chinese-funded reconstruction projects in Sri Lanka; it not only offered free feasibility studies but also exaggerated likely economic benefits.
16. Debunking the Myth of 'Debt-trap Diplomacy', How Recipient Countries Shape China's Belt and Road Initiative, Chatham House, 14 December 2020, https://www.chathamhouse.org/2020/08/debunking-myth-debt-trap-diplomacy/4-srilanka-and-bri.
17. Simon Mohsin, BRI- 10 years on, and Bangladesh, The Financial Express, November 20, 2023, https://thefinancialexpress.com.bd/views/bri-10-years-on-and-bangladesh.
18. Sreeparna Banerjee, Revamping BRI in post-coup Myanmar, 8 December 2022, ORF, https://www.orfonline.org/expert-speak/revamping-bri-in-myanmar-post-coup
19. Sarah Lain, The Potential and Pitfalls of Connectivity along the Silk Road Economic Belt, in Marlene Laruelle ed – China's Belt and Road Initiative and its Impact in Central Asia, The George Washington University, Central Asia Program, 2018, pp. 1-10.

20. For a detailed analysis through figures on how much investment has been done in Central Asia plz see Farkhod Aminjonov et al, BRI in Central Asia: Overview of Chinese projects, Central Asia Data Review 20 (2019) 1-5. OSCE Academy in Bishkek.
21. Greening the Belt and Road Projects in Central Asia: A Visual Synthesis, Zoi Environment Network, https://zoinet.org/wp-content/uploads/2018/01/BRI-Layout-WEB.pdf
22. Ibid.
23. Sahakyan Mher, China and the South Caucasus in a Multipolar World Order 2.0, Security, Diplomacy, Economy and Cyberspace, Routledge, New York, ISBN 978-1-003-35258-7, OCLC 1353290533.
24. On Kuwait's perspective of the Belt and Road Initiative, Al-Yahya underscored that Kuwait is "one of the first countries with a special connection to the Silk Road, and we remain committed. This vision will materialize in the near future."
25. Kuwait-China relations continuously developing: Kuwaiti FM, 19 December 2024, http://www.china.org.cn/world/Off_the_Wire/2024-12/19/content_117617661.htm
26. Nicola Casarini, The Future of the Belt and Road in Europe; How China's Connectivity Project is Being Reconfigured across the old Continent – and What it means for the Euro-Atlantic Alliance.
27. Macao SAR 25: Why is richer-than-ever Macao still ambitious for more?19 December 2024, http://www.china.org.cn/china/Off_the_Wire/2024-12/19/content_117618285.htm
28. Chinese, Egyptian foreign ministers hold strategic dialogue in Beijing, 13 December 2024, http://www.china.org.cn/china/Off_the_Wire/2024-12/13/content_117606970.htm
29. Africa has much to gain from a Contained BRI, Institute for Security Studies, Online web URL: https://issafrica.org/iss-today/africa-has-much-to-gain-from-a-more-contained-bri
30. COIDIC was launched in September 2016 at the 2nd Invest in Africa Forum in Guangzhou, China. The main business of COIDIC is the early stage development of Public Private Partnership (PPP) infrastructure projects, handling financial, engineering and legal aspects of project preparation. COIDIC undertakes projects from concept phase through bankability to create a supply of projects ready for construction, thereby directly addressing the scarcity of properly prepared projects ready for financial close. COIDIC's first focus is project preparation in Africa, and soon it expects to expand its operations to contribute to China's One Belt, One Road (OBOR) program, with the goal of becoming an influential global "project incubator platform" for essential infrastructure development.

31. Interview: Robust Tanzania-China ties pave way for extensive cooperation, says Tanzania's Zanzibar senior tourism official, 14 December 2024, http://www.china.org.cn/world/Off_the_Wire/2024-12/14/content_117608039.htm
32. Aparna Divya and Salman Ali, Brazil-China Partnership: Redefining the Belt and Road Initiative in Latin America, 30 December 2024, The Diplomat, https://thediplomat.com/2024/12/brazil-china-partnership-redefining-the-belt-and road-initiative-in-latin-america/
33. China-Latin America trade reaching new heights, China Daily, Zhao Ruinan, 3 March 2023, http://www.chinadaily.com.cn/a/202301/03/WS63b38e17a31057c47eba763b.html
34. Xiconomics: From Chancay to Shanghai: new voyage of common development, 19 December 2024, Online URL http://www.china.org.cn/world/Off_the_Wire/2024-12/19/content_117618448.htm
35. China has been Peru's largest trading partner and largest export market for 10 consecutive years. From 2016 to 2023, bilateral trade has grown at an average annual rate of 14.6 percent, reaching USD 37.69 bn last year. This mirrors the increasingly closer economic links between the two nations. The Chancay Port project is likely to stimulate new business ventures and joint investments between Chinese and Peruvian companies.
36. Diana Roy, China's Growing Influence in Latin America, Council on Foreign Relations, 10 January, 2025. https://www.cfr.org/backgrounder/china-influence-latin-america-argentina-brazil-venezuela-security-energy-bri
37. Win-win cooperation key word in China-Latin America relations: spokesperson, Xinhua, 18 February 2025, Beijing, https://english.news.cn/20250218/e9f6ed0765044bf5b0fd65b0ac3eac20/c.html
38. Ibid.
39. Pongphisoot (Paul) Busbarat, Alvin Camba, Fadhila Inas et al, How Has China's Belt and Road Initiative Impacted Southeast Asian countries?, https://carnegieendowment.org/posts/2023/12/how-has-chinas-belt-and-road-initiative-impacted-southeast-asian-countries?lang=en
40. Angela Tritto, Statism and state activism in response to China's belt and Road Initiative: Indonesia and Malaysia's approaches to developing the EV sector, 13 January 2025, SAGE Journals, Online URL:https://doi.org/10.1177/10245294241311417.
41. Ibid.
42. Hoang Thi Ha, Late to the Party: Vietnam and the Belt and Road Initiative, FULCRUM, December 14, 2023, https://fulcrum.sg/late-to-the-party-vietnam-and-the-belt-and-road-initiative/
43. Andrew Wheeler: How Trieste could become the Singapore of the Adriatic in Asia Shipping media – Splash 247, February 19, 2019.

44. Richard Ghiasy and Rajeshwari Krishnamurthy, China's Digital Silk Road; Strategic Implications for the EU and India, IPCS, Special Report#208, August 2020, p. 6.
45. Ibid.
46. David Ho, COVID-19 won't have long-term impact on BRI, 26 March 2020, China Daily, http://www.chinadaily.com.cn/a/202003/26/WS5e7c0e74a310128217282227.html
47. Anu Anwar, Belt and road Initiative: what's in it for China? 30 Oct 2019, Economics, Politics & International Relations, East-West Centre, https://eastwestcenter.org/news/eastwest-wire/belt-and-road-inititave-whta%E2%80%99s-in-it-china.
48. Indo-Pacific countries include- Australia, Bangladesh, Canada, Indonesia, Israel, Japan, Seychelles, Singapore, South Korea, Sri Lanka, the UK, and the US among others (40).
49. Tim Marshall, The Indo-Pacific is an idea whose time has come, Engelsberg Ideas, https://engelsbergideas.com/notebook/the-indo-pacific-is-an-idea-whose-time-has-come/?gad_source=1
50. Darshana M. Baruah, India in the Indo-Pacific: new Delhi's Theatre of Opportunity, 30 June 2020, Carnegie Endowment for International Peace, https//carnegieendowment.org/reserach/2020/06/india-in-the-indo-pacific-new-delhis-theatre-of-opportunity?lang=en
51. Walter Ladwig, The Ind0-Pacific in Indian Foreign Policy, 30 April 2024, RUSI, https://rusi.org/explore-our-reserach/pubications/polcy-briefs/indo-pacific-indian-foreign-policy
52. Walter Ladwig, Opcit.
53. https://www.ansi.org/trade-development/standardization/regions/indo-pacific
54. 美国对印太地区的持久承诺：本届政府印太战略发布两周年, 9 February 2024, Online URL, https://mp.weixin.qq.com/s?__biz=MjM5MDA2NDk0MA==&mid=2651319512&idx=1&sn=e2ec2cda735750d38ae9a55fc89b452a&chksm=bdb9c49b8ace4d8d8da7d43050830c74149776eedb6f4f483613eb9a56fac3cdea381fe18cf0&scene=27
55. Ibid. "But as we strengthen our cooperation to advance our shared values and interests and meet the challenges we face, we see the PRC of China becoming more authoritarian at home, more assertive internationally, undermining human rights and international law, and trying to change the international order. We see that North Korea continues to expand its illicit nuclear weapons and ballistic missile programs."

56 US Department of State, Department Reports and Publications, https://www.state.gov/united-states-finland-consultation-on-the-indo-pacific/

57. Canada's Indo-Pacific Strategy, https://www.international .gc.ca/transparency/indo-pacific -indo-pacifique/index.aspx?lang+eng
58. For more information on Korea's Indo-Pacific Strategy please See, ßhttps://www.mofa.go.kr/enng/wpge/m_26382/contents.do
59. For more information see the document—Joint Communication to the European Parliament and the Council; the EU Strategy for cooperation in the Indo-Pacific issued by the European Commission.
60. Manoj Kewalramani, China as a rising norm entrepreneur, Examining GDI, GSI and GCI, ISEAS (Yusof ISHAK Institute), Trends in Southeast Asia, Issue 2, 2024.
61. Wang Yi: The US Indo-Pacific Strategy is Bound to be a Failed Strategy, 22 May 2022, MOFA, PRC, https://www.fmprc.gov.cn/eg/wjbzhd/202205/t20220523_10691136.html
62. Ibid.
63. https://amti.csis.org/chinese-investment-in-the-maldives-appraising-the-string-of-pearls/ Chinese Investment in Maldives: Appraising the String of Pearls. Accessed on April 28, 2021.

2

The BRI and China's Charm Offensive in the Maldives

Eshita Rudra

In 2014, Chinese President Xi Jinping visited the Maldives for the first time in 42 years and promoted his foreign policy initiative. The Maldives, located in the Indian Ocean, can be a significant partner in strengthening China's presence in the Indian Ocean Region (IOR), furthering Chinese President Xi Jinping's Belt and Road Initiative/One Belt One Road (BRI/OBOR). It is, hence, significant to study the bilateral relations and evolving dynamics in the Indian Ocean between China and the Maldives. China is trying to enhance its foreign economic relations through the Maritime Silk Road Initiative (MSRI) in the Indian Ocean region and secure a foothold in South Asia, driving India to reemphasise New Delhi-Male ties. China aims to consolidate its influence in the maritime backyard. The Maritime Silk Road Initiative is the maritime dimension of the Belt and Road Initiative or the One Belt One Road. The Maldives, under President Abdulla Yameen, shifted its foreign policy from the traditional "New Delhi first" outlook to a more welcoming approach towards China. The Maldivian leadership under Yameen's administration accelerated high level visits between Malé and Beijing. By leaning towards Beijing, the Maldives, under Yameen's administration, secured financial assistance for developing infrastructure. But the non-transparent nature of these funds and fear of Maldives being unable to repay them has stoked concerns in New Delhi about Male falling into a debt-trap, thus giving Beijing access to the Maldives' assets. The Maldives' location in the middle of the Indian Ocean, straddling the significant international shipping lanes, elevates its geopolitical significance. Infrastructure development through the Maritime Silk Route (MSR) initiative will help to strengthen China's presence in the Indian Ocean Region. The great power geopolitics in the Indo-Pacific maritime arc in the 21st century is making it imperative for the two Asian giants to forge and maintain a long-term partnership across the Indo-Pacific. New Delhi must carefully act to manage South Asian littorals drifting away from its orbit. Reassuring neighbours requires a thoughtful inclusive and extended neighbourhood foreign policy commensurate with a sustainable growth plan for the smaller neighbours. A comprehensive and sustainable alternative on connectivity and infrastructure impacting the lives of the local population might help India regain its lost image.

The shift in power distribution across the international system shapes the domestic and international policies to be implemented in small states. For a small state, band-wagoning and hedging are two strategies available to manage ties with major powers. Browning argued that small states are "isolated variables in the sea of anarchy, being buffeted by powerful waves of others' actions". In international politics, small states are considered objects of international relations rather than subjects. It is hereby attempted to make a case study on Maldives-China relations as Beijing promotes its 21st century major foreign economic policy Belt and Road Initiative (BRI/OBOR).

President Xi Jinping, after coming to power, pledged to make China a strong maritime state. In 2013, Xi Jinping, during a state visit, unveiled his dream project in Kazakhstan, and the maritime dimension of the initiative was launched in Indonesia. It is imperative to study Beijing's engagement with small littorals in the Indian Ocean through economic, military, and cultural interactions, which determine the behaviour of the littorals, as well as implications towards India's sphere of influence in the region. The concluding part contends that a geopolitical rivalry has already taken shape in the Indian Ocean between China and India. New Delhi requires a thoughtful neighbourhood foreign policy along with an active implementation of the same to maintain dominant power status in the region.

Beijing's anchorage in South Asia

China's changing economic profile due to economic reform and opening-up policies adopted in the 1970s made it an export-oriented economy. From a USD 390.28 billion economy in the 1990s, China has now become a USD 14342.90 billion economy. In 1995, the value of China's imports and exports of goods totalled USD 280.9 billion or 3 per cent of global trade. In 2018, China's total trade in goods had jumped to USD 4.6 trillion or 12.4 per cent of global trade. By 2018, it became the largest trading partner to about 128 countries out of 190. This huge bulk of trade requires Beijing to protect it from unplanned encounters and threats emerging at far-flung areas. China is also the 2nd largest net importer of crude oil, and the bulk comes from West Asia. Therefore, Beijing's vital interest lies in peaceful and stable high seas. To secure its oil import and trade from threats emerging at the high seas, China is looking to strengthen its presence in the Indian Ocean region (IOR). It becomes inevitable then for Beijing to forge ties and strategic partnerships with smaller developing countries in South Asia. In recent years, China has been actively engaging with the South Asian states through investment in robust infrastructure development in the region.

A 2018 paper of the Asian Development Bank stipulates that the region suffers from severe shortages of quality infrastructure, which can be seen as a serious challenge to its progress as the fastest growing sub region in the world. The paper further elaborates on how South Asia is falling behind most other regions, such as East Asia, Latin America, and the Caribbean. There are large deficits in transport and connectivity and a general deterioration in the condition of roads. South Asia also lags behind in cross-border infrastructure investment. The report further extrapolates that in order to provide adequate high-quality infrastructure, South Asia will require to engage more private finance.[1]

In 2013, Chinese President Xi Jinping launched a foreign policy initiative known as the One Belt One Road (OBOR)/Belt and Road Initiative (BRI) in Kazakhstan. The Belt and Road Initiative (BRI) aims to promote and strengthen China's foreign economic relations through infrastructure build-up, opening connectivity networks, such as highways, bridges, and airports etc. China seeks to provide loans to developing nations from accumulated surplus capital under this initiative.

Initially, when the project was launched, it was postulated that the Belt would run through land across Asia and Europe while the road would be constituted by the maritime dimension of the project, known as the Maritime Silk Route (MSR). To understand China's BRI project under Xi Jinping, it is necessary to enhance an understanding about the foreign policy tenets and concepts endorsed by the Chinese government. The "period of strategic opportunity", often promoted and mentioned in speeches by the Chinese leaders and officials, focuses on economic opportunities. However, the inordinate focus on China's rapid increase in military build-up makes it important to note that the "period of strategic opportunity" implies the notion of economic development and not the path to arms race. China aims at being a regional superpower on the basis of a strong economy and does not put much emphasis on being perceived as a gun- wielding military power.

China's BRI project has received an overwhelming response from many countries that are in dire need of capital to boost their infrastructure. China has even provided financial aid to regimes that sometimes do not abide by the rules of the IMF and other infrastructure development financing institutes, since these local regimes desire to stay in power by accepting grants from Beijing. China has forged close ties with political parties and heads of states, establishing an enduring presence in South Asia.[2] China's penetration in the region is an issue of concern for India as Beijing might reduce New Delhi's position as the dominant power in this region. Already, the bilateral relations between the two Asian powers are afflicted with unresolved border disputes. While the Himalayas are already a zone of conflict between the two, gradually, the maritime domain is also becoming a zone of contest for primacy.

Jhonson argues that despite the growing realisation for a more coordinated approach between foreign and domestic policies on advancing foreign economic relations, internal reform policies continue to remain a priority under the Xi Jinping administration as well. Historically, it was under the paramount leader, Deng Xiaoping, that China embarked upon a course of economic reforms in the 1970s. As long as internal reforms to enhance economic development continue to be listed as a high priority for Chinese policymakers, maintaining a low profile while hiding capabilities and biding time will remain fundamental for China. Sceptics, however, believe that China's BRI is geopolitically motivated, which might challenge India's sphere of influence in South Asia and ultimately aims at containing India's outreach.

China's presence in South Asia has been slowly upscaled since the mid-2000s when the Chinese leaders began to realise that their country's dependence on the Strait of Malacca could leave it vulnerable to external aggression. China's growing economic strength gives Beijing leverage to push forward a Sino-centric economic architecture across Asia, Europe, and Africa. The BRI is a huge infrastructure investment project that could enable a seamless web of connectivity, consequentially boosting trade and growth in the region.

China's increasing footprint in the Indian Ocean is making New Delhi jittery as Beijing deepens its ties with each of its neighbours. The 19th Party Congress report of the Chinese Communist Party (CPC) reiterates that "no matter what stage of development China reaches it defends its increasing presence in IOR is an attempt to build an economic community with a common destiny, or shared future, emphasizing its efforts are towards maintaining internal stability and development." This has resulted in a security dilemma between Beijing and New Delhi as both are now vying for their respective spheres of influence.[3]

India and China in the Indian Ocean region

To New Delhi's dismay, China has steadily increased its trade with other South Asian nations. In the last two decades, China has established itself as a major trade partner of South Asia. Until 2005, China and India still had some parity in the South Asian region in terms of overall trade volume. However, at present, China's trade in South Asia has a surplus balance in comparison to India. Beijing's trade with Bangladesh and India remains proportional for both exports and imports. On the other hand, Beijing's imports from Pakistan and Afghanistan have declined drastically. Chinese exports to Pakistan and Afghanistan increased from USD 13 billion and USD 300 million in 2014 to USD18 billion and USD 541 million, respectively.[4] China has replaced India as the largest trading partner of Bangladesh[5] and has also gradually increased its trade with other South Asian nations, such as the Maldives, Sri Lanka, Nepal, and Afghanistan. Policymakers in China consider that penetration in South Asia, through economic integration across the region, is crucial to consolidate China's presence and manage any challenges emanating from rival powers.[6]

China's presence in numerous South Asian small developing nations, by building roads, railways, bridges, ports, and airports, is becoming a reality that the Indian leadership and policymakers need to accept while charting the course of India's foreign policy. While exports to China from the region have been staggering, imports from China have been growing since 2012 in Myanmar and since 2014 in the Maldives, Bangladesh, as well as Pakistan. Sri Lanka was heavily dependent on India due to the Indo-Sri Lanka Free Trade Agreement (ISFTA). However, post- 2013, exports to Sri Lanka from China and India are at par. China's burgeoning trade relations with smaller South Asian nations is an indication of the region's significance to further/ promote the BRI.[7] A large percentage of China's trade with Pakistan accounts for China's high trade volume in South Asia. Although China's trade volume remains large, barring China-Pakistan trade, Beijing's trade with South Asia in 2018 is relatively lower at USD 12.87 billion.[8] China's influence in the region still may not be at par with that of New Delhi; however, it is substantive enough not to be neglected by India anymore.

Beijing's BRI got acceptance among the South Asian smaller nations as they are in dire need of financing aid for infrastructure development, notwithstanding the debt trap debate. As China steps up engagement with the region through the BRI, it can extend financial assistance through the Asian Infrastructure Investment Bank (AIIB), replacing other existing financial aid institutions providing grants to developing nations. Sceptics argue that the MSRI infrastructures are driven primarily with strategic objectives while hardly reaping any economic benefits. However, with a few exceptions, Beijing and the recipient countries have demonstrated that these projects are capable of facilitating trade in the latter and across the region.[9] Most countries from SAARC depend on developed nations as destinations for trade where protectionism is minimal. As tariff barriers and trade protectionism gets strengthened in the US and other European nations due to US-China decoupling, Beijing is looking for economic integration in other regions. Alyssa Ayres argues that despite China gradually overtaking India in South Asia in trade, Beijing is yet to displace India in the region in terms of security provider and defence.[10]

Nevertheless, the Maritime Silk Route (MSR), the maritime part of the BRI, promises an array of opportunities for developing countries in South Asia to transform their economy and connectivity networks. According to estimates, about USD1-4 trillion is available in BRI funding to build new roads, railways, ports, and other infrastructure. An estimate of the World Bank suggests that to mitigate the infrastructure gap, a minimum investment of USD 1.7 trillion is required. China's dependency on the Indian Ocean is growing owing to its huge import of crude oil from West Asia and trade across South Asia, West Asia, and Africa. Due to lack of quality infrastructure, exporting and importing containers are more expensive in South Asia than in East Asia. In 2014, Chinese President Xi Jinping visited the Maldives to promote his major foreign policy initiative, the OBOR/BRI. During a three-nation tour in South Asia, President Xi promoted the MSRI in the Maldives, Sri Lanka, and India.

The Maldives: A significant pearl in the Indian Ocean

The Maldives is a small island nation located in the Indian Ocean. It is mostly a destination for honeymooners. It is the smallest Asian nation with an area of 300 sq. km and has a population of 530,953 people. Amongst the Maldivian population, around 98 per cent are Sunni Muslims. The island nation straddles important international shipping lanes (ISL) as it is a dispersed island nation in the Indian Ocean, providing only two shipping passages on the north and south. These shipping lanes are the arteries to maritime trade between the Gulf of Aden and Hormuz in West Asia and the Strait of Malacca.[11] Tourism is the prominent industry of the Maldives. Around 1200 coral islands make up the Maldivian archipelago. The island nation is connected via important shipping routes in the Indian Ocean. Recently, the small island nation gained the attention of the Chinese leadership in Beijing as a "pearl" in the Indian Ocean. The Maldives, a South Asian island nation, which completely depends on tourism, took China's MSRI as an opportunity to develop infrastructure for its tourism industry.

Figure 2.1: The Maldives Exclusive Economic Zone

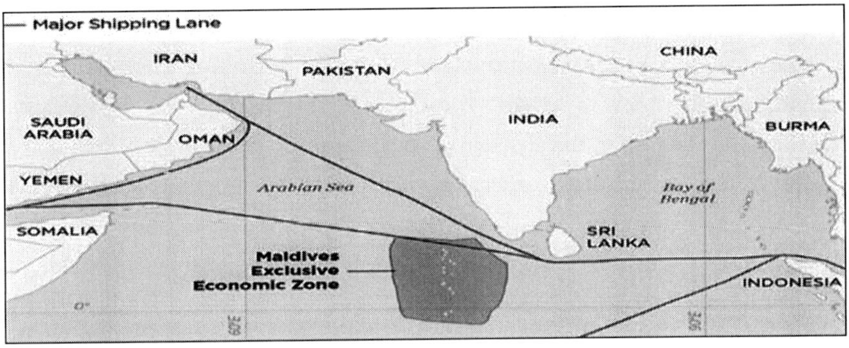

Source: Heritage Foundation Research.

In mid-2011, at the outset of the political turmoil in the Maldives, Politburo Standing committee member Wu Bangguo, a high-ranking Chinese leader, visited Malé. In November 2011, China opened its first embassy in the Maldives. After President Nasheed was deposed in September 2012, President Waheed flew to Xinjiang to meet Prime Minister Wen Jiabao to secure developmental aid. A month later, Li Changchun was welcomed in Malé. The gradual increase in interaction between the leadership of the two states made New Delhi jittery and raised concerns about Malé tilting towards China.[12]

The Maldives has traditionally been New Delhi's friend. The small island nation suffered political turbulence in 2012-2013. Due to domestic political problems, India-Maldives relations suffered considerably. The Maldivian government ended a contract with the Indian company, GMR, to renovate Male airport and the contract was given to a Chinese company. Under President Abdulla Yameen, the Maldives' foreign policy shifted away from its traditional "India First" outlook. It was during President Waheed's tenure that the Maldives started drifting towards China. Under President Yameen, the Maldives took a pro-China turn. The shift in the Maldives' foreign policy outlook is a reflection of Chinese President Xi's promotion of the MSRI in Male, which opened an alternative source for Maldivian leadership to secure financial assistance from Beijing to invest in building infrastructure. Although President Abdulla Yameen, after his election and swearing in, paid a three-day visit to India and promised that ties with New Delhi are "far more precious" and "will precede any other relationship", Yameen deviated from his words and heralded a new era of Sino-Maldives ties.[13]

Yameen's administration even went as far as undertaking a constitutional amendment in order to exploit the opportunity that China's MSRI was offering. The cabinet, in the absence of the opposition party, took a decision to amend Male's Constitution on land ownership by foreigners. It became only the second amendment to the Constitution, overturning a prohibition on land ownership by foreigners and allowing them to purchase land in the Maldives if investment is more than USD 1 billion.

Chinese investment in the Maldives

Since tourism is the main industry in the Maldives, Beijing is eyeing to fund projects that would facilitate the growth of this industry. In the Maldives, the infrastructure projects funded by China are mostly in Malé and the adjacent town of Hulhumalé; the two are commercial and administrative centres of the island nation. The Maldivian government has allocated a large amount of money in developing the area.[14] China has invested in the expansion of the Velana International Airport in Malé and the construction of the Sinamalé bridge connecting it to Hulhumalé. China's export- import bank has funded the expansion of the Velana International Airport. The expansion contract of Velana International Airport was given to Beijing Urban Construction Group, terminating the contract with India's GMR.[15] Earlier, only the terminal was to be constructed, but later on, China agreed to build the whole airport and a second runway as Chinese tourists vacationing in Maldives have been on the increase.[16]

Currently, the Sinamalé bridge, also named as the China-Maldives Friendship Bridge, is being built at a total cost of RMB1.26 billion, with 57.5 per cent of the cost being covered by a grant from the Chinese government. Of the remaining, 36.1 per cent of the cost is in the form of a preferential loan from the Chinese government, and the remaining 6.4 per cent is to be borne by the Maldivian state. All loans are to be repaid with interest to China by the Maldives. Besides the Velana International Airport which has been constructed with Chinese investment, the Hulhumalé Phase II housing project is being carried out with Chinese investment. A fourth project being constructed is a link road between the Hulhulé and Hulhumalé.

Recently, there has been a huge increase in the number of Chinese tourists visiting the Maldives. China is leasing 17 of the 1200 islands of the Maldives. The Sinamalé bridge, built between the islands of Male, Hulhule and Hulhumale in the Maldivian archipelago, has made it possible for Malé's taxi drivers to pick up passengers right from the airport entrance. The bridge built between these islands in the Maldivian archipelago has led to a boom in property and commercial developments on the nearby island of Hulumalé, easing congestion in the capital for its 140,000 residents. In terms of the utility of the bridge, it can be seen as a boost to the Maldives' tourism sector and could be claimed as yet another exemplary connectivity infrastructure funded by China. The idea of linking Male with larger Hulhumale by bridge was first put forward in 2007. Former President Mohammad Nasheed tried to initiate the project, but as he lost the election, the project stalled. It was under Yameen's administration that the construction of the bridge finally kicked off.[17]

Further on, Feydhoo Finolhu is a tiny island with an area of 0.5 square miles, located 3 nautical miles from the Maldivian capital, Malé. A resort is being built at the Feydhoo Finolhu island. The initial speculation was that the island was being used for strategic purposes as a Chinese company bagged the island at a low price of USD 4 million. Since the island is strategically located, monitoring traffic to and from the international airport in Malé can be done easily. A Chinese company bought the islet and started dredging, filling work. It was being contemplated that the wharf or airstrip to be constructed could be used for dual purposes. However, as the resort in Feydhoo Finolhu neared completion by August 2020, doubts about the Finolhu resort's commercial purposes were cleared. Another Chinese developer is building a resort in the Kunavaashi islands, 35 nautical miles from Malé.[18]

Yameen's administration and Sino-Maldives relations

Soon after coming to power, Abdulla Yameen broke away from the traditional "New Delhi first" foreign policy of Malé, forging ties with Beijing. President Abdulla Yameen borrowed millions from China to boost the economy of the Maldives. By 2018, Chinese investments in the Maldives had reached USD 1.5 billion.[19] Though it is not a significant amount, given that China-Maldives bilateral relations started warming up in 2011-2012, it can be seen as a considerable investment from China within a short period. Yameen's tenure saw a rise in Chinese investments and a boost in the economy.

In September 2018, President Ibrahim Mohammed Solih unseated Mr. Yameen, promising to restore democracy in the Maldives. President Ibrahim Solih, in a joint coalition with former President Mohammed Nasheed, who re-entered politics as Speaker, brought charges against Abdulla Yameen of receiving illicit payments from the Chinese government.[20] Due to non-transparent transactions between Yameen's government and China, his administration was seen to adopt authoritarian measures. Under his administration, state repression, intimidation, and surveillance made the political environment in the Maldives unstable. President Yameen had declared a state of emergency after the Supreme Court ordered the release of nine Opposition leaders who criticised Yameen's government for accepting loans from China that would push the country into the debt trap.[21]

As the new government under President Solih took charge, it looked into the Maldives' economic reserves. According to an interview given by former Maldivian President Nasheed, Male owes China between USD 1.1–1.4 bn, which is a huge amount to be paid back to China by a small island nation given that the Maldives' GDP is around USD 4.03 billion, according to official data from the World Bank. The GDP growth rate started rising following the influx of Chinese investment in the country during the Yameen administration.[22] If revenue generation falls short, the Maldives might struggle to repay the loan by 2022-23 and would eventually face the same fate as Sri Lanka. It is illustrative that Sri Lanka, another island nation in the Indian Ocean, borrowed funds from China to reconstruct the country after the civil war ended.[23] Another media report exposed that the Chinese debt amount was USD 3.1 bn. The figure included government-to-government loans, money given to state enterprises, as well as private sector loans promised by the Maldivian government. In 2020, the Maldivian economy, which relies on tourism, was hit hard by coronavirus, cutting down foreign tourists by 55 per cent by the end of June, and estimates were that the country might lose more than USD 700m, which is more than a third of income from tourism.[24]

Challenges to furthering the BRI in South Asia

A survey on the challenges faced by the BRI was conducted by Zhang Hua and Jiang Chen, scholars from the China Academy of Social Sciences. The survey was published on China.com.cn and analysed and summed up more than 60 countries that are located in the BRI- promoted region. It was published consecutively for 30 weeks and contained 60 articles. Zhang Hua and Jiang Chen contend that the internal political development of states located under the canopy of the BRI influences the smooth functioning of the overall BRI strategy. Many states which have the potential to facilitate the BRI are facing various challenges at the international level, namely, major power geopolitical tussle, domestic leadership connections, democratic political transitions, ethnic conflicts, and other myriad challenges. The political challenges of these BRI facilitating countries are a serious obstacle to "going out" and amalgamation of local firms by Chinese firms.[25]

Employment of Chinese nationals exacerbates the local unemployment situation

Recipient countries dependent on financial aid often complain that construction projects under the OBOR, despite huge investment, only employed Chinese workers in construction work and do not generate local employment, leading to rising social discontent. Unemployment is already a key social security challenge in most developing nations of South Asia and China's BRI apparently does not ameliorate existing conditions. Moreover, the loans often create an asymmetric economic dependency between China and other recipient nations, which is used by Beijing to secure its political objectives that are often tied with foreign economic aid.

The construction of the Sinamalé or China-Maldives Friendship Bridge started at the end of 2015 and took 33 months for completion. Chinese engineers and workers were engaged in its construction.[26] This created an anti-Beijing sentiment in Male. China has replicated the practices of its state-owned enterprises (SoEs) in the recipient nations. Chinese construction companies bring along their entire workforce from engineers to workers. A key development challenge in the Maldives is inclusive growth and a sustainable growth model. Despite this, the Maldives has successfully tapped its natural assets and built up a resort- based tourism industry as the main source of economic growth and foreign exchange, but it has limited options in other sectors while being heavily dependent on imported labour, both skilled and unskilled. It can be argued that the BRI, often championed as Xi Jinping's foreign economic initiative, is a re-labelling of the previous Chinese SoE's "Going Out" (走出去*zouchuqu)* strategy.

Like the Sinamalé bridge, during President Mahinda Rajapaksa's tenure, Sri Lanka built the controversial Hambantota port with China's financial assistance, investing about USD 1 billion. In December 2017, after Sri Lanka defaulted in paying its debts, Colombo had to hand over the port to China on a 99- year lease. Reports suggest that Sri Lanka's foreign debt increased from 36 per cent of its GDP in 2010 to 94 per cent in 2015. Almost 95 per cent of government revenue of Sri Lanka went into servicing its debt, and for this, it needed USD 1.5 billion from the International Monetary Fund (IMF). Although Sri Lanka has stated that the security of the port will remain with Sri Lanka, in the long- term it implies the consolidation of Chinese presence in the Indian Ocean.[27] Another example is the BRI flagship initiative in South Asia—the China Pakistan Economic Corridor (CPEC) in Pakistan—under which China has 17,177 soldiers deployed to protect Chinese nationals working on construction projects.[28] All these BRI projects have become a security concern for New Delhi as China is stealthily consolidating its position in the Indian Ocean by executing these projects.

Li Qingyan surmises that there are new situations cropping up in South Asia, which are going to impede further penetration of the BRI in South Asia. After the initial phase of launching the OBOR, what is important for China is the integration of land and sea routes connectivity in the region. However, due to political instability in South Asia, the BRI is facing challenges, especially as India, the dominant power in South Asia, has opposed China's BRI from the very beginning. Subsequently, this has led to a downward spiral in the bilateral relations between India and China, reaching its lowest during the Doklam incident in 2017. The incident completely sabotaged the mutual trust between India and China. Howsoever, India, owing to a strong government and an economic reboot, is regaining its regional influence.[29] Li Qingyan further contends that owing to internal reforms in economic policies under the Modi government, such as reforms in the Goods and Services Tax, a GDP growth rate of 7.2 per cent, and a strong government, New Delhi has pushed the boundaries of foreign policy.[30] After the Modi government implemented the Goods and Services Tax reform, India's GDP growth rate reached 7.2 per cent and a strong government has made it possible to rejuvenate New Delhi's foreign relations.

External commitments of Beijing hampered by its internal priorities

Beijing's efforts of proactive economic diplomacy have been hampered by the country's economic policies that are perceived in the region as self-serving. Even as China's phenomenal growth has brought increased prosperity to the region, it has fuelled anxieties among China's neighbours about competition and overdependence. What Beijing promotes as "win-win" cooperation is perceived in the region as benefitting only China.[31] China's external commitments or the CCP leadership's pledges during high level visits are often not realised due to China's internal priorities.

The Maldives' internal challenges: Implications in furthering the Maritime Silk Road Initiative (MSRI)

The radicalisation of Maldivian youth is a challenge that not only poses threat to the Maldivian society but also the stability of the region. During Yameen's tenure, many Maldivian youth were recruited into the Islamic State.[32] Under the Yameen administration, the Maldives has seen the rise of radical Islam. In order to secure popular support, Yameen criticised his opponent as an anti-Islam candidate. These developments led to the outflow of foreign investments from the country, and due to the declining state of ease of doing business, the country does not provide investors' with a suitable business environment. A research article by Yang Siling points out that democratic polity is becoming an obstacle in cooperation between China and South Asian nations participating in the BRI. The article observes that in South Asia, most of the states have democratic governments. As in a democracy, there are power transitions due to which BRI projects often suffer from an uncertain political environment, instability is another factor—often it is seen that a new government might terminate contracts and policies adopted by preceding governments. Divided interests within political parties are perceived as a challenge in executing the BRI in South Asia. Yang Siling highlighted concerns about how often opposition political parties raise an issue with the BRI projects, specially relating to debt trap or illegitimate payments from Chinese firms or governments, to unseat the ruling party.[33] For example, in the case of the Maldivian BRI projects, Ibrahim Solih's government accused Yameen's administration of graft charges. The observations made by Yang Siling are not without proof as there has been a decline in the business environment in the Maldives due to political turmoil. A media report on a Chinese website mentioned the Maldives as slipping to 116th position in the Doing Business report, 2015, published by the World Bank. In 2020, Maldives again slipped further to 147th rank on the same index.

Despite the declining ease of business environment, the Chinese report provides a positive outlook on investment in the Maldives. The report enumerates several investment friendly conditions that make the Maldives worthwhile for China to invest in, such as its geostrategic advantageous location and established business and corporate laws.[34] Further, the absence of exchange control legislation enables both residents and non-residents to freely import and export capital. Foreign direct investment (FDI) requires approval from the government and permission is easily obtainable in the Maldives. In fact, there is no restriction on repatriation of profits.[35] The overall trade policy adopted by the Maldives is open and aims at maintaining a conducive environment for commerce and economic activity.[36]

In 2015, in an emergency sitting of Majlis without the presence of the opposition, Yameen's administration decided to enter into a free trade agreement (FTA) with China. The opposition party—the Maldivian Democratic Party (MDP)—claimed that the national security committee vetted China's proposition of a free trade agreement in 10 minutes and further evoked concerns that the nation would eventually come under the Chinese debt trap and national strategic assets would come under stress. Economic considerations about the development of the Maldives prompted Yameen's administration to consider China's proposition of a FTA.[37] The Maldives became the second country in South Asia to sign a free trade agreement with China.[38] For China, the Maldives' location in the Indian Ocean makes bilateral relations significant to further propagate the Maritime Silk Route (MSR) in South Asia.

Rising concerns in New Delhi: The Maldives is vulnerable to Beijing's debt trap

The drifting away of other smaller South Asian states from the "New Delhi First" foreign policy and the growing presence of Beijing in New Delhi's strategic backyard is a concern for New Delhi.[39] New Delhi, under its "Neighbourhood First" foreign policy, has extended support to build the Maldives' economy and has restored stability in the country promptly, as and when required by the Maldivian government. Around a half of India's external trade and a bulk of its energy imports transit the International Shipping Lanes where the Maldives is naturally placed like a "toll gate" between two major chokepoints.[40] Moreover, its geographical proximity to the western coast of India, for obvious reasons, might create tension in New Delhi when Chinese warships dock in Male for friendly visits, which include the training session for the Maldivian National Defense Force and visits to the military base at Girifushi.[41] This expanding Chinese presence is a nightmare for New Delhi, given the Maldives's minimal distance from India's naval bases. INS Venduruthy is stationed approx. 800 km away from Girifushi.

China's interaction in South Asia cuts into New Delhi's sphere of influence

The Centre for Global Development considers that among the South Asian smaller nations, the Maldives is most vulnerable to debt under China's BRI. As a country transitions from the status of low income developing nation to middle income developing nation, it faces difficulties in availing concessional loans from the international development finance system.[42] On reaching the per capita income level of a middle income country, the debt repayment schedule gets tightened. Samaranayake points out that the Maldives' debt to China is about 8.6 per cent of its total debt and 27 per cent of its external debt.

Howsoever, Samaranayake also highlights that in the case of small states, debt-trap diplomacy of China is often highlighted, but what is often overlooked is that under the "middle income trap", a developing small state often is unable to pay its debt on schedule.[43] Samaranayake contends that for such states, China is considered as a fallback option and not a primary source of assistance. The leadership across countries in South Asia still perceive India as the dominant power and as the net security provider. Even though China's economic activity in the region is galloping, Beijing might find it hard to displace New Delhi's sphere of influence. This would be enhanced by India's reach in the region as an economic and military power across swathes of the Indian Ocean.

India's influence in the region has been on the decline as trade and commercial activity with its neighbours has slowed down. India's trade growth with South Asian countries between 1991 and 1999 was minimal. In 2008, India's trade with its neighbours reached a decade-high of almost USD 13.45 billion. Following a dip in 2009 due to the global financial crisis, India's trade with its neighbours doubled in the next five years, reaching USD 24.69 billion in 2014. The slowdown in India's exports to South Asia in 2015 and 2016 coincided with a 13 per cent decline in India's global trade from USD 19 trillion in 2014 to USD 16.5 trillion in 2015. There was a revival of intra-regional trade in 2017, reaching its peak at USD 24.75 billion, and picking up further in 2018 when it rose to USD 36 billion.

Figure 2.2: China-India Trade in South Asia

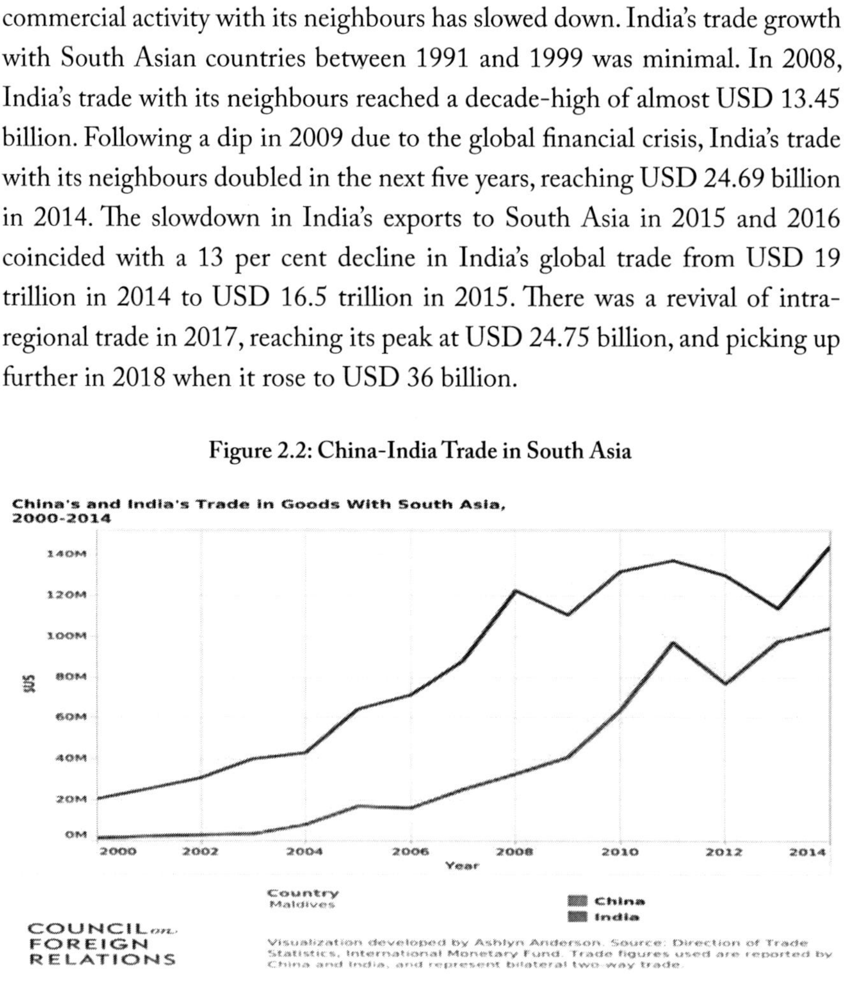

Source: Council on Foreign Relations.

Although there are several intra-regional trade agreements, such as the South Asian Association of Regional Cooperation Preferential Free Trade Agreement (SACPTA) and the South Asian Free Trade Agreement

(SAFTA), they have failed to promote intra-regional trade. The existing trade barriers push the cost of trading in South Asia much higher.[44] Meanwhile, driven by an export- oriented trade, China, since the last two decades, has made a breakthrough in the region. This certainly has given New Delhi a jolt.

India re-engaging in the neighbourhood

As an offshoot of these realistic considerations, Indian Prime Minister Narendra Modi has been reemphasising India's diplomatic ties with its South Asian neighbours. Recently, New Delhi has been reengaging with its smaller neighbouring states in South Asia. In 2015-16, New Delhi extended funds to Bhutan in order to maintain its influence in the country. Nepal was given USD 1 billion for post-earthquake reconstruction. It underpins the thought that India can still assert itself in its traditional sphere of influence and be a counterweight to China.[45] Afghanistan Prime Minister Haneef Atmar met both Prime Minister Modi and Foreign Affairs Minister S. Jaishankar, following which, India, for the first time in 20 years, participated in the Afghan talks. The Indian leadership wished the Pakistani Prime Minister, Imran Khan, a speedy recovery from COVID-19.[46] Prime Minister Modi visited the Maldives and Sri Lanka in 2019 after commencing his second term. He was making up for the lost opportunities by reassuring a "Neighbourhood First" foreign policy to the smaller neighbouring states.[47]

Following Modi's visit to the Maldives, a team from the Exim Bank also visited the island nation and signed a Line of Credit Agreement for USD 400 million for the Greater Male Connectivity Project (GMCP). The GMCP is a 6.7 km bridge and causeway network connecting Male, Villingili, Gulhifalhu, and Thilafushi.[48] The team also held discussions to assess the progress on seven other mega projects for which a USD 800 million Line of Credit was extended. The projects include developing an international airport at Gulhifalhu, water supply and sewerage networks, roads and storm water drainage in Addu atoll, a cancer hospital in Hulhumale, expanding the Hanimaadhoo Airport, and a cricket stadium in Hulhumale.[49] Foreign Minister Jaishankar also visited New Delhi's Indian Ocean neighbours, the Maldives and Mauritius. Amid the Covid-19 pandemic situation, the Indian Foreign Affairs Minister visited both the countries as part of India's maritime security agenda. Both the countries decided to upgrade security and defence partnerships in order to combat terrorism. India also committed assistance in upgrading Male's maritime surveillance capabilities. India also promised help in developing and maintaining a Maldives National Defense Force Coast Guard Harbour at Sifavaru. After his meeting with the Maldivian defence and foreign minister, Jaishankar referred to the Maldives as a "reliable security partner".[50] A race for infrastructure development is an indicator of geopolitical rivalry between India and China. Indian strategic analyst Manoj Joshi contends the Maldives is highly significant for India's national security given its geographical proximity. "There's nothing India can do in the Maldives to affect Chinese security, but there's a lot Chinese can do in the Maldives to affect Indian security."[51] He contends the increased frequency in visits by Indian leadership and officials indicate New Delhi's renewed attention in its maritime backyard.

Another obstruction to China in furthering BRI projects in South Asia is negative perception. Several policy makers in India believe that there are loopholes in Chinese arguments in promoting the BRI in South Asia, particularly in India. Jacob argues that Chinese discourse on promoting the BRI in the region pushed India to think of different ways to promote regional connectivity, such as the Bangladesh-Bhutan-India-Nepal (BBIN) connectivity project announced by the Modi government. Jacob also states that any progress in the South Asian Association of Regional Cooperation is dependent on India-Pakistan dynamics. This is more pertinent as Chinese Premier Li Keqiang, during his visit to India in May 2013 to launch the Bangladesh-China-India-Myanmar Economic Corridor (BCIM-EC), instead of discussing the intricacies of making BRI projects operational, went to Pakistan to launch the China-Pakistan Economic Corridor (CPEC) passing through Pakistan-occupied Kashmir, thereby challenging India's territorial sovereignty.[52] Without addressing India's sensitivities, Beijing launched the China-Pakistan Economic Corridor. Therefore, the BRI actually undermined India's position in South Asia.[53] Also, in 2017, Chinese warships docked in the Maldives for a training session, which began to indicate that India's status as a dominant power and primary regional partner of the Maldives had been challenged.[54] However, China has its own concerns about the successful implementation of the BRI in South Asia as most of the South Asian states have military ties with India. Also, since New Delhi is the net security provider in the region, the geographically smaller states in the region are obliged to take into account New Delhi's security concerns.[55]

Recently, however, it has been observed that Maldivian President Yameen welcomed Beijing's involvement in the Maldives' internal crisis in order to stay in power. Amid the political crisis in the Maldives when President Abdulla Yameen ordered the arrest of judges of the Supreme Court of the country along with the former President and declared a state of emergency, what seemed an internal power struggle had wider geopolitical ramifications and spiralled into a power struggle between India and China.

Conclusion

The Indian Ocean region has today become a theatre of power struggle between India and China. By engaging with the smaller southern states and littorals, Beijing has slowly moved into the Indian Ocean region. China's economic assistance under the BRI projects to promote infrastructure build-up in the Indian Ocean littoral region can be seen in the light of '*biding time as it builds up its capability*' to rival India's sphere of influence. Beijing is mindful of the fact that while an overt Chinese military presence in the region might push the smaller Indian Ocean littoral states to come together against China, a more benign approach would create room for manoeuvre. The way forward for New Delhi is to maintain stability in the Indian Ocean region and encourage the smaller South Asian states to receive financial assistance from foreign countries, but in a more transparent and democratic way. Also, New Delhi itself needs to extend strategic assistance to the smaller littoral states, elevating the living conditions of the population in these states. Maintaining close communication with the leadership to build trust through diverse capacity building would be another priority for India. Besides this, India also needs to actively implement a maritime security strategy.

Notes

1. Shortage of Quality Infrastructure in South Asia Impedes Growth—ADB, https://www.adb.org/news/shortage-quality-infrastructure-south-asia-impedes-growth-adb. Accessed on July 7, 2021.
2. Chinoy, Sujan R. (2019) Round Table Discussion on "China's Policy Towards South Asia: Implications for India.

3. Xiaoping, Yang, https://warontherocks.com/2018/04/when-indias-strategic-backyard-meets-chinas-strategic-periphery-the-view-from-beijing/. Accessed on April 20, 2021.
4. Chinoy, Sujan R. (2019) Round Table Discussion on China's Policy Towards South Asia: Implications for India, https://idsa.in/event/rt-chinas-policy-towards-south-asia-120719. Accessed on June 6, 2021.
5. India losing ground in trade with Bangladesh, https://www.eastasiaforum.org/2011/08/20/india-losing-ground-to-china-on-trade-with-bangladesh/
6 https://thediplomat.com/2019/03/chinas-vision-for-the-belt-and-road-in-south-asia/#:~:text=Theper cent20longper cent2Dtermper cent20Chineseper cent20vision,andpercent20evenpercent20thepercent20Eurasianpercent 20continent.
7. China's Trade with India's neighbours has grown stronger since 2005. Delhi must catch up, https://theprint.in/opinion/chinas-trade-with-indias-neighbours-has-grown-stronger-since-2005-delhi-must-catch-up/433327/
8. India's limited trade connectivity with South Asia https://www.brookings.edu/research/indias-limited-trade-connectivity-with-south-asia/
9 https://www.csis.org/analysis/chinas-maritime-silk-road-initiative-economic-drivers-and-challenges
10. Anderson, Ashlyn and Alyssa Ayres Economics of Influence: China and India in South Asia, https://www.cfr.org/expert-brief/economics-influence-china-and-india-south-asia
11 https://idsa.in/askanexpert/what-is-the-geo-strategic-importance-of-maldives what is the geostrategic importance of Maldives to India?
12 https://foreign.gov.mv/index.php/en/mediacentre/news/1375-member-of-the-politburo-standing-committee-of-cpc-arrives-in-maldives
13 https://www.heritage.org/global-politics/report/china-and-the-maldives-lessons-the-indian-oceans-new-battleground
14 https://amti.csis.org/chinese-investment-in-the-maldives-appraising-the-string-of-pearls/ Chinese Investment in Maldives: Appraising the String of Pearls. Accessed on April 28, 2021.
15 https://amti.csis.org/chinese-investment-in-the-maldives-appraising-the-string-of-pearls/ Chinese Investment in Maldives: Appraising the String of Pearls. Accessed on April 28, 2021 .
16 https://www.globalsecurity.org/military/world/indian-ocean/mv-forrel-prc.htm
17. Chinese Investment in the Maldives: Appraising the String of Pearls https://amti.csis.org/chinese-investment-in-the-maldives-appraising-the-string-of-pearls/

18 https://amti.csis.org/chinese-investment-in-the-maldives-appraising-the-string-of-pearls/

19 https://globalriskinsights.com/2018/07/indias-concerns-over-the-strengthened-china-maldives-relations/

20 https://www.bbc.com/news/world-asia-52743072

21 https://www.thehindu.com/news/international/maldives-court-orders-arrest-of-former-president-abdulla-yameen-over-alleged-corruption/article26304101.ece

22 https://tradingeconomics.com/maldives/gdp#:~:text=GDPpercent20inper cent20Maldivespercent20ispercent20expected,accordingpercent20topercent 20ourper cent20econometricper cent20models. Maldives GDP

23 https://www.bbc.com/news/world-asia-52743072 Ethirajan Anbarasan, China debt dogs Maldives bridge to prosperity. Accessed on May 1, 2021.

24 https://economictimes.indiatimes.com/news/international/world-news/chinese-debt-casts-shadow-over-maldives-economy/articleshow/78172615.cms?from=mdr Chinese debt casts shadow over Maldives economy

25 http://www.china.com.cn/opinion/think/2015-04/17/content_35347672.htm 一带一路投资风险研究之马尔代夫张华姜晨。

26 https://www.chinadaily.com.cn/a/201909/04/WS5d6e0b92a310cf 3e3556972e_1.html

27 https://thediplomat.com/2018/09/china-expands-its-footprint-in-sri-lanka/ https://thediplomat.com/2019/01/rajapaksas-town-a-visit-to-hambantota/

28 https://www.thenews.com.pk/print/82009-17177-soldiers-deployed-for-security-of-Chinese-workers-of-CPEC

29 https://www.ciis.org.cn/yjcg/xslw/202007/t20200710_1073.html

30 Ibid.

31. Jhonson Christopher K., (2016 March) President Xi Jinping's "Belt and Road" Initiative A practical assessment of the Chinese Communist Party's Roadmap for China's Global Resurgence A Report of the Freeman Chair in China Studies. Centre for Strategic and International Studies.

32. Wright, Oliver Islamic State: The Maldives- a recruiting paradise for Jihadists https://www.independent.co.uk/news/world/asia/islamic-state-maldives-recruiting-paradise-jihadists-9731574.html Trouble in Paradise https://www.aljazeera.com/program/101-east/2019/10/31/maldives-trouble-in-paradise

33 http://www.cssn.cn/gjgxx/gj_ytqy/202011/t20201113_5216125.shtml一带一路倡议维度中的

34. Hua, Zhang, Jing Chen 一带一路投资风险研究之马尔代夫http://www.china.com.cn/opinion/think/2015-04/17/content_35347672.htm

35. World Trade Organization Trade Policy Review Body 2009.

36. Ibid.

37. Mallempati, Dr. Samatha, The Visit of President of Maldives to China, Indian Council for World Affairs March 2018 https://icwa.in/show_content.php?lang=1&level=3&ls_id=2359&lid=1626
38. Maldives Parliament Approves FTA with China-But with no opposition present *The Wire*, https://thewire.in/diplomacy/maldives-parliament-approves-fta-china-amidst-opposition-boycott. Accessed on 30 November 2017.
39. Ramachandran, Sudha The China-Maldives Connection https://thediplomat.com/2018/01/the-china-maldives-connection/
40 https://idsa.in/askanexpert/what-is-the-geo-strategic-importance-of-maldives
41 https://edition.mv/news/4072 Three Warships of Chinese Navy on friendly visit to Maldives.
42. Samaranayake, Nilanthi China's Engagement with Smaller South Asian Countries, https://www.usip.org/sites/default/files/2019-04/sr_446-chinas_engagement_with_smaller_south_asian_countries.pdf
43. Samaranayake, Nilanthi China's Engagement with Smaller South Asian Countries, https://www.usip.org/sites/default/files/2019-04/sr_446-chinas_engagement_with_smaller_south_asian_countries.pdf
44. Sinha Riya, Sareen Niara India's limited trade connectivity with South Asia, https://www.brookings.edu/research/indias-limited-trade-connectivity-with-south-asia/
45. Economics of influence: China and India in South Asia. https://www.cfr.org/expert-brief/economics-influence-china-and-india-south-asia
46. From Kabul to Islamabad and Dhaka, Modi asserts India Influence in South Asia will match China, https://www.youtube.com/watch?v=Wgc3rqtQ1Kg&t=13s
47 https://thediplomat.com/2019/06/modi-regaining-lost-opportunities-in-the-maldives-and-sri-lanka/ Upadhyaya, Shishir Modi Regaining Lost Opportunities in the Maldives and Sri Lanka
48 https://economictimes.indiatimes.com/news/economy/finance/india-signs-line-of-credit-pact-with-maldives-for-financing-major-connectivity-project/articleshow/78617443.cms India signs Line of Credit Pact with Madives for financing major connectivity project
49 https://www.southasiamonitor.org/region/indias-exim-bank-extends-400-mn-line-credit-maldives India's Exim Bank extend $400 million Line of Credit to Maldives.
50 https://thediplomat.com/2021/02/jaishankar-reaches-out-to-delhis-indian-ocean-partners/ Rajagopalan, Rajeswari Jaishankar reaches out to New Delhi's Indian Ocean partners. Accessed on April 2021.
51 https://edition.cnn.com/2020/11/24/asia/maldives-india-china-bridges-intl-hnk/index.html

52. Jacob, T Jabin "What does India think of China's "Belt and Road" Initiative"? https://icsin.org/uploads/2018/01/18/d19243ff5a8988734f076f02a59e55ca.pdf. Accessed on May 23, 2021.
53. Ibid.
54 https://thediplomat.com/2018/03/the-maldives-crisis-and-the-china-india-chess-match/
55. Samaranayake, Nilanthi China's Engagement with smaller South Asian Countries, https://www.usip.org/sites/default/files/2019-04/sr_446-chinas_engagement_with_smaller_south_asian_countries.pdf

References

Anderson, Ashlyn and Alyssa Ayres, "Economics of Influence: China and India in South Asia", Council for Foreign Relations, https://www.cfr.org/expert-brief/economics-influence-china-and-india-south-asia. Accessed on April 2021.

"China's Trade with India's neighbours has grown stronger since 2005. Delhi must catch up", https://theprint.in/opinion/chinas-trade-with-indias-neighbours-has-grown-stronger-since-2005-delhi-must-catch-up/433327/

"Chinese Investment in Maldives: Appraising the String of Pearls", (September 4, 2020), Asia Maritime Transparency Initiative, https://amti.csis.org/chinese-investment-in-the-maldives-appraising-the-string-of-pearls/. Accessed on April 28, 2021.

"Chinese debt casts shadow over Maldives economy", *The Economic Times,* https://economictimes.indiatimes.com/news/international/world-news/chinese-debt-casts-shadow-over-maldives-economy/articleshow/78172615.cms?from=mdr. Accessed on May 29, 2021.

"China Maldives Friendship Bridge brings convenience for locals", https://www.chinadaily.com.cn/a/201909/04/WS5d6e0b92a310cf3e3556972e_1.html Xinhua 2019. Accessed on May 2021.

Ethirajan, Anbarasan (September 2020), "China debt dogs 'Maldives bridge to prosperity'", https://www.bbc.com/news/world-asia-52743072, *BBC News.* Accessed on June 8, 2021.

Funaiole, Mathew P. and Jonathan E. Hillman, Centre for Strategic and International Studies (2018), "China's Maritime Silk Road Initiative Drivers and Challenges", https://www.csis.org/analysis/chinas-maritime-silk-road-initiative-economic-drivers-and-challenges. Accessed on April 20, 2021.

Hua Zhang and Jing Chen, "Study on BRI Investment challenges in Maldives" 一带一路投资风险研究之马尔代夫 Think China.com http://www.china.com.cn/opinion/think/2015-04/17/content_35347672.htm. Accessed on April 2021.

"Islamic State: The Maldives a recruiting paradise for Jihadists", September 2014, https://www.independent.co.uk/news/world/asia/islamic-state-maldives-recruiting-paradise-jihadists-9731574.html. Accessed on April 2021.

Jhonson, Christopher K., (March 2016), "President Xi Jinping's "Belt and Road" Initiative: A practical assessment of the Chinese Communist Party's Roadmap for China's Global Resurgence", Centre for Strategic and International Studies. Accessed on May 2021.

Kumar, Sunaina and Angela Stanzel (2018), "The Maldives Crisis and China India Chess Match", *The Diplomat,* https://thediplomat.com/2018/03/the-maldives-crisis-and-the-china-india-chess-match/. Accessed on June 2021.

Li Qingyan, "New Developments in South Asia will impact the functioning of BRI in the region李清燕南亚局势新动向对"一带一路"在南亚推进的影响", 29 October 2018, China Institute of International Studies, https://www.ciis.org.cn/yjcg/xslw/202007/t20200710_1073.html

"Maldives Court orders arrest of former President Abdulla Yameen over alleged corruption", 2019, *The Hindu,*https://www.thehindu.com/news/international/maldives-court-orders-arrest-of-former-president-abdulla-yameen-over-alleged-corruption/article26304101.ece. Accessed on June 3, 2021.

"Maldives Parliament Approves FTA with China-But with no opposition present", *The Wire,* 30/11/2017, https://thewire.in/diplomacy/maldives-parliament-approves-fta-china-amidst-opposition-boycott. Accessed on April 2021.

Mallempati, Dr. Samatha, "The Visit of President of Maldives to China", Indian Council for World Affairs (March 2018), https://icwa.in/show_content.php?lang=1&level=3&ls_id=2359&lid=1626. Accessed on April 2021.

"Member of the Politburo Standing Committee of CPC arrives in Maldives", 19th October 2012, https://foreign.gov.mv/index.php/en/mediacentre/news/1375-member-of-the-politburo-standing-committee-of-cpc-arrives-in-maldives Ministry of Foreign Affairs Republic of Maldives. Accessed on June 2021.

Ramchandran, Sudha (September 11, 2018), "China Expands Its Footprint in Sri Lanka", *The Diplomat,* https://thediplomat.com/2018/09/china-expands-its-footprint-in-sri-lanka/. Accessed on April 2021.

Ramachandran, Sudha (October 28, 2020), "The China-Maldives Connection", *The Diplomat,* https://thediplomat.com/2018/01/the-china-maldives-connection/. Accessed on May 2021.

Sahoo, Pravakar (August 20, 2011), "India losing ground in trade with Bangladesh", East Asia Forum, https://www.eastasiaforum.org/2011/08/20/india-losing-ground-to-china-on-trade-with-bangladesh/

Samaranayake, Nilanthi, "China's Engagement with Smaller South Asian countries", https://www.usip.org/sites/default/files/2019-04/sr_446-chinas_engagement_with_smaller_south_asian_countries.pdf. Accessed on April 2021.

"Shortage of Quality Infrastructure in South Asia Impedes Growth—ADB", (2018), Asian Development Bank, https://www.adb.org/news/shortage-quality-infrastructure-south-asia-impedes-growth-adb. Accessed on June 7, 2021.

Singh, Antara Ghoshal (2019), "China's Vision for the Belt and Road in South Asia: What progress has BRI made in South Asia thus far", *The Diplomat,* https://thediplomat.com/2019/03/chinas-vision-for-the-belt-and-road-in-south-asia/#!#:~:text=Thepercent20long-termpercent20Chinesepercent20vision, andper cent20evenper cent20theper cent20Eurasianper cent20continent

Sinha, Riya and Niara Sareen (May 26, 2020), "India's limited trade connectivity with South Asia", https://www.brookings.edu/research/indias-limited-trade-connectivity-with-south-asia/, Brookings. Accessed on April 28, 2021.

Singh, Abhay Kumar (June 03, 2019), "What is the geostrategic importance of Maldives to India?", https://idsa.in/askanexpert/what-is-the-geo-strategic-importance-of-maldives, Manohar Parrikar Institute of Defence Studies and Analyses. Accessed on April 17, 2021.

Singh, Malvika (July 9, 2018), "India's concerns over the strengthened China-Maldives relations", https://globalriskinsights.com/2018/07/indias-concerns-over-the-strengthened-china-maldives-relations/ Global Risk Insights. Accessed on May 29, 2021.

Smith, Jeff M. (October 28, 2020), "China and the Maldives Lessons from the Indian Ocean's New Battleground", The Heritage Foundation, https://www.heritage.org/global-politics/report/china-and-the-maldives-lessons-the-indian-oceans-new-battleground. Accessed on April 2021.

"17,177 soldiers deployed for security of Chinese workers of CPEC", December 15, 2015, https://www.thenews.com.pk/print/82009-17177-soldiers-deployed-for-security-of-Chinese-workers-of-CPEC, *The News International.* Accessed on May 2021.

"Three Warships of Chinese Navy on friendly visit to Maldives", 2017, *The Edition,* https://edition.mv/news/4072. Accessed on June 2021.

"Trouble in Paradise", 2019, *Al Jazeera,* https://www.aljazeera.com/program/101-east/2019/10/31/maldives-trouble-in-paradise. Accessed on May 2021.

Yang Siling, Source: Indian Ocean Economic Cluster Research China Social Sciences Internet, http://www.cssn.cn/gjgxx/gj_ytqy/202011/t20201113_5216125.shtml. Accessed on May 2021.

Yang, Xiaoping (April 20, 2018), "When India's Strategic Backyard Meets China's Strategic Periphery: The View from Beijing", https://warontherocks.com/2018/04/when-indias-strategic-backyard-meets-chinas-strategic-periphery-the-view-from-beijing/, *War on the Rocks.* Accessed on May 20, 2021.

3

China's BRI and Responses from Provinces: The Case of Fujian Province

Md. Yasin

The Belt and Road Initiative (BRI) is an ambitious Chinese plan to improve the country's economy and further its geopolitical interests by improving its connectivity with Europe and the rest of Asia. The BRI—a signature project of President Xi Jinping—is envisioned to advance Beijing's economic and political interests. Following its announcement in 2013, a wide range of geopolitical and geostrategic studies on the BRI have surfaced, but not many studies have covered the role of provincial governments and their response to the BRI. While it is the international aspects that drive a grandiose BRI, there is a need to understand how Chinese provinces have responded to this initiative. What are the gaps between the central government's policy formulation and implementation at the provincial level, and where does Fujian province stand as the 'core area' of the Maritime Silk Road? This study argues that the notion of the Chinese central government's sole ability to design the BRI as a grand strategy is incorrect. Rather, the BRI is ingrained in China's subnational practices and bears huge implications on its provinces. The pronouncement of Chinese President Xi Jinping's signature project, 'One Belt, One Road' (一带一路*yidaiyilu*), begs the question: is there any major takeaway from China's foreign policy strategy? It would appear so.

With Xi Jinping as President, Beijing has put forward a series of project and plans, including the most ambitious BRI, comprising the 'Silk Road Economic Belt' (SREB) that goes to Europe via Xi'an, Xinjiang, Central Asia, Moscow, Rotterdam, and Venice, and the '21st Century Maritime Silk Road' (MSR), connecting China with South Asia, Southeast Asia, East Asia, and the Mediterranean via the South China Sea, the Indian Ocean, and the Arabian Sea. The BRI mainly involves large-scale investment and infrastructure projects aimed at consolidation, cooperation of China's outreach, and restrengthening connectivity between China and the world. While Beijing's official rhetoric points to 'common development' and 'win-win' for all parties concerned, as well as the idea of a 'community with a shared future for mankind', several analyses indicate China's desire to play a greater role by perfecting its 'going-out strategy' (*zouchuqu*), leveraging its economic clout, and challenging the existing US-led global order. China has, in a nutshell, envisaged the BRI as an instrument to advance its national interests, including the logic of domestic economy, reducing its excessive and unnecessary investment, and subsequently, shifting the industrial overcapacity to outside China's borders.

The BRI is one manifestation of China's governing philosophy that the country has held since the 1990s. The Chinese leadership had long continued the policy of 'concealing strengths and biding its time' (韬光养晦*taoguangyanghui*) prescribed by then paramount leader, Deng Xiaoping. However, with Xi Jinping in office, China embarked on a major foreign policy overdrive, bringing its vision for building a 'community with shared future for mankind' (人类命运共同体*renleimingyungongtongti*) as a cornerstone of its (peripheral) diplomacy and geopolitical calculus that revolves around the Eurasian space and beyond. It is evident from the speeches and writings of Chinese leaders and policy advisors that a conceptual modification as well as a new direction of Chinese policy has surfaced—'Striving for Achievement'[1] (奋发有为*fenfayouwei*)—to realise the 'China dream' at a global stage (Xuetong, 2014; Zhongying, 2020; Yanqing, 2013; Hongying, 2014; Xinhua). With China's growing economic strength and diplomatic dexterity, Beijing started combining new ideas (China Dream), new institutions (AIIB), and new projects (BRI) to promote its new vision of global governance (William A. Callahan. 2016, p.1). In 2017, Beijing formally proposed a 'new outlook of global governance' (*xinxingquanqiuzhiliguan*) (Pang Zhongying, 2020, p. 11), and the BRI evidently fits well within this vision. But, apart from the factors driving a grandiose BRI, how do Chinese provinces respond to this initiative? What are the gaps between the central government's policy formulation and implementation at the provincial level, and where does Fujian province stand as the 'core area of MSR'? This paper attempts to answer some of these questions.

Contrary to the traditional view that the BRI is the initiative of China's top leadership and is driven by important international aspects, this study argues that various domestic factors have been instrumental in the making of the BRI, and on many occasions, it is just a continuation of existing policies or revival programmes, for instance, the 'Great Western Development' (西部大开发*xibudakaifa*) or local governments preferred varied narratives or interpretation of the strategy to advance their own interests. Thus, contrary to the notion of the BRI being a top-down coherent grand strategy of the central government, there are 'yawning gaps' (Naughton, 2016, p. 43) between policy intent of the central government and implementation by China's provinces, most notably in Fujian, Guangdong, and Yunnan. In other words, a '*de facto* federalism' existed in China's policy operations vis-à-vis the BRI. The argument is based on novel insights from a case study of Fujian's involvement in the BRI policymaking-bargaining and implementation.

The BRI: Definition, Decision-making and Domestic Dynamics

The BRI is an ambitious Chinese plan to improve its economy and further its geopolitical interests by improving its connectivity with Europe and the rest of Asia. There are two major projects within this plan: the 'Silk Road Economic Belt' (SREB) and the '21st Century Maritime Silk Road' (MSR) that President Xi Jinping elaborated during his state visit to Central Asia (Kazakhstan) in September 2013 and to Indonesia in October 2013. The initiative envisions to 'promote connectivity, tap market potential, promote investment and consumption, create demands and job opportunities, enhance people-to-people and cultural exchanges, and mutual learning' between China and Eurasian countries (NDRC 2015). According to "Vision and Actions on Jointly Building Silk Road Economic Belt and 21st Century Maritime Silk Road" (hereafter V&A Document), the SREB is designed to create a network of rail routes and overland roads, and oil and natural gas pipelines, by bringing together Western China and Europe via Xi'an, Xinjiang, Central Asia, Moscow, Rotterdam, and Venice. The MSR, on the other hand, focuses on connecting China with South Asia, Southeast Asia, East Asia, and the Mediterranean via the South China Sea, the Indian Ocean and the Arabian Sea, by building a network of ports and other coastal infrastructure projects (NDRC, 2015). Moreover, as part of Beijing's grand strategy, the BRI is envisioned to play a key role in China's relations with its neighbours and beyond.

There are two categories of engagement vis-à-vis the BRI: economic and diplomatic. The economic affairs are conducted under the aegis of the Ministry of Finance and Commerce (MOFCOM), the National Development and Reform Commission (NDRC), and the Central Bank, while the Ministry of Foreign Affairs is responsible for the diplomatic affairs. To this end, the decision adopted at the 3rd Plenary Session of the 18th CPC Central Committee on November 12, 2013, stated, 'We will set up development-oriented financial institutions, accelerate the construction of infrastructure connecting China with neighbouring countries and regions, and work hard to build a Silk Road Economic Belt and a Maritime Silk Road, so as to form a new pattern of all-round opening'.[2] Subsequently, the Memorandum of Understanding for the Asian Infrastructure Investment Bank (AIIB) was signed in October 2014, and the Silk Road Fund was set up in November the same year. Thus, the colossal scope of the BRI project is to be financed by newly established financial institutions, such as the AIIB (USD 100 billion), along with the USD 40 billion Silk Road Fund, and Chinese banks, such as the Export-Import Bank. In total, Beijing is expected to spend nearly USD 1 trillion on the initiative (*The Economist*, 2015).

Following Xi Jinping's announcement in 2013, a wide-ranging variety of geopolitical and geostrategic studies on China's BRI have surfaced. This initiative is a 'well thought-out grand strategy … to reclaim (China's) geopolitical dominance in Asia … (realize) China dream … (challenge) the US dominance…and create a Chinese-centered order' (Bhattacharya, 2016, p. 310). Furthermore, it is described as 'a grand global strategy for achieving the "Chinese Dream" (Rumi Aoyama, 2016, p. 3). Lee, Wainwright, and Glassman (2018, p. 427) have encapsulated the purposes of the BRI into three major narratives: the BRI as a 'geo-economic or commercial project to facilitate a cross-continental flow of capital, commodities, labour, and resources through infrastructure construction or a "spatial fix" to China's industrial overcapacity problem'; a strategic move for realising Beijing's ambition in 'classical and realist geopolitical fashion'; and as 'a geopolitical-economic strategy to not only counter US imperialist efforts to isolate China but also to promote South-South cooperation'.

To this end, Shi Yinhong (2015) sees the BRI as containing a component of 'strategic economy' (*zhanluejingji*) as well as 'strategic military' (*zhanluejunshi*). As cited by Swaine (2015, p.15), a group of military and civilian observers underscore military-related strategic implications of the BRI, which include 'the need to strengthen the security of maritime and land transport routes, to reduce territorial disputes, enhance anti-terrorism efforts, and deepen the joint exploitation of strategic resources'. Chinese scholar Wang Yiwei (2015, p. 2) opines that the BRI is 'a road of friendship and prosperity, a road of exchange and mutual respect', which offers 'new standards of globalization' (p. 29) contrary to the globalisation of 'Western civilization'. Yong Wang (2016, pp. 3-5) argues that the combined challenges of China's economic slowdown, US pivot to Asia (later renamed as 'rebalancing strategy'), and deterioration of relations with neighbouring countries following the Global Financial Crisis of 2008 may be considered the crucial drivers for the BRI initiative. Zhao Lei (2015) sees the BRI (culturally) as playing a role in 'China's civilizational rise', while Zheng Yongnian (2015, pp. 197-200) views it as a moral alternative in which China is guiding the values of the post-American global 'zeitgeist' (shidaijingshen时代精神).

Although the geopolitical and geostrategic analyses point to an ambitious initiative of the Chinese central government to advance Beijing's geopolitical interests, they have largely left the dominance of domestic interests and the supremacy of subnational dimensions unrecognised. Nevertheless, the works of Tim Summers, Baogang He, Jie Yu, Sumie Yoshikawa, Mingjiang Li, Lee Jones, and Jinghan Zeng have encapsulated some of the prominent domestic factors with case studies of Yunnan, Guangdong, and Guangxi provinces.

Decision-Making

> *'There is no small issue in diplomacy, all power belongs to the Central Committee.'*
>
> – Zhou Enlai.

While the international ramifications of China's rise are taking shape, it is prudent to examine Beijing's policymaking process in general and the parties involved, particularly regarding the BRI. Lampton (2001, p. 32) describes the decision-making for Chinese foreign affairs as 'a system in which an increasingly professionalized, complex, and conflict-ridden bureaucracy has coexisted with a still very powerful, personalized senior-dominated elite'. However, a decade later, Jakobson and Knox (2010, p. 24) reasoned that apart from the Party and the People's Liberation Army (PLA), other new foreign policy actors on the margins included local governments, Chinese state-owned enterprises and energy companies, financial and research institutions, the media, and netizens. On complications of the BRI and Beijing's foreign policy decision-making, Jie Yu (2018, p. 2) rejects the prevalent assumption that China is a 'static' and 'authoritarian' state where only the top elites command policy. While this perception might appear true under Mao, it is certainly not the case in contemporary China. Another significant yet unrepresented feature, Jie stresses, is the domination of domestic interests. The BRI is majorly intended to soothe the anxieties and concerns related to China's excessive industrial capacity. Chinese provinces, therefore, strive to influence foreign policymaking process through 'trailblazing',[3] 'carpetbagging'[4] or 'resisting'[5] the implementation of policies formulated by the central government. For example, while China's Yunnan province trailblazed by promoting the idea of 'Malacca Dilemma' and convinced Beijing to subsequently construct oil and gas pipelines from Kyaukpyu port (Myanmar) to Yunnan's Kunming city (Wong, A. 2018, p. 739), Hainan carpetbagged China's South China Sea policies by upgrading Sansha City to advance its parochial interests (Ibid., pp. 746-8), and during the 2009 Kokang conflict in Myanmar's borderlines, the elites of Yunnan resisted the central government's order to shut the border (before Beijing's subsequent and direct intervention) (Ibid., p. 752). Thus, China's political and policy procedures can be labelled as '*de facto* federalism' and the provincial government 'has its own power resources to initiate policy within its jurisdiction and influence the formation and implementation of policies of the central government' (Zheng, 2007, p. 14). Under the BRI, while China's provinces are obliged to implement the top-down national strategy, they are also at liberty to interpret the policy in accordance with their provincial interests.

While the Western bureaucratic system is defined and characterised by various government ministries and departments, the Chinese decision-making process interlaces between the Party and the Government. There is no doubt that the most powerful seven Chinese Politburo members set the standards for key strategy or long-term policy goals, and particular policy processes are initiated and implemented by different ministries and corporations. However, following a process of decentralisation in decision-making in 1978, various stakeholders have been competing for departmental/ministerial interests, as well as for resources and greater budgetary power (Yu, 2018, p. 227).

After the announcement of the grand strategy, the Chinese central government appointed its top leaders and core members for the leading group of the BRI. Zhang Gaoli, the vice premier and a member of the Politburo Standing Committee of the CPC, was appointed the head of the leading group. Other members included Wang Huning, the mastermind behind President Xi Jinping's power; Wang Yang, who served as the Party Secretary of Guangdong until December 2012 and was one of the four vice premiers of China; Yang Jiechi, the State Councilor for Chinese foreign affairs; and Yang Jing, the Secretary General of the State Council. Apart from the small leading group, there are multiple ministries and (state-owned) corporations holding a share of votes that impact BRI projects, thus making the bureaucratic system opaque and overarchingly uncertain. Therefore, China needs to perfect the framework with reasonable consistency that must be brought into practice persistently to persuade partners (Ibid., p. 230).

Domestic Dynamics

The single most important phenomenon in the 21st century is, perhaps, the rise of China, both economically and politically (Grosse, 2021, p. 4). In marked contrast from the post-World War II era, China, the world's second largest economic power, rivals the US, the largest economic power. Analysts have recurrently stated that China is now the largest trading partner for more than 120 countries, and its investment in Asia is precipitously increasing. Michael Swaine (2015, p.1) argues that the BRI is designed to 'leverage China's growing economic power and influence in order to strengthen and expand cooperative interactions, create an integrated web of mutually beneficial economic, social and political ties, and ultimately lower distrust and enhance a sense of common security'. In addition, the BRI is one of the 'three great national strategies' (三大战略*sandazhanlue*) along with the Beijing-Tianjin-Hebei integration plan and the Yangtze River Economic Belt to create a new pattern of coordinated regional development with orderly and free flow of elements (Government Work Report, 2016).

It is an established fact among China's analysts that the primary aim of the CPC is to remain in power with absolute authority and complete control, and therefore, it needs social stability. The CPC is thus required to maintain an agreement or a 'social contract' with the Chinese people that is premised on the CPC's aptitude and ability to deliver economic growth and employment.[6] Jie Yu (2018, p. 3) argues that one of the negative legacies left by Deng Xiaoping's 'reforms and opening up' policy is the regional imbalance in economic development, and the BRI is positioned as a key policy to reduce this disparity and to connect existing revival programmes, such as *'Develop the West, Raise the Central Region and Revitalize The Old Northeast Industrial Bases'*.

Against this backdrop of Chinese regional developmental imbalance and economic slowdown, the demarcation of Chinese regions in the V&A Document is quite significant. China's regions (alternatively, the domestic factor) are covered in a separate section of Beijing's V&A Document in which four key areas are delineated: north-western and north-eastern regions comprising Xinjiang, Shanxi, Gansu, Ningxia, Inner Mongolia, Heilongjiang, Jilin, and Liaoning provinces; southwestern regions including Guangxi, Yunnan, and Tibet; coastal regions including Shanghai, Fujian, Guangdong, and also Hong Kong, Macao and Taiwan; and inland regions, such as Sichuan, Henan, Hunan, and Hubei. Section VI, titled 'China's Regions in Pursuing Opening-Up', clearly highlights that it will 'fully leverage the comparative advantages of its various regions…strengthen interaction and cooperation among eastern, western and central regions…improve the openness of the Chinese economy (to advance BRI)'.

Consequently, Premier Li Keqiang, during his annual Government Work Report[7] at the Great Hall of the People, said that the Chinese government would 'integrate the development of the Silk Road Economic Belt and the twenty-first century Maritime Silk Road with the development and opening up of related regions' (*The Wall Street Journal*, 2015, p. 26). Also, at the first conference on BRI Construction Work on February 1, 2015, Zhang Gaoli said that the construction of the BRI was a major decision made by the Party Central Committee and the State Council in 'coordinating the overall domestic and international situations…(it is necessary) to give full play to the role of multilateral, bilateral, regional and sub-regional cooperation mechanisms… all regions and departments should strengthen organization…give full play to the initiatives of *local* [emphasis mine], departmental and market entities'.[8] However, the coordination does not always go as per the central government's wishes.

The BRI initiative has brought new focus to the existing debate between decentralisation and centralisation in China. To this end, President Xi's referral to the great Emperor Han Wudi and his centralised governance model in Astana indicated the central government's willingness for more centralisation within China (Mierzejewski, 2021, p. 6). Moreover, the BRI is placed in a way so as to assist and complement the concept of horizontal relations between provinces and strengthen intra-provincial cooperation by further narrowing disparities between inland and coastal provinces. The vertical management of the central government, on the other hand, includes 'coercion, bargaining and reciprocity' (Zheng Yongnian, 2007; Dominik Mierzejewski, 2021, p.7). Apart from being at liberty to establish local markets, the authority of approving foreign investment also lies with the provincial level governments (Zhu, 2008, pp. 272-273).

Zheng Yongnian (2007) probed central-local relations in China through three dimensions. The first model is the cellular approach that offers limited interaction, where the centre is dependent on local governments for implementing its policies. The second model—the structural one—points to the institutionalised relations between the central-local governments through fiscal policy. The central argument is that a consensus in decision-making is achieved by means of bargaining, and this model describes central-local relations as 'the function of discrete strategic interactions' between two parties (Mierzejewski, 2021, p. 12). In this regard, the bond between the business community and officials is very crucial, and the BRI's provincial 'go global' strategy advanced support to and cooperation between these two bodies (Zheng Yongnian, 2017, pp.108-109). The last model is pluralist, in the sense that it provides a platform for both the central and local governments to view relations from the perspective of the interest groups. The model also dictates that China's development hinges upon the greater policy support and the 'first-in-trial' right (先行先试权*xianxingxianshiquan*), which is based on what is often referred to as the 'new special zone' (Mierzejewski, 2021, p.13). Also, perhaps more importantly, the bargaining process is an arrangement in which neither the central government nor the local government(s) enjoys total victory or total failure, and in addition, reserves a few prerequisites: the irreducible power of both the central authority and local officials over one another; the basis of the centre's power over provinces (coercion); the provinces' power over the centre (intermediary role); and mutual interdependence and indispensability-protracted conflicts (Li, 2003, pp. 44-45).

The following section looks at the local governments' interpretation and implementation of the initiative to successfully fulfil their own provincial interests. As a case study, this chapter focuses on Fujian Province's approach towards the BRI's 'Maritime Silk Road'.

The MSR and the Fujian Province

Coastal provinces make up 14 per cent of Chinese land but are home to 40 per cent of the population, more than 60 per cent of the country's GDP, and 90 per cent of its foreign trade, including more than 70 per cent of energy imports (Wang Fang, 2017, p. 65). Evidently, there is a gap in China's regional development. Hence, the BRI creates new space for regional economic development to reshape China's economic geography. In the Government Work Report (2016), Premier Li Keqiang explicitly pointed out the need to promote domestic regional development. Also, the BRI conforms to the needs of China's factor flow transformation and industrial transfer.

Following the release of the V&A Document by the NDRC, Fujian has been assigned the central position of the MSR by the Ministry of Foreign Affairs and the Ministry of Commerce, with the State Council's approval. According to the V&A Document, Fujian proposed to support Quanzhou's construction of the '*Haisi*' (海丝) pilot zone, support the establishment of Fuzhou New District, accelerate the construction of Pingtan Comprehensive Experimental Zone; and strive to start the construction of a number of major projects, such as Jiyongquan Railway and Fuxia High-speed Railway. Moreover, *Guancha* (April 13, 2015) noticed that it was the first time an official map was released by the CCTV during its coverage of the report, and the map included the southern route of the MSR to Southeast Asia.

China's 'Maritime Silk Road' goes to the Mediterranean Sea via the South China Sea, the Indian Ocean, and the Arabian Sea. Soon after the announcement of the MSR, the city government of Fuzhou set up a USD 1.6 billion (RMB10 billion) fund to boost China's MSR development (*China Daily*, 2014). With the announcement of China's 13th Five-Year-Plan in November 2015, Fujian was identified to be the core area for building the 21st century MSR (*Beijing Review*, 2019).

Fujian has nine prefecture-level cities under its jurisdiction, among which six are listed in the BRI. These six cities—according to the analysis made by Huang Duan, Deputy Director of the Fujian Provincial Government Development Research Center—are also listed as "strategic fulcrums for maritime cooperation" (海上合作战略支点).[9] Quanzhou has been confirmed as an extension of "Made in China" (中国制造2025) and positioned as the "21st Century Maritime Silk Road Pioneer Zone" (21世纪海上丝绸之路先行区). Xiamen has identified 39 key 'OBOR' projects in six areas, namely, infrastructure, investment promotion, foreign investment, maritime cooperation, tourism and exhibition, and cultural exchanges, while Fuzhou Development and Reform Commission Office stated that it previously established a leading group for the promotion of "*Haisi*" in the Fuzhou Bureau of Commerce. It is estimated that Xiamen and nine countries along with the MSR will strive to reach USD 34 billion in imports and exports.[10]

The Fifth Plenary Session of the 18th Central Committee of the Communist Party of China (2012) emphasised that reforms and opening-up are the only ways for the country to develop and prosper. The report from the Fujian Provincial People's Government Research Group of Development Research Center (2017, p. 21) highlighted that while recognition of Fujian as the starting point of the MSR remained at the forefront of the country's export-oriented economy, large disparities and differences in the level of opening-up within the province have remained. For example, the export-oriented development in coastal regions, such as Fuzhou, Xiamen, Quanzhou, and Zhangzhou, under the dual effects of preferential policies and market forces, are in dominant positions in the province—as is evident from the scale of Xiamen's foreign trade (2010–2015) that basically accounted for half of that of the province. The opening-up of other coastal areas, such as Putian and Ningde, has been relatively delayed. Indeed, there is a significant gap between these coastal zones and inland mountainous areas, such as Nanping, Sanming, and Longyan. Thus, the BRI vision, with origins in Chinese provincial development plans, 'is a state-led spatial fix to provide infrastructure to facilitate the development of networks of capital across the Eurasian continent' (Tim Summers, 2016, p. 1637).

Since Fujian was formally designated as the core area of the Maritime Silk Road (海丝*Haisi*), it has become a major strategic task for the province to effectively implement the glorious mission assigned to it by the central government, opines Cai Yongzhi (2017, p. 187), a professor at the Fujian Provincial Party School of the Communist Party of China (CPC). Following the policy announcement, Fujian has actively used the policy advantages of being the core area of '*Haisi*' to increase 'bringing in' (*yinjinlai*) and 'going out' (*zouchuqu*) (Ibid.).

Historically, Fujian has been an important starting point of the ancient (Maritime) Silk Road. Fuzhou, Quanzhou, and Zhanghou are among the six provinces and nine cities that have jointly applied for '*Haisi*'. Quanzhou Port, formerly known as '*Citong* Port', was the starting point during the Tang Dynasty and later became 'the largest port in the East' during the Song and Yuan Dynasties; Fuzhou Changle Port was a depot (supply port) for Zheng He's seven voyages to the West; Zhangzhou Yue Port was the only legal foreign trade point during the late Ming Dynasty (Cai Yongzhi, 2017, p.187). Fujian has evidently been a key active participant of the MSR from the Tang Dynasty to modern times. In recent times, however, some departments have dared not explore or innovate in actual work, and instead, have towed the line to "wait, rely, and demand" (*deng, kao, yao*) preferential policies from higher authorities (Ibid., p.189). In terms of attracting foreign investment, the central government has not given enough value and attention to the positioning of the core area of Fujian's '*Haisi*' (p.189). It is, therefore, indicative that whilst the central government formulates the BRI project, local governments continue to influence and reshape them in the process of implementation.

Conclusion

China's Belt and Road Initiative—reminiscent of the ancient Silk Road—is a grandiose infrastructure project that would foster connectivity between China and Europe. It has the potential to yield substantial economic and diplomatic gains for Beijing and could reorientate a major portion of the world economy towards China. Equally significantly, China's growing confidence over advancements in many aspects of economic prosperity, compared to both the developed world and other developing neighbours, in the last four decades has given rise to its 'China Dream' campaign (Zheng, Shiping) and the BRI is positioned to fulfil this dream.

Contrary to general assumptions and the traditional view that the BRI is a coherent policy of the Chinese central government, provincial players could 'influence' or 'reinterpret' the policy implementation to advance their parochial interests. The V&A Document highlights Fujian province as a pivotal player, which competed with other coastal provinces to position and project itself as the 'starting point' of the MSR and an important hub. In a bid to do so, Fujian's officials lobbied central authorities to put emphasis on energy security. This also exhibits an economy-driven and development-oriented provincial focus rather than a singular focus by Beijing to only advance its geopolitical interests. This is not to claim that Beijing does not aim to break the perceived United States' 'encirclement' in the Asia-Pacific; the economic underpinnings and colossal scale of the BRI are clearly major drivers for Beijing. For example, investment and trade in strategic areas will help Beijing to diversify its transport network. However, it is imperative to remember that various domestic factors are instrumental in the making of the BRI, while local governments' preferred narratives or interpretation of the strategy are meant to advance their own interests.

Soon after President Xi's proposal of the BRI project, provincial governments launched their campaigns to infuse local interests and agendas. The case study of Fujian and its officials' response to the BRI further demonstrates the role of provincial agencies in Beijing's foreign policy. Contrary to the general perception of unequivocal control by the central government in China, provincial governments are also at liberty to influence policy implementation, albeit this discretionary power primarily lies in the economic domain. While central agencies control capital, licensing, project authorisation and so on, the provincial governments develop their own plans for policy implementation. Therefore, it is not erroneous to say that the BRI appears to be a hybrid top-down policy by the central government and bottom-up implementation by the local authorities.

Notes

1. 'Striving for Achievement' (SFA) is indeed an assertive strategy in nature. Celebrated Chinese IR scholar, Yan Xuetong (2014: 167) claims that the tenets of SFA are mainly illustrated by the four Chinese characters of '*qin* (being close), *cheng* (credible), *hui* (benefiting) and *rong* (inclusive). The assertiveness of SFA is evident in Chinese expressions or phrases, e.g. 'Jiji Jinqu' (积极进取'energetically enter/get in'), 'Gengjia Zhudong' (更加主动'take greater initiative'), 'Gengjia Jiji' (更加积极'being even more active').
2. "Decision of the Central Committee of the Communist Party of China on Some Major Issues Concerning Comprehensively Deepening the Reform", http://www.dzwww.com/2013/gghl/jd/. Accessed on March 25, 2021.
3. *Trailblazing* is basically creating facts on the ground. The province creates new policy ideas on specific issues that constitute broader foreign policy and proactively persuades Beijing to adopt them. It involves lobbying the centre, often in collaboration with state-owned enterprises or the military. Wong, A. 2018. "More than peripheral: How provinces influence China's foreign policy". *The China Quarterly*, p. 738.
4. *Carpetbagging* is adapting national policy to suit local ends. This occurs when the province publicly echoes central rhetoric but pursues different priorities; it captures central policy by enacting new local policies under existing frameworks, Ibid.
5. It happens when a province perceives that a foreign policy has adverse effects on its local interests, it can resist by refusing to adopt central directives. Ibid., pp. 738-39.
6. At a meeting to discuss the decline of the communist regime in Romania, Deng Xiaoping said: "We'll be like this, if we don't carry out reforms and bring about benefits to the people." Cited in Marsh, C. 2005. *Unparalleled Reforms: China's Rise, Russia's Fall, and the Interdependence of Transition*. Maryland. Lexington Books, p. 106.
7. Chinese State media describes it as China's version of the U.S. State of the Union address.
8. "Zhang Gaoli: Put efforts to achieve a good start for the BRI construction" (Zhang gaoli: nuli shixian 'yidai yilu' jianshe lianghao kaiju), *Renminwang* 01/02/2015, http://cpc.people.com.cn/n/2015/0202/c64094-26488560.html. Accessed on May 30, 2021.

9. "CCTV releases the authoritative 'OBOR' layout, Fujian will become a pioneer area in the docking plan" (Yangshi fabu quanwei 'yidai yilu' bantu Fujian duijie fang'an zhong quanzhou jiangcheng xianxingqu). *Guancha.* 13/04/2015. https://www.guancha.cn/Neighbors/2015_04_13_315767_1.shtml and https://www.guancha.cn/Neighbors/2015_04_13_315767_2.shtml Accessed on June 1, 2021.
10. Ibid., p. 2.

References

Aoyama, R. (2016), "One Belt, One Road: China's New Global Strategy", *Journal of Contemporary East Asia Studies*, 5(2), pp. 3-22.

Bhattacharya, Abanti (2016), "Conceptualizing the Silk Road Initiative in China's Periphery Policy", *East Asia,* 33(4), pp. 309-328.

Callahan, W.A. (2016), "China's 'Asia Dream': The Belt Road Initiative and the new regional order", *Asian Journal of Comparative Politics*, 1(3), pp. 226-243, doi:10.1177/ 2057891116647806.

"China NPC 2015: The Reports", *The Wall Street Journal*, 4 March 2015, https://www.wsj.com/articles/BL-CJB-26104. Accessed on May 22, 2021.

Fujian Provincial People's Government Research Group of Development Research Center. 2017. *Based on the Construction of the 21st Century Maritime Silk Road Core Area, Accelerating the Dislocation Development and coordinated Development of Open Economy in Fujian.* Development Research. (04), pp. 21-29.

"Fund to boost China's maritime Silk Road development", *China Daily*, 19 May 2014, http://www.chinadaily.com.cn/business/2014-05/19/content_17518605.htm. Accessed on April 28, 2021.

Grosse, R. et al. (2021), "China's Rise, World Order, and the Implications for International Business", *Management International Review*, 61, pp. 1-26.

Jakobson, L. & Knox, D. (2010), "New Foreign Policy Actors in China", *SIPRI Policy Paper 26,* https://www.sipri.org/sites/default/files/files/PP/SIPRIPP26.pdf, Accessed on May 15, 2021.

Lampton, David M. (2001), "China's foreign and national security policy-making process: is it changing and does it matter?" In David M. Lampton (ed.), *The Making of Chinese Foreign and Security Policy in the Era of Reform, 1978-2000.* Stanford, CA: Stanford University Press, pp. 1-36.

Lee, Seung-Ook, Wainwright, Joel, & Glassman, Jim (2018), "Geopolitical economy and the production of territory: The case of US-China geopolitical-economic competition in Asia", *Environment and Planning A* 50(2), pp. 416-436. doi:10.1177/ 0308518X17701727.

Li Yifan (2019), "A new Voyage", *Beijing Review*, 12 September, http://www.bjreview.com/Nation/201909/t20190909_800177974.html, Accessed on May 10, 2021.

Liu, Yanqing [刘砚青] (2013b), *"Cong taoguang yang hui dao fen fa you wei, zhongguojueqishi buke dang"* (From taoguang yang hui to fen fa you wei, the trend of China's rise cannot be blocked), [从韬光养晦到奋发有为, 中国崛起是不可挡]. *ZhongguoJingjiZhoukan (China's Economic Weekly)*, November 11.

National Development and Reform Commission (NDRC), Ministry of Foreign Affairs and Ministry of Commerce of the People's Republic of China (PRC), 2015, *Vision and Actions on Jointly Building Silk Road Economic Belt and 21st Century Maritime Silk Road.* Beijing.

Naughton, B. (2016), "Shifting Structures and Processes in Economic Policy-Making at the Centre". In *China's Core Executive: Leadership Styles, Structures and Processes Under Xi Jinping*, edited by Sebastian Heilmann and Matthias Stepan, pp. 40-43. Berlin: MERICS.

Pang Zhongying (2020), "From Tao Guang Yang Hui to Xin Xing: China's Complex Foreign Policy Transformation and Southeast Asia".

Shi Yinhong (2015), "China's complicated foreign policy", European Council on Foreign Relations, Commentary, March 31, 2015, https://ecfr.eu/article/commentary_chinas_complicated_foreign_policy311562/

Swaine M. (2015), "Chinese Views and Commentary on the 'One Belt, One Road' Initiative", *China Leadership Monitor*, No. 47, pp. 1-24.

Tim Summers (2016), "China's 'new silk roads': Sub-national regions and networks of global political economy", *Third Quarterly*, 37 (9), pp. 1628-1643.

Wang Hongying (2014), "From 'TaoguangYanghui' to 'YousuoZuowei': China's Engagement in Financial Minilateralism", CIGI Papers, No. 52, December.

Wang Yiwei (2015), *One Belt, One Road: Opportunities and Challenges [Yidaiyilu: Jiyuyutiaozhan]*, Beijing: Renminchubanshe.

Wang Yong (2016), "Offensive for defensive: the belt and road initiative and China's new grand strategy", *The Pacific Review*, DOI: 10.1080/09512748.2016.1154690.

Yan, Xuetong (2014), "From Keeping a Low Profile to Striving for Achievement", *The Chinese Journal of International Politics*, 7(2), pp.153–184.

Zhao Lei (2015), *One Belt, One Road: China's Civilizational Rise [Yidaiyilu: Zhongguo de wenmingxingjueqi].* Beijing: Zhongxinchubanshe.

Zheng Yongnian (2007), *De Facto Federalism in China: Reforms and Dynamics of Central-Local Relations*. Singapore: World Scientific.

Zheng Yongnian (2015), *30 Years into the Future: Key Issues for the New Normal of Reform [Weilaisanshinian: Gaige xinchangshexiadeguanjianwenti].* Beijing: Zhongxinchubanshe.

Zheng, Shiping, 'Rising confidence behind the "Chinese dream"', *Journal of Chinese Political Science*, 19: 1, 2014, pp. 35-48.

4

China's BRI: Revisiting the Labyrinth Post a Decade

Gunjan Singh

The One Belt One Road Initiative (OBOR)/Belt and Road Initiative (BRI) was announced by the Chinese President, Xi Jinping (XJP), in March 2013. It has two major parts: one is focussed on the land and is known as the Silk Road while the other targets the sea routes and is known as the Maritime Silk Road. It is a grand plan with the objective to build major infrastructure networks connecting prominent markets. It has been almost a decade since the grand infrastructure and connectivity project officially began. As per reports, by March 2022, 146 countries and 32 international organisations had joined the BRI.[1] In fact, the BRI is a grand initiative which plans to look at international development and a network of infrastructure with China at its centre. A report by the Chatham House describes China's objectives, surmising that "it is an effort to develop an expanded, interdependent market for China, grow China's economic and political power, and create the right conditions for China to build a high technology economy".[2] In 2017, Chinese President Xi Jinping promised a total investment of USD 124 bn dollars in the BRI.[3] As per Xi Jinping, "the pursuit of the Belt and Road Initiative requires a peaceful and stable environment. We should foster a new type of international relations featuring win-win cooperation; and we should forge partnerships of dialogue with no confrontation and of friendship rather than alliance. All countries should respect each other's sovereignty, dignity and territorial integrity, each other's development paths and social systems, and each other's core interests and major concerns".[4] According to Refiniti, by the year 2021, there were already 3,220 BRI projects with a combined value of USD 3.49 trillion.[5]A lot has been written and discussed about the hopes and aspirations associated with the BRI. Several countries became a part of the BRI with the hope of getting access to infrastructure development and Chinese investments.

However, not all has been as smooth as that hoped for by Xi Jinping or the Chinese Communist Party (CCP). Over the last decade, the BRI has been mired in controversies and challenges. One of the major challenges has been the issue of debt trap diplomacy which has been associated with it. In addition, the outbreak of the COVID-19 pandemic further derailed the projects and made a dent in the progress of the initiative. In November 2022, while attending the Asia Pacific Economic Cooperation (APEC), Xi Jinping announced that China will be holding the Third Belt and Road Forum in 2023. He also asserted that the forum will provide the much-needed boost to the BRI.[6] Since the outbreak of the Covid- 19 pandemic, China was following a strict zero-covid policy, which restricted any travel inside or outside the country. Such announcements were primarily undertaken to show the commitment of the CCP towards the BRI. The ongoing Russia-Ukraine conflict had further added hurdles to the progress of the BRI. It would be interesting to take note of the status of this grand initiative after a decade, and the same is attempted herewith.

Now that the Third Belt and Road Forum has already taken place and China has committed to further strengthen the BRI, the paper will try to discuss how the BRI has changed over the last 10-12 years. Is it still the beacon of hope for the smaller nations or has it become a major challenge for the same? The paper will attempt to discuss the trajectory of changes that have occurred over the years with respect to the BRI. It is also imperative to analyse the Chinese government's response towards the BRI in light of the mounting challenges.

Background

The BRI was officially announced in 2013 by Xi Jinping during his visit to Kazakhstan. It is a project which aims to connect Asia with Europe. During his speech, Xi had said[7]:

> "In order to make our Eurasian countries have closer economic ties, deeper mutual cooperation, and broader development space, we can use innovative cooperation models to jointly build the "Silk Road Economic Belt". This is a great cause that benefits the people of all countries along the way. We can start from the following aspects, from point to point, from line to piece, and gradually form a regional cooperation."

After four years of announcing the BRI, Beijing organised the First Belt and Road Forum in May 2017. During the First Belt and Road Forum, Xi Jinping said[8]:

> "In the autumn of 2013, respectively in Kazakhstan and Indonesia, I proposed the building of the Silk Road Economic Belt and the 21st Century Maritime Silk Road, which I call the Belt and Road Initiative. As a Chinese saying goes, "Peaches and plums do not speak, but they are so attractive that a path is formed below the trees." Four years on, over 100 countries and international organizations have supported and got involved in this initiative. Important resolutions passed by the UN General Assembly and Security Council contain reference to it. Thanks to our efforts, the vision of the Belt and Road Initiative is becoming a reality and bearing rich fruit."

To follow it up, Beijing organised a Second Belt and Road Forum, which was held in April 2019. During the Second Belt and Road Forum, Xi Jinping said[9]:

> "The joint pursuit of the Belt and Road Initiative (BRI) aims to enhance connectivity and practical cooperation. It is about jointly meeting various challenges and risks confronting mankind and delivering win-win outcomes and common development. Thanks to the joint efforts of

> all of us involved in this initiative, the decisions of the first BRF have been smoothly implemented. More than 150 countries and international organizations have signed agreements on Belt and Road cooperation with China. From the Eurasian continent to Africa, the Americas and Oceania, Belt and Road cooperation has opened up new space for global economic growth, produced new platforms for international trade and investment and offered new ways for improving global economic governance. Indeed, this initiative has helped improve people's lives in countries involved and created more opportunities for common prosperity."

The Third Belt and Road Forum was organised in Beijing on October 17 and 18, 2013. During the Third Belt and Road Forum, Xi Jinping said[10]:

> "What has been achieved in the past 10 years demonstrates that Belt and Road cooperation is on the right side of history. It represents the advancing of our times, and it is the right path forward. We need to remain clear-eyed and undisturbed in a volatile world, and we need to be keenly aware of our responsibility for history, for the people and for the world. We should jointly address various global risks and challenges, and deliver a bright future of peace, development, cooperation and mutual benefit for future generations."

The major argument driving the BRI was connectivity and infrastructure. Xi had a vision of major networks across the world connected through ports, roads, bridges, railways, and pipelines, which will run through and across Central Asia as well as South Asia. He believed that such a network will help in promoting international use of the Chinese currency while helping in increasing connectivity and creating markets. He also envisioned developing almost 50 Special Economic Zones and investing in the development of major ports across East Asia, South Asia, and Southeast Asia.[11]

Most of the speeches delivered by Xi Jinping about the BRI focus on the idea of promoting 'win-win' relations and also on how it is going to benefit the countries that decide to become part of the grand initiative. It is an attempt to showcase that the BRI has a strong and dedicated economic agenda with an aim to help countries develop and learn from the Chinese economic growth experience. It was also evident that China wanted to export the Chinese infrastructure growth to other countries. One major example is high-speed railways. China has built more high-speed rail networks than the whole world combined. As per data, Beijing's expansive railway network transports around 10 million people per day and grows by 3,600 kms per year. Till date, the network has handled around 20 billion passenger trips as 8,700 bullet trains operate every day in China.[12] It was largely believed that after the demand got saturated domestically, Beijing used the BRI to export its domestic capacities and extended major subsidies to the importing countries.[13]

From the very beginning, the OBOR/BRI was a very attractive project for the smaller nations in the world as most of the smaller countries face challenges in gaining any kind of investment or loans for infrastructure growth from major investment organisations. With the announcement of the BRI, China became a viable alternative and it was no surprise that almost 150 countries actively enrolled as participants in the BRI. Many countries like Sri Lanka, Nepal, the Maldives, Malaysia, and Bangladesh welcomed investments under the banner of the BRI. To celebrate the decadal growth of the BRI, a book, titled *Walk Along the Road: Ten Years of BRI*, was published in Malaysia in January 2023, which found abundant endorsement by the Chinese.[14]

However, most of the countries which joined the BRI faced major challenges with respect to repayments and thus, the debates surrounding debt-trap diplomacy gained momentum. In addition to this, there are other challenges faced by the BRI. Over the last ten years, the OBOR has not gained the kind of impetus or held as much water as Beijing would have expected.

Major Challenges

The Belt and Road Initiative, as envisaged by China, was to be an economic project connecting countries and in the process, helping them to develop economically and culturally. However, soon after the project was launched, there were a number of issues which proved to be a threat for the image of the BRI. Several countries raised concerns regarding corruption, environmental degradation, debt-trap, and other hidden economic challenges of the market. These challenges have adversely affected the ongoing projects and diminished proposals about new projects and investments under the BRI banner.

Debt-Trap

One of the major challenges that the BRI faces is an attempt to counter the idea of debt-trap proliferated in the international discourse. In a number of cases, the loans and investments extended by China under the BRI have faced logistical issues. The countries at the borrowing end, which have been economically smaller and weaker in the past, over time, have faced constraints in repaying the loans or in payment of instalments; this was very much expected. India had, in fact, raised similar concerns from the very beginning. In a statement outlining the Indian stand on not participating in the BRI, New Delhi stated its various concerns, the most prominent being the fear of debt- trap. To quote, the Indian side "listed several concerns behind the venture, noting that any initiative promoting connectivity between countries must not create unsustainable debt burdens for communities".[15]

The smaller nations though, in need of infrastructure development and investments, did not possess a similar resource capacity to be able to repay the loans in the stipulated time period. Hambantota Port became one of the major examples of what went wrong with the BRI investments and how it adversely affected the sovereignty and fiscal economy of the smaller nations. The leasing of the port by China for 99 years (some reports state that it can be further extended by an additional 99 years) has raised major questions about the feasibility of Chinese loans while raising issues of safeguarding the sovereignty of the smaller nations. The fact that Beijing is going to operate and manage the Hambantota port and the port city around it for almost a century gives China access to Sri Lankan land and also gives it a stake in the domestic politics of Colombo. It is no surprise that the recent financial crisis in Sri Lanka is also being linked to the BRI and the recurrent default in repayment of the Chinese loans and investments. This is also a strong geopolitical leverage which Beijing has acquired. With access to ports and a strong foothold in South Asia, China has transformed the narrative around the BRI. The initiative is, thus, designed to be used by China to extend its geopolitical ambitions, especially in South Asia, and instrumentalised towards containing Indian influence.

The massive increase in Sri Lankan debt and its default on loan payments has affected the geopolitics of the Indian Ocean region. In the last few years, a number of Chinese ships have visited and docked at the Hambantota port, adding to India's unease, the most recent being the Chinese satellite survey ship that docked in August 2022. Some experts have also argued that the way Beijing is using the Hambantota port is a clear indication of how it wants to use most of the infrastructure being built under the BRI. Most of the ports, bridges, railways, and roads will be eventually used by China to strengthen its geopolitical ambitions.[16]

This has raised some scepticism amongst smaller South Asian countries. Not only Sri Lanka but also others have started revisiting their commitments to the BRI projects. In the last few years, there have been several studies on the feasibility and sustainability of the BRI projects amongst the smaller nations with reference to their national conditions. According to Brad Parks, "A growing number of policymakers in low- and middle-income countries are mothballing high profile BRI projects because of overpricing, corruption and debt sustainability concerns."[17] This highlights that Sri Lanka has proved to be a major eye-opener for the countries in South Asia about the dangers of the BRI and debt- trap. To add to this, according to AidData, a large number of projects have been cancelled between 2013 and 2021—USD 11.58 bn worth of projects in Malaysia, USD 1 bn worth in Bolivia, and USD 1.5 bn worth in Kazakhstan.[18] These reports underscore one of the major trends visible today as far as the BRI is concerned.

Another prominent example of the weakening attractiveness of the BRI is Nepal. Nepal was one of the first countries in South Asia to officially join the BRI. However, things have not moved in a positive direction. As per a recent article, since Nepal joined the BRI in 2017, no project has been completed under the BRI; initially, nine projects were mooted, which later gained in number but not in substance. Due to geopolitical considerations, these projects have either been stalled or left incomplete after the feasibility study. The Nepalese government has been wary of the challenges posed by the debt trap. In order to boost the pending BRI projects, the recently appointed Chinese ambassador to Nepal, Chen Song, said, "I am ready to work closely with Nepali friends from all walks of life, gather walks of life, gather wisdom and pool strength to bring more benefits to the two peoples, and jointly write a new chapter of the 'China-Nepal Strategic Partnership of Cooperation Featuring Ever-lasting Friendship for Development and Prosperity'".[19]

Apart from South Asia, China has also lent and invested huge amounts of money in the African nations under the BRI projects. However, a number of African countries have also started questioning the viability of the BRI projects. In October 2018, Sierra Leone decided to cancel a Chinese project for an airport outside the capital city of Freetown. The value of the project was around USD 318 mn. This was the first instance of an African nation cancelling a project with China.[20] In addition to these countries, Pakistan, Malaysia, Myanmar, and Bangladesh have also started reconsidering their BRI projects. Some of the projects have been renegotiated or cancelled.[21]

Another aspect of the debt trap or debt crisis is that it can force the countries to "leasing back major projects or collateralizing a high percentage of their loans, which means more countries could become economically dependent on China". This is also a challenge for borrower countries as it can help Beijing to gain political influence.[22]

In the last few years, a number of countries that were very keen and excited about investing under the BRI have started revisiting or cancelling the initial projects. This indicates that there is a trust deficit regarding the agenda driving the OBOR/BRI today. The narrative of 'win-win' was cleverly used to sell the idea of the BRI, however, it is becoming obvious that the primary goal of China is to gain geopolitical leverage. It has also proved to be a major tool in the hands of China to extend its influence in the domestic politics of a number of countries. Such actions challenge the sovereignty of the smaller nations and thus, further weaken their international standing.

The COVID-19 Pandemic and its Impact on the functioning of the BRI

The outbreak of the COVID-19 pandemic in 2020 adversely affected the global economic system and supply chains. The epicentre of the outbreak was Wuhan, China. The way Beijing handled the information about the virus in the initial days affected the handling of the virus worldwide. The immediate instinct of the CCP to censor and hide information prevented the Chinese government from sharing it with the world in the initial days. This aggravated the global criticisms targeting Beijing. The fact that Donald Trump named it the 'Chinese Virus' further affected the Chinese position internationally.

The pandemic's after-effects can still be felt across the world and even a few years post-Covid, most of the smaller nations are still struggling to come out of its impact. The global lockdowns have pushed a number of countries to the brink of bankruptcy while challenging their existing economic models. To add to this, the massive loss of life and danger to human security has reduced Beijing's credibility.

However, it is not like China was itself immune to the effects of the pandemic. During the pandemic, Beijing also suffered heavily in economic terms and the focus of government expenditure was largely concentrated on the domestic realm and sought to manage the spread of the infections. China suffered an economic slowdown, which tarnished the image of "Chinese deep pockets" and constricted China's spending capacities. The true extent of the impact of the pandemic on the BRI was very obvious in 2020, when Wang Xiaolong, the director general of the Foreign Ministry's International Economic Affairs Department said that around "a fifth of the Chinese projects under the BRI were seriously affected by the pandemic".[23] This argument was underscored by an ANI report, which concluded that Beijing decided to reduce its investments under the BRI in the period between 2020 and 2025 due to the Covid-19 pandemic and for domestic reasons. The report further highlights, "In view of the grim economic situation at home, Chinese BRI engagement is expected to reach at the levels that were in 2018-2019. There is also a recognition of the Chinese Ministry of Commerce (MOFCOM), which put a break on fast overseas expansion in its 14th Five-Year Plan (FYP) for 2021 to 2025: it plans for China to invest USD 550 billion (that includes non-BRI countries), down 25 per cent from USD 740 billion in the 2016-2020 period".[24]

Another reason for slowing down of extending loans to other countries under the BRI is that the countries are not now sure that the BRI can help in generating sufficient economic growth. As reported by some scholars, "With less margin for error in the face of a global economic recession, BRI has likely entered a new phase of smaller, more rigorous lending to projects that have greater chances of success. BRI's smaller scale means that the benefits and risks of BRI are likely to be reduced moving forward."[25]

Thus, one can conclude that the Covid-19 pandemic has had a significant impact on the future of the BRI. With weakening economic growth across the world, there is a shift in China's focus, which is redirected to domestic ventures. Even the partner countries are more concerned about reviving their economies. The break of the supply chains has further intensified the debates around domestic development simultaneously encouraging multiple supply chains. In a sense, the Covid lockdown has bared the challenges of an interconnected economic world order with Beijing at its centre.

Corruption

Another major challenge which the BRI faces today is that of corruption. It is not a misnomer that the governments under the BRI are accused of illegal and undemocratic ways of functioning and utilising money by giving bribes and favours in order to stay in power. As per a Wall Street Journal Report, the Chinese government, in order to extend its investments and undertake construction, sometimes resorts to corruption and is not averse to using unofficial routes of communication and business. The mega projects promoted under the BRI need environmental clearances, domestic support, government approvals, banking channels etc. In order to expedite this process, the government often avoids the normal channels as they might prove to be time-consuming. Time is of the essence and thus, breaking or bending some rules and laws has become an acceptable norm.[26]

Another aspect that has come to surface is that under the BRI projects, funds have been primarily directed to countries which are high on the corruption index, thus, not making exceptions as far as countries prone to corruption are concerned. It has been reported that in a number of countries, leaders have projected inflated costs for the BRI projects while accepting bribes and kickbacks from the Chinese.[27] Another ANI report discusses how under the garb of the BRI, various "Chinese companies under the BRI designed to make profits for Chinese companies at cost of recipient country's natural resources".[28]

The Chinese government has also been criticised for having double standards when it comes to corruption. It is known that China, under Xi Jinping (XJP), has been clamping down on corruption domestically and has undertaken several enquiries and has punished officials across the ranks. However, when it comes to discussion on corruption related to the BRI, China has adopted a very different tone. It holds the position that corruption should be regarded as the domestic challenge of the respective countries. In case of Kyrgyzstan, the Chinese ambassador had said, "The investigation is an internal affair of Kyrgyzstan and we do not interfere."[29] Such incidents, however, showcase the long- standing Chinese foreign policy tool of not engaging in domestic policies of other countries.

It should be understood that there is a covert element of duplicity involved in the Chinese undertakings. In fact, with respect to BRI projects, corruption and debt trap can be juxtaposed. This link has been highlighted by Inside Over: "In many cases the countries due to heavy corruption in the projects have failed to repay the loan to China and have fallen into the 'Debt Trap'."[30] Such incidents have not helped the Chinese case. The information regarding corruption and environmental degradation has made BRI projects greatly unpopular among the domestic population. This sentiment is highlighted by Brooke Russel in a project by AidData. He states, "Host country policymakers are mothballing these high-profile BRI projects because of corruption and overpricing concerns, as well as major changes in public sentiment that make it difficult to maintain close relations with China."[31] Consequently, these sentiments have led to protests and in some cases, cancellation of the committed projects.

Ukraine War

Another challenge has been the ongoing Ukraine war, which has also affected the BRI unfavourably. It was initially expected that the war would destabilise the region and thus, will have an impact on the regional economic relations. It is no surprise then that the Chinese international public image suffered due to abnormal relations between these countries. According to an American think tank group, Rhodium Group, "China reported 19 cases of interest payment waivers and other loan conditions in 2021, a significant jump from previous years."[32]

The negative impact of the ongoing conflict was felt by China as well. Beijing tried to look for ways to overcome this challenge and circumvent Russian-Ukrainian interference in its economic dealings in the region. One major step undertaken by China was in June 2022. Beijing had sent a delegation to the Central and East European (CEE) nations to convince them that the ongoing Russia-Ukraine war will not affect their economic engagements. However, the response towards these delegations has been pretty lukewarm, with Poland even refusing to meet the Chinese delegation.[33] This highlights the fact that the Ukrainian crisis, which has affected the global economic balance, has also impacted the BRI, and Beijing is looking for ways to bring the project back on track.

Conclusion

In recent years, the BRI has been facing several challenges and hurdles. To counter these narratives, the Chinese media is in full swing, publishing positive articles and interviews marking the "initial decade of BRI". In recent announcements, Beijing had also asserted that the BRI will be given major attention, especially in the near future beginning in the year 2023. As per an article in the *China Daily*, "China-led visions, including the Belt and Road Initiative, will be a major highlight of Beijing's diplomatic agenda over the next several years to ensure they better serve the common good of the international community."[34] In another article in the state-owned newspaper, the *Global Times*, massive praise was heaped on the freight trains launched under the BRI. The article quotes Liang Haiming, Dean of the Belt and Road Institute, at Hainan University, "The train has created a new passage between China, Central Asia, East Asia, Southeast Asia, and the European continent. It is also building a new landscape in global trade that will lead to win-win cooperation with countries and regions along the BRI."[35]

Such media propaganda further underscores the fact that China is aware of the problems within the architecture of the OBOR/BRI, and the government is using its propaganda department to drive confidence in the ongoing as well as the upcoming projects under the BRI. However, the question which remains is whether such pronouncements can manage to mitigate or even reduce the already negative sentiments associated with the Chinese BRI.

Another major step undertaken by China is the announcement of the Global Development Initiative (GDI). The GDI was announced by Xi Jinping in September 2021 while addressing the United National General Assembly (UNGA). There are assumptions that the GDI is proposed as an extension of the BRI. Xi Jinping had described the GDI as "global public good". It is also being regarded by some scholars "as an 'Expansion of BRI', while others have considered it as a 'booster dose to BRI' which is facing challenges and backlash in various regions/countries of the world".[36] Given the Chinese history of wordplay, can one argue that the GDI is just a new term to package the existing BRI projects. In the last few years, the BRI has been affected by a number of challenges and negative reporting. It is no surprise that the Chinese government is trying to counter these with terms like the GDI, which appears to be more benign and caters to the Chinese agenda.

Notes

1. "About the Belt and Road Initiative (BRI)", https://greenfdc.org/belt-and-road-initiative-about/. Accessed on November 2, 2022.
2. "What is China's Belt and Road Initiative (BRI)?", Chatham House, September 18, 2021, https://www.chathamhouse.org/2021/09/what-chinas-belt-and-road-initiative-bri. Accessed on November 6, 2022
3. "What is China's Belt and Road Initiative (BRI)?", Chatham House, September 18, 2021, https://www.chathamhouse.org/2021/09/what-chinas-belt-and-road-initiative-bri. Accessed on November 6, 2022.
4. "Full text of President Xi's speech at opening of Belt and Road forum" Xinhua, May 14, 2017, http://www.xinhuanet.com/english/2017-05/14/c_136282982.htm. Accessed on October 24, 2024.
5. "Xi Jinping's third term: After a decade of building the Belt and Road, where does China go from here?" by Tho Xin Yi, CNA, October 14, 2022, https://www.channelnewsasia.com/asia/china-belt-and-road-initiative-xi-jinping-third-term-2993856. Accessed on November 6, 2022.
6. "Xi announces 3rd Belt & Road forum to be held in 2023, calls on Asia-Pacific to up cooperation to new height" by Wang Cong, Bai Yunyi and Yang Ruoyu in Bangkok Global Times, November 19, 2022, https://www.globaltimes.cn/page/202211/1279916.shtml. Accessed on November 20, 2022.
7. "Promoting People's Friendship and Creating a Better Future" Belt and Road Initiative Hong Kong, September 7, 2013, https://www.beltandroad.gov.hk/important-speeches_20130907_tc.html. Accessed on November 6, 2022.
8. "President Xi's Speech At Opening Of Belt And Road Forum, USC-US China Institute, May 14, 2017" May 14, 2017, https://china.usc.edu/president-xis-speech-opening-belt-and-road-forum-may-14-2017. Accessed on November 6, 2022.
9. "Xi Jinping Attends the Opening Ceremony of the Second Belt and Road Forum for International Cooperation (BRF) and Delivers a Keynote Speech" April 27, 2019 http://www.beltandroadforum.org/english/n100/2019/0429/c22-1391.html. Accessed on November 6, 2022.
10. "Full text of Xi Jinping's keynote speech at 3rd Belt and Road Forum for Int'l Cooperation" Xinhua, October 18, 2024, https://english.news.cn/20231018/7bfc16ac51d443c6a7a00ce25c972104/c.html. Accessed on October 24, 2024.

11. "China's Massive Belt and Road Initiative" by Andrew Chatzky *and* James McBride, Council on Foreign Relations, January 28, 2020, https://www.cfr.org/backgrounder/chinas-massive-belt-and-road-initiative. Accessed November 6, 2022.
12. "High-speed rail showcasing China's rapid modernization" By Liu Zhiqiang, People's Daily Online, September 14, 2024, http://en.people.cn/n3/2024/0914/c90000-20219764.html. Accessed on October 24, 2024.
13. "China's Belt and Road: Implications for the United States", by Jennifer Hillman and David Sacks, Council on Foreign Relations, March 2021, https://www.cfr.org/report/chinas-belt-and-road-implications-for-the-united-states/findings. Accessed on November 20, 2022.
14. "Book launch in Malaysia marks BRI milestone anniversary" China Daily, January 14, 2023, https://global.chinadaily.com.cn/a/202301/14/WS63c22aa8a31057c47eba99ad.html. Accessed on January 14, 2023.
15. "China has designs to spread money and influence across the world — India isn't having it" by Nyshka Chandran, CNBC, May 15, 2017, https://www.cnbc.com/2017/05/15/china-has-designs-to-spread-money-and-influence-across-the-world--india-isnt-having-it.html. Accessed on November 7, 2022.
16. "Why a Chinese ship's arrival in Sri Lanka has caused alarm in India and the West" by Lauren Frayer, NPR, August 19, 2022, https://www.npr.org/2022/08/19/1118113095/sri-lanka-china-ship-hambantota-port. Accessed on November 7, 2022.
17. "China's Belt and Road plans losing momentum as opposition, debt mount -study" by David Stanway, Reuter, September 29, 2021, https://www.reuters.com/world/china/chinas-belt-road-plans-losing-momentum-opposition-debt-mount-study-2021-09-29/. Accessed on November 8, 2022.
18. "China's Belt and Road plans losing momentum as opposition, debt mount -study" by David Stanway, Reuter, September 29, 2021, https://www.reuters.com/world/china/chinas-belt-road-plans-losing-momentum-opposition-debt-mount-study-2021-09-29/
19. "China sends in new ambassador to revive stalled BRI projects in Nepal" January 11, 2023, https://infra.economictimes.indiatimes.com/news/ports-shipping/china-sends-in-new-ambassador-to-revive-stalled-bri-projects-in-nepal/96904945. Accessed on January 14, 2023.
20. "Africa cancels a Belt and Road Initiative project for the first time" by Dipanjan Ray Chaudhary, The Economic Times, October 25, 2018, https://economictimes.indiatimes.com/news/international/world-news/africa-cancels-a-bri-project-for-the-first-time/articleshow/66363312.cms?utm_source=contentofinterest&utm_medium=text&utm_campaign=cpp. Accessed on November 8, 2022.

21. "Fears of excessive debt drive more countries to cut down their Belt and Road investments" by Nyshka Chandran, CNBC, January 18, 2019, https://www.cnbc.com/2019/01/18/countries-are-reducing-belt-and-road-investments-over-financing-fears.html. Accessed on November 8, 2022.
22. "China's Belt and Road: Implications for the United States", by Jennifer Hillman and David Sacks, Council on Foreign Relations, March 2021, https://www.cfr.org/report/chinas-belt-and-road-implications-for-the-united-states/findings, Accessed on November 20, 2022.
23. "Majority of China's BRI projects abroad adversely affected by COVID-19 pandemic: Official" The Economic Times, June 28, 2020, https://economictimes.indiatimes.com/news/international/business/majority-of-chinas-bri-projects-abroad-adversely-affected-by-covid-19-pandemic-official/articleshow/76673279.cms?utm_source=contentofinterest&utm_medium=text&utm_campaign=cppst. Accessed on November 8, 2022.
24. "China Slows BRI investments amid Ukraine war, Covid-19 pandemic" ANI, https://www.aninews.in/news/world/europe/china-slows-bri-investments-amid-ukraine-war-covid-19-pandemic20220805231841/. Accessed on January 14, 2023.
25. "China's Belt and Road: Implications for the United States", by Jennifer Hillman and David Sacks, Council on Foreign Relations, March 2021, https://www.cfr.org/report/chinas-belt-and-road-implications-for-the-united-states/findings. Accessed on November 20, 2022.
26. "The Belt and Road Initiative Is a Corruption Bonanza" by Will Doig, Foreign Policy, January 15, 2019 https://foreignpolicy.com/2019/01/15/the-belt-and-road-initiative-is-a-corruption-bonanza/, Accessed on November 9, 2022.
27. "Is The BRI A Corruption Magnet?" The ASEAN Times, October 10, 2018, https://theaseanpost.com/article/bri-corruption-magnet. Accessed on November 20, 2022.
28. "BRI designed to make profits for Chinese companies at cost of recipient country's natural resources: Report" ANI, December 29, 2021, https://www.aninews.in/news/world/asia/bri-designed-to-make-profits-for-chinese-companies-at-cost-of-recipient-countrys-natural-resources-report20211229063157/. Accessed on January 16, 2023.
29. "Is The BRI A Corruption Magnet?" The ASEAN Times, October 10, 2018, https://theaseanpost.com/article/bri-corruption-magnet. Accessed on November 20, 2022.
30. BRI designed to make profits for Chinese companies at cost of recipient country's natural resources: Report" ANI, December 29, 2021, https://www.aninews.in/news/world/asia/bri-designed-to-make-profits-for-chinese-companies-

at-cost-of-recipient-countrys-natural-resources-report20211229063157/. Accessed on January 16, 2023.

31. "One-third of BRI projects facing major implementation problems: Report" Times of India, October 3, 2021, http://timesofindia.indiatimes.com/articleshow/86721888.cms?utm_source=contentofinterest&utm_medium=text&utm_campaign=cppst. Accessed on January 16, 2023.
32. "China goes easy on foreign lending as BRI loans mounts" The Economic Times, September 21, 2022, https://economictimes.indiatimes.com/news/defence/china-goes-easy-on-foreign-lending-as-bri-loans-mounts/articleshow/94359467.cms?utm_source=contentofinterest&utm_medium=text&utm_campaign=cppst. Accessed on November 20, 2022.
33. "Russia-Ukraine conflict affects China's BRI projects in Central and Eastern European countries" The Economic Times, June 29, 2022, https://economictimes.indiatimes.com/news/international/world-news/russia-ukraine-conflict-affects-chinas-bri-projects-in-central-and-eastern-european-countries/articleshow/92531504.cms?utm_source=contentofinterest&utm_medium=text&utm_campaign=cppst. Accessed on January 14, 2023.
34. "BRI, other China-led visions high on 2023 agenda" by Zhang Yunbi, China Daily, December 26, 2022, https://www.chinadaily.com.cn/a/202212/25/WS63a85e60a31057c47eba6083.html. Accessed on January 14, 2023.
35. "As BRI enters 10th year of development, China-Europe freight train set to see 'explosive growth' in 2023" By Tao Mingyang in Erenhot, Li Xuanminand Yin Yeping Global Times, January 12, 2023, https://www.globaltimes.cn/page/202301/1283707.shtml. Accessed on January 14, 2023.
36. "One Year of China's Global Development Initiative: High on Rhetoric, Low on Substance?" by Sanjeev Kumar, ICWA, September 14, 2022, https://www.icwa.in/show_content.php?lang=1&level=3&ls_id=7916&lid=5287. Accessed on January 15, 2023.

5

Geopolitical Contestation in the Indo-Pacific and the Belt and Road Initiative: An Evolving Great Game in the Maritime World

Vishal Rajput

Introduction

In the realist school of thought, international politics is considered a matter of geopolitical and geostrategic contestation for the nation-states. Since the advent of the Westphalian world order, where allies and adversaries keep changing depending upon the national interests of the involved powers, immediate and long-term gains are defined by the confluence of interchange between these powers. From the great wars during the Middle Ages to the recent post-Cold war period, nations have exercised their influence and aim to be at the helm to set the rules and order, either at the global or the regional level. John Mearsheimer, an offensive realist, holds that the need for security, and ultimately, for survival, makes states aggressive power maximisers. States do not cooperate, except during temporary alliances, but constantly seek to diminish their competitors' power and enhance their own. The process of contestation for 'global or regional dominance' is inevitable in international power politics where every nation-state tries to secure its national interests on the one hand, and attempts to expand and broaden them on the other. During the colonial period, Great Britain and other colonial powers fought for control over foreign territories, which was linked to the burgeoning of their powers. The retreat of the colonial era, particularly after the Second World War, gave rise to the bi-polar rivalry between the former Soviet Union and the US. The war ultimately resulted in the triumph of the latter and then there was the dawn of *Pax Americana* and a 'Unipolar World Order'. Over a period of time, the unipolarity was challenged by rising regional powers where China donned the role of being the first among equals and was perceived by the US as the prime challenger to its global dominance. China is already confronting the US on the economic front and now, in the geostrategic space, the former is challenging the latter on several fronts. Keeping in mind the long US dominance over the maritime world in the 'Indo-Pacific', China's rise can no longer be denied.

Whereas, on the other hand, China sees the Indo-Pacific construct as a propaganda tool of the US to isolate China in the region and with an aim to consolitdate US' allies in the region to resurrect its influence that had slightly waned at the expense of China. When its adversaries are leaving no stone unturned to constrain its influence, China, too, is adapting a strategy to encircle the US and its allies through its signature project—the One Belt One Road/Belt and Road Initiative. In pursuit of the BRI, China is leveraging the support of like-minded partners and resorting to an anti-US block where on the top, Russia is providing complete support to China in counter-balancing the strategies of the US. Moreover, with the outbreak of the novel coronavirus which hugely impacted the course of international affairs and diplomacy over the past few years, it is necessary to see international politics in the shadow of the COVID-19 pandemic. The present study explores the Indo-Pacific as an important 'geopolitical and geostrategic' site for greater power politics between the US and China. It attempts to look into the ongoing contestation of the Indo-Pacific and the Belt and Road Initiative through the neo-realist framework. This paper examines China's maritime moves under the apparatus of the BRI in the Indian Ocean and the Indo-Pacific while at the same time, consolidating her strategic interests, and considers the moves from the vantage point of 'Offensive Realism'. Employing this school of thought in understanding the Sino-US and Sino-Indian interaction gives us unique insights, which make evident, through a pattern of regular offensive outlook of China, its intentions to dominate and to create a challenging environment for the US and in its neighbourhood (India, Philippines, Vietnam, Japan) and for other concerned powers. The school of offensive realism believes that international politics is characterised by anarchy of states, as states do not recognise any authority over each other; neither is there any central authority governing the behaviour of states. In such a system of anarchy, states compete with each other for security, market, and influence. Security, in turn, could be achieved only by acquiring power.[1] Thus, states are bent on increasing their relative powers against their political rivals. The pursuit of power-seeking states is relentless as their ultimate aim is to achieve hegemony at least in their region and ultimately, to challenge the status quo of the international order.[2]

On assessing China's moves through this lens of offensive realism, this study traces the growing competition for regional security, stable market, and expanding influence in its neighbourhood along with the Indian Ocean. According to offensive realism, nation-states are power maximisers, and they are always in search of opportunities to augment their relative power vis-à-vis their peer competitors. Historically speaking, the only way to augment a state's power was to conquer territories, but in the contemporary world, this is no longer the case. Moreover, in contemporary times, control over oceans and the maritime world has become extremely crucial keeping in mind the rising economic interdependence, growing integration of the global society, and in core economical terms, the fact that much of the world's trade is dependent on these water bodies. The 'Rimland Theory' of Nicholas Spykman (Deudney, n.d.) consolidated the relevance of the maritime world and the strategic role of the adjoining littorals in controlling the world. Interestingly, this theoretical development made the Heartland theory obsolete. Hereafter, countries in the Indo-Pacific started prioritising their overarching engagement with the maritime world. In fact, there is a direct correlation between a country's naval prosperity and economic development, more so for trading states like China.[3]

The Indo-Pacific: A Global Geostrategic Theatre

In strategic terms, the Indo-Pacific comprises the Indian Ocean and the Pacific Ocean, conjoined through its main trading channel, the Strait of Malacca. The primary reasons for the sudden rise in the strategic importance of the Indo-Pacific are the declined phase of US influence, rapid burgeoning of the Chinese hard power manifestation, and now, the US' quest for resurgence (Das, 2019). Moreover, a maritime analyst and former naval officer of the Indian Navy, Abhijit Singh, has defined the Indo-Pacific as an integrated theatre that combines the Indian Ocean and the Pacific Ocean and the land masses that surround them. Even though it is still an evolving concept, most analysts see it as an idea that captures the shift in power and influence from the West to the East. Its geographical expanse is still undefined, but it is said to range from the coast of East Africa, across the Indian Ocean, to the Western Pacific, including countries like Japan and Australia. It is both a strategic as well as an economic domain, comprising important sea-lines of communication that connect the littorals of the two oceans. Since it is primarily a maritime space, the Indo-Pacific is associated with maritime security and cooperation.

The power play in the Indian Ocean and the Indo-Pacific region sheds light on the unfolding geostrategic paraphernalia between two power blocks. Alfred Thayar Mahan, the great US naval strategist, observed over a century ago that "*whoever controls the Indian Ocean dominates Asia. This ocean is the key to the seven seas. In the twenty-first century the destiny of the world will be decided in these waters*" (Ghosh, 2004). The observation becomes prophetic when the unfolding of recent events in the region and the importance of the Indian Ocean are analysed in terms of trade and commerce as well as other strategic influences. The Indian Ocean's strategic geopolitical landscape has made it an epicentre of contemporary geopolitics and the great game. On a larger scale, India and China are likely to drive this geopolitical conflict in the near future, but various other small players and regional organisations, like the ASEAN and QUAD, may have higher stakes and more potential to influence the massive shift happening in this part of the world and the course of events thereof.

As far as trade and commerce are concerned, the region is important as the Indian Ocean offers major sea routes connecting the Middle East, Africa, and East Asia with Europe and Asia.[4] It accounts for 50 per cent of the world's container traffic and 30 per cent of the world's trade traverses via the Indian Ocean (Abraham, 2015). About 66 per cent of the world's seaborne trade in oil transits through the Indian Ocean (Bana, 2016). The Indian Ocean is home to four important waterways, namely, the Suez Canal (Egypt), Bab-el-Mandeb (Djibouti-Yemen), the Straits of Hormuz (Iran-Oman), and the Straits of Malacca (Indonesia-Malaysia). It is estimated that about 55 per cent of the world's known oil reserves and around 40 per cent of gas reserves are located in the Indian Ocean region (Salman Khurshid, Putting out to sea a new vision, 2013).

From the geostrategic perspective, the Indo-Pacific has become a battleground for conflict between the two global superpowers: the US and China.[5] Until now, the US, being the predominant power and having significant business interests in the region, took upon itself the responsibility of ensuring the protection of SLOCs where other regional powers, like India, Indonesia, Australia, and Japan, were supporting and assisting the US in keeping the region 'free and open' for economic trade. However, with the Middle East emerging as the US' top priority over the last two decades, its dominance was eroded from the region and China started consolidating and strengthening itself as a regional power to replace the US. However, the US is now rejuvenating itself in the Indo-Pacific region along with its allies, especially India, which possesses multi-faceted geostrategic characteristics that have the potential to be the counterweight to China and limit Chinese ambitions in the region. Moreover, former President of the US, Barack Obama, had formerly noted that India has the capability to play a larger role as an Asian power and that America would welcome it.[6] Not only this, in the last days of Trump's presidency, the US had declassified the US Strategic Framework for the Indo-Pacific. With regards to India, the US sees it as a major security partner/"preferred partner" to counterbalance China (Zeeshan, 2021). It is now an appropriate time for India to take advantage of the opportunity to secure a strategic deterrence against China in case of any conflict in the Himalayan region, such as the Doklam Standoff; India could achieve this by creating a blockade in trade and energy supply routes.

As far as the Indian Ocean is concerned, domestically, China was heavily criticised by its think tanks for not being proactive enough in the region. The newly released 'Blue Book', published by the Chinese Academy of Social Sciences, had criticised Beijing for not having a clear-cut Indian Ocean strategy. The book emphasises that the 'changing dynamics of international relations necessitates that China play a more proactive role in affairs of the region'.[7] Brahma Chellaney, a noted expert on China, also opines that China's latest white paper emphasises an expanded role for her navy beyond her naval backyard (Chellaney, 2015). Thus, one can clearly foresee a likely contestation in the Indian Ocean as both countries try to expand their sphere of influence in the region. Moreover, Coral Bell, an Australian international relations scholar, in her paper titled 'The end of the Vasco da Gama Era', propounded that "The Indian Ocean is likely to become an arena of complex naval rivalries."[8]

China's Naval Foray in the Indo-Pacific

Ab initio, China has traditionally been a continental power rather than a seafaring nation. Until the Song Dynasty, China was always interested in the land route and left the maritime route to be used by the Srivijayans and never made direct contact with the maritime world, let alone active engagement in the Indian Ocean (Medcalf). Except for a brief period in the 15th century when Admiral Zheng He undertook his historic seven voyages beyond China's shores, little had been known about China's maritime exploits.[9] The period between 1405 and 1433 was the golden phase of Chinese naval history in which it became a major actor in international politics. A total of seven expeditions passed westwards through the Straits of Malacca, calling at ports on the Malay Peninsula, Sumatra, Bengal, Ceylon, Southern India, Persia, Arabia, and East Africa. Subsidiary expeditions pushed as far north as Jidda on the Red Sea and the Mozambique Channel between Madagascar and the African continent.[10] These expeditions primarily were political in character, designed to persuade rulers of the Indian Ocean to submit to the suzerainty of the Chinese emperor, which had deep ramifications. This endeavour has always modified the nature and pattern of economic and political power. Chinese naval technology made great strides under the patronage of the imperial government (Ibid.) in this period. These expeditions were a landmark in China's maritime history, demonstrating increasing Chinese military prowess. It was the first time that the Chinese navy had ventured beyond its shores and made its presence felt west of the Straits of Malacca. However, this Chinese naval odyssey was abruptly terminated in 1433, as it was felt that the operational costs far exceeded the revenue earned from these expeditions. Maritime affairs did not receive much attention from subsequent dynasties

(Ming and Qing dynasties) (Cheng, 2011). Even after the establishment of the People's Republic of China (PRC), not much attention was devoted to the maritime world as the PRC opted for a closed economy. However, since 1978, when China opened its economy to the outside world, considerable importance began to be attached to the maritime sphere (Ibid.).

Remarkably, the infamous legislation called the "Law Concerning Territorial Water and Adjacent Regions", passed in February 1992, led to the advent of Chinese aggressive maritime adventures in the 'South China Sea' and 'Southern Ocean', which are popularly known as *Nanhai* and *Nanyang* in the Chinese mainland. The passing of Chinese maritime laws also coincided with the US' withdrawal from the Philippines. The strategic shift helped China in its ascendency at the expense of the erosion of US influence.[11]

Consequently, China's economic prosperity is today directly linked to her naval capabilities since much of the world's trade is conducted through seas. Furthermore, the Chinese economy is export- oriented and almost 60 per cent of its exports are seaborne.[12] In this context, it becomes pertinent for China to streamline her maritime infrastructure to sustain the growth and enhance its strategic access and political leverage. China's economy has grown at a rapid pace since it began its economic reforms, which includes the energy sector as energy is one of the most significant prerequisites for development. Usually, there is a direct connection between the energy consumption patterns and the income of a nation. The more economically developed a nation is, the higher are its energy requirements.

However, China's strategic vulnerability is compounded by the fact that 90 per cent of its oil imports are transported via the Indian Ocean, through narrow choke points, namely, the Hormuz and Malacca Straits.[13] This overdependence on the Malacca Strait is popularly referred to as the "Malacca Dilemma".[14] Geographically, the Malacca Strait is a very narrow strait between Indonesia and Malaysia that connects the Indian Ocean with the South China Sea. The strait is very shallow—at some places, the water is barely 23 metres deep. It is also very narrow—at some places, the strait is barely 1.5 to 2 kilometres wide. However, it is one of the busiest waterways in the world. This strategic dilemma was captured by an article in a Chinese newspaper in 2004, which stated that "it is no exaggeration to say that whosoever controls the Straits of Malacca will have a stronghold on the energy route to China".[15] China fears that if its shipments are blockaded at Malacca, it has to re-route them through Sunda or Lombok Straits despite their geographical unsuitability as the latter themselves are vulnerable to blockades. Recently, however, a researcher of the Chinese Ministry of Commerce's think tank, Mei Xinyu, opined that the Malacca Dilemma would be replaced with the 'Indian Dilemma' in the near future. Infact, China's vulnerability has actually transcended much beyond the peripheries of the Strait of Malacca. He propounded, "In order to cut off and had supplies from the gulf to China, they just need to advise Gulf countries to close oil wells, they don't need the Malacca Strait."[16] This persistent Chinese fear is in consonance with Mearsheimer's offensive realism, which says that "great powers fear each other. They regard each other with suspicion, and they worry that war might be in the offing. They anticipate danger."[17]

According to former Admiral Arun Prakash, who had been India's Naval Chief then and had very closely observed China's naval manoeuvres in the Indian Ocean, "China fears that in the event of confrontation, its economy could be held hostage through the threat of interdiction at sea. This has prompted her to secure footholds in the Indian Ocean where its naval forces could find sustenance and support for extended deployments away from home."[18]

China's presence in the Indian Ocean has been interpreted by experts to various degrees. On the one hand, a group of experts believes that this presence is limited to safeguarding its trade and commercial interests.[19] On the other hand, the other group believes that this presence is aimed at gaining a superior power in the region so that the power deferential keeps its strategic position secure[20] (Malik M., 2011) (Jae-Hyung, 2002). Keeping this in mind, an article was published in *Pacific Journal,* articulating the contours of China's Indian Ocean Strategy where it came out with a sixteen-character (Chinese language characters) guideline: "Select locations meticulously, make deployments discreetly, give priority to cooperative activities and penetrate gradually."

It cautioned that China would pursue expansion quietly and with a slow pace, primarily with an intent to maintain the balance of power in the Indian Ocean. The aforementioned assemblage refers to the Chinese maritime drive in the Indian Ocean at present (Macaes, p. 72). Chinese strategists believe that 'slow penetration' would not startle or pre-empt India and the US while China tries to establish maritime hegemony.

Bypassing the Malacca Dilemma or Quest for Great Power Status: The Role of the Maritime Silk Road

To understand China's recent emerging role in the Indo-Pacific, especially in the context of withdrawal of the US presence, one needs to assess China's utilisation of the void created by US' declined influence. From a realist perspective, it makes sense that China's adoption of an offensive stance is more meaningful in maintaining its prominence in the region. Even the Malacca dilemma is so critical for China that merely a defensive stance would not be sufficient to secure its national interests. Considering these aspects, China embarked on its reinvigoration, and in an effort to strengthen its national territories, occupied the shoals, built artificial islands in the South China Sea, enabled them with strategically capable airstrips, erected radars, deployed a massive fleet of vessels to regularly guard its waters, and has allegedly even attempted to frequently and aggressively violate the maritime boundaries of its neighbours (Madhav, Ibid., p. 6). Mearsheimer opines that "great powers are constantly searching for opportunities so as to gain power over their rivals with hegemony as their final goal."[21] He further goes on to say that "a great power that has a marked advantage over its rivals are likely to behave more aggressively because it has the capability as well as incentive to do so"(Ibid., p. 33). Moreover, it has been observed by various scholars that China has intentions of expanding its foothold in the maritime domain to threaten the US naval presence in case of future confrontation or a low-level conflict or any multilateral engagement of the US with other regional powers, such as India, Australia, and Japan, who perceive Chinese expansion as a threat to their national interests. The strategic interest of China is leading it to gradually emerge as a powerful player in the Indo-Pacific to assert its influence, thereby securing its trade at choke points. China's Indian Ocean policy also has to be seen from this perspective.

Moreover, President Xi Jinping aims to gain a larger presence over the Eurasian region and the Indo-Pacific in particular under the canopy of its billion dollar project—the Belt and Road Initiative, having both land and maritime dimensions. So as far as geopolitics is concerned, the BRI/OBOR is akin to a global order that aims to replace the western principles with Chinese ones and puts China at the heart of world trade and prosperity.

The BRI consists of both a Belt and a Road, indicating the former as 'land routes' and the latter as a 'maritime connectivity' belt. As far as the Road is concerned, the 2017 document of Vision for Maritime Cooperation under BRI proposed three routes for the Maritime Silk Road: first, the China-Indian Ocean-Africa-Mediterranean Sea Blue Economic Passage, linking China-Indochina Peninsula Economic Corridor, running westward from the South China Sea to the Indian Ocean, and connecting the China-Pakistan Economic Corridor (CPEC) and the Bangladesh-China-India-Myanmar Economic Corridor; second, the "blue economic passage" of China-Oceania-South Pacific, travelling southward from the South China Sea into the Pacific Ocean. Third route encompasses the China-Arctic Ocean-Europe economic passage which is envisioned linking Europe via the Arctic Ocean.

Figure 5.1: Map of the Indian Ocean Region Illustrating the Maritime Silk Road Security Implications and Investments

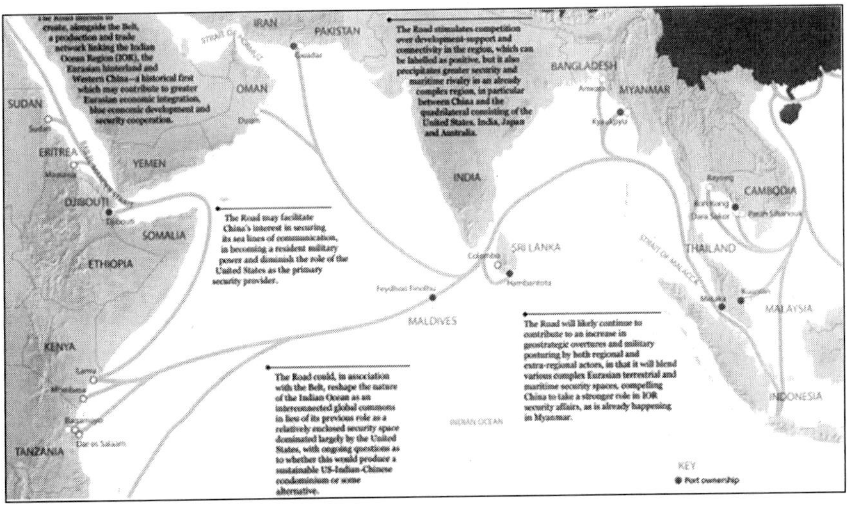

Source: SIPRI.

It has been reported that the Maritime Silk Road is going to help in the advancement of Chinese national interests in the South China Sea in myriad forms. Firstly, it will develop certain pressure points which might coax the disputed parties to resolve their issues with China at once and will offer rewards to the countries falling in line with China, as could be seen with reference to the Chinese strategy with Cambodia and the Philippines in 2012.

Secondly, the cooperative projects will be aimed at the reduction and possibly, erosion of territorial tensions in the region. And lastly, the institutional linkages will help in fostering the 'new convention' that maritime affairs and disputes should be handled and resolved directly by the concerned parties, without the involvement of any mediator or outside actor, such as the US.[22] Moreover, China passed a law in 2016, aiming to postulate a comprehensive legal framework intended to provision for the use of the civilian assets to support military logistics operations and seek assistance from all Chinese industries to provide supplies and aid to the Chinese navy in case of any conflict and eventuality.[23]

A former Indian diplomat, Subhash Kapila, has asserted, "*China's Maritime Silk Road enterprise is not an economic response but a strategic and military response to the United States 'Strategic Pivot to Asia Pacific' and India's 'Look East Policy' assuming more proactive contours as 'Act East Policy' incorporating Indian Navy presence in the South China Sea and Western Pacific. China if it was a responsible member of group of Major Global Powers should have collaborated with them in maintaining security and stability in the South China Sea and the Indian Ocean. Regrettably, its demonstrated track record was the opposite and hence invited countermeasures.*

China forgets that the above-mentioned strategic responses by the United States and India which find equal resonance with Japan and Australia were the logical responses to China's not so benign military rise and China's aims to evict the United States from the Western Pacific and a double encirclement of India both in the Himalayan Borders in the North and open a new maritime flank in the South in the Indian Ocean (Kapila, 2018)."

Other strategic analysts are of the opinion that the Chinese Maritime Silk Road is going to pose a strategic challenge to the Indo-Pacific security if its maritime grid gets connected to the CPEC, and China's push for a similar corridor emanating from Yunnan connecting with the shores of Myanmar will provide the former a strategic maritime access to the Indian Ocean. Although China purported these corridors for economic development alone, in the true sense, these are strategic highways paving the way for direct access to the Indian Ocean through the Bay of Bengal and the Arabian Sea. The Chinese Maritime Silk Road Project is a key instrument in achieving its global maritime ambitions as enshrined in China's Maritime Strategy Doctrine of 2015. Moreover, Chinese strategists know that if China is not able to expand its distant maritime influence, then it will not get the desired recognition and respect of being a global power.

It is being argued that China, in order to offset the Malacca dilemma and expand its geopolitical influence, has adopted a three-pronged strategy (Ji, 2008, p. 74): First, China is looking for alternate supply routes through the construction of pipelines via Myanmar and Pakistan. Secondly, China is trying to secure military bases in and around these choke points and establish militarised islands, a strategy that has been often described as 'String of Pearls' in the defence circles. In the South China Sea, China has been bullying other regional countries over the maritime boundaries and ownership of islands. China has illegally demarcated a vaguely defined 'nine-dash line' and it has moved ahead with the establishment of two new districts in Paracel and Spratly Islands, giving them the Chinese names of Xisha and Nansha.[24] It was evident that the site is in dispute with Vietnam and is a clear violation of the China-Vietnam Agreement on the Basic Principles Guiding the Resolution of Maritime Issues in October 2011.[25] Finally, China has been trying to transform the PLAN into a 'blue water navy' capable of safeguarding SLOCs and other overseas assets.

China views Myanmar as a gateway to get access to the Indian Ocean. It is for this reason that Beijing is toiling hard to establish a strategic network of rail, road and air transport connecting Yunnan Province located in the southwest part of China to Myanmar. Myanmar, thus, is the most convenient land bridge to the Indian Ocean for Beijing, both for its acquisition of trade routes as well as security.[26] Various strategists regard 'pipeline supply' as a safer and cheaper mode of transporting oil. China is busy constructing a network of gas and oil pipelines in Myanmar and another pipeline from Maday Island to Yunnan Province. This move will help China in transporting the oil coming from Africa and the Middle East, a move designed to bypass the Malacca dilemma. However, one could well argue that the oil supply could still be strangled by India in open sea areas (see Map 1). In case of a clash, India could still create a blockade before the ships reach Myanmar's shores.

In this regard, the Gwadar port under the CPEC holds the key to China's strategy to bypass the Malacca Strait. China plans to import oil from the Middle East and create storage of oil in the refineries at Gwadar. Thereafter, the refined oil would be sent to China through roads, pipelines, or railway.

For Beijing, the strategic value of Gwadar is due to the fact that it is located just 240 miles away from the Strait of Hormuz. China's quest to secure its oil supply hinges on two things—the Gwadar port and its subsequent linkage with the Karakoram highway. In fact, the Karakoram highway along with Gwadar port together form the linchpins of the long-standing relationship between China and Pakistan (Singh, 2007).

Map 5.1: Map showing China's Strategy of 'String of Pearls'

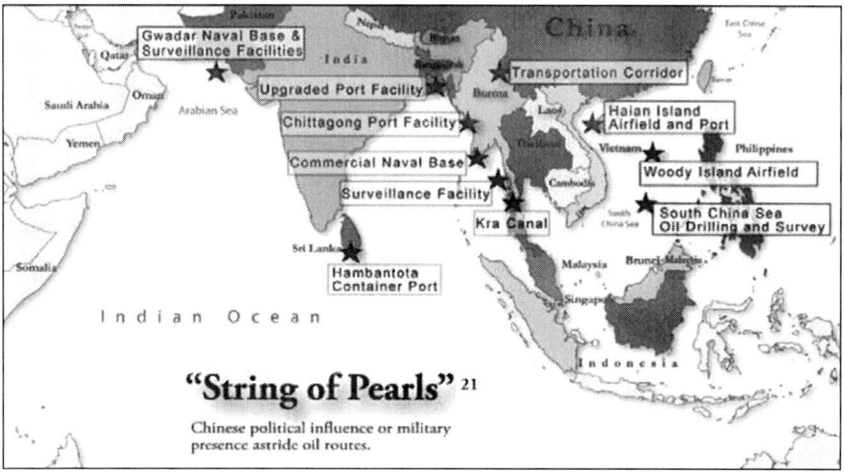

Source: IJBSR, 2017.

The second strategy, which has been heatedly debated in Indian strategic circles, is known as 'String of Pearls' (See Map 1). The concept was floated in 2005 by Booz Allen Hamilton—a US-based think tank—and it soon became a buzzword in the strategic circles.[27] The 'String of Pearls' is supposedly "a nexus of Chinese geopolitical influence or military presence along its stretched sea lanes of communication."[28] These "Pearls" extend from the coast of China through the littorals of the South China Sea, the Strait of Malacca, across the Indian Ocean, and on to the littorals of the Arabian Sea and the Persian Gulf. China is busy building strategic relationships with countries lying along the Sea Lines of Communication (SLOCs) that connect Beijing to the Middle East. "The list of these pearls include upgraded military facilities in Hainan Island, advanced airship on Woody Pherson Island located in a parallel archipelago, which is about 300 nautical miles east of Vietnam, construction of deep water port in Sittwe (Burma), construction of naval base in Gwadar (Pakistan), container shipment facility in Chittagong, intelligence gathering facility on Islands in Bay of Bengal near the Malacca strait, Hambantota port in Sri Lanka apart from porting rights in Aden (Yemen), Salah (Oman) and Djibouti."[29]

Third, the strategy adopted by China to mitigate its energy woes is to modernise its navy. Policymakers in China have realised that the best way to guard SLOCs or protect its maritime assets abroad is to have a powerful navy. It is for this reason China is investing heavily so as to modernise its navy. Beijing wishes to transform the PLAN (People's Liberation Army Navy) into a 'blue navy', which will have the capability of conducting military operations far beyond its coastlines. "In April 2013, China came up with a white paper titled, '*The Diversified Employment of China's Armed Forces*', which referred to the PLAN, as China's mainstay for maritime security operations involving overseas energy and resources, strategic sea lines of communication (SLOCs) (Len, 2015)." Obviously, Beijing has embarked upon a massive naval transformation. This is done so as to transform what was essentially a coastal navy into a blue water navy that has the capability to dominate the region, deny entry to a superior force, carry out belligerent operations, and undertake distant deployments so as to protect its SLOCs. In its quest for acquiring blue water navy status, China has embarked upon an Aircraft Carrier Programme. China's first aircraft carrier, Liaoning, was inducted into the PLAN in September 2012 (Krishnan, 2014). Beijing's deployment of aircraft carriers would go a long way in strengthening the PLAN and protecting its maritime security. Moreover, China is developing technologically advanced new generation submarines capable of thwarting the American military advantage, in particular, and challenging its adversaries if the latter ever threaten its SLOCs. These submarines have nuclear arsenals on board and are capable of patrolling the Indian Ocean at all times, gathering intelligence of the adversary's strategic assets, testing its capability to go deep down, and more importantly, practising military drills in case of war eventuality.[30] However, the culmination of these events has resulted in the emergence of a nuclear arms race in the Indian Ocean in particular, and the Indo-Pacific in general, where along with the US and China, other regional powers, like India, Japan, Australia, and Russia, are also developing submarines capable of targeting each other's mainland strategic assets. Although a direct nuclear confrontation is less likely to happen, the region will remain in a state of permanent coercion, which could be summarised as the 'stability-instability paradox'.

All these strategic moves strengthen the arguments around China's hegemonic ambitions. Although China has always upheld its rhetoric of peaceful rise officially, its military build-up needs to be understood as an instrument that renders minimal aggression so as to prevent a coalition of affected states congregating against it. According to Mearsheimer's reasoning, one can summarise: "On the other hand, a state bent on aggression is likely to emphasize its peaceful goals while exaggerating its military weakness, so that the potential victim does not build up its own arms and thus leaves itself vulnerable to attack."[31]

Assessing India's Strategic Options To Counter Chinese Influence in the Indo-Pacific

The Indian Ocean strategy is central to India's strategic and economic interests and pivotal in its foreign policy. Geographically, India enjoys a strategic preeminence in the Indian Ocean. India's triangular wedge-shaped landmass extends some 1500 miles into the Indian Ocean. It has a western coastline of over 1400 miles and an eastern coastline of 2000 miles and is thus uniquely positioned to control the Arabian Sea in the west and the Bay of Bengal in the east.[32] Additionally, India also has over 1000 islands and atolls accounting for over 1300 miles of coastline (Ibid.). As per UNCLOS (United Nation Convention on Laws of Seas), India's long coastline gives it a huge exclusive economic zone worth 1.37 million square miles (Ibid.).

Keeping in mind the strategic facet, the Indian Ocean is of critical importance to India, so much so that India's first Prime Minister, Jawaharlal Nehru, emphasised, "whatever happens in the whole Indian Ocean region affects and is affected by India. It simply cannot help it." Moreover, India's former Deputy Prime Minister, Sardar Patel, also once remarked that "the geographical position and features of India makes it inevitable to have a strong navy to guard its long coastline and to keep a constant vigil on the vast expanse of the sea that surrounds us."[33] However, despite the importance given to the Indian Ocean by the founding fathers of the Indian nation- state, the advice received very less attention by later leaders. This was due to a myriad of factors.

However, currently, there are two external catalysts, which are propelling the Indian policymakers to maintain a sound maritime policy. The first motivation is China's inroads into the Indian Ocean via its much-touted Belt and Road Initiative and its quest for the Blue Water Navy to strengthen its position in the Indian Ocean; the other is the tacit support of the US, which wants India to play a major role in the region.

China's naval foray has forced India's policymakers to come up with a comprehensive and futuristic maritime strategy. India's maritime draft, released in 2004 under the caption, "Freedom to Use Seas: India's Maritime Military Strategy", takes note of this expanding Chinese foothold in the Indian Ocean region. It states, "The Chinese Navy is set on the path to becoming a blue water force. It has an ambitious modernization program. Notable amongst those is the renewed interest in the aircraft carrier program, the nuclear submarines and the ballistic/cruise missile projects along with the attempts to gain a strategic toe-hold in the IOR."

The last few years have proved eventful for the Indian Navy as the reactor of the indigenously built nuclear- capable submarine, Arihant, went critical, and the first indigenously built aircraft carrier, Vikrant, was finally unveiled. INS Arihant "marks the first step towards completing the third component of the triad of air, land based and sea based deterrent forces envisaged in India's nuclear doctrine." When INS Vikrant was commissioned on September 2, 2022, India joined a select group of nations that have their own aircraft carriers, an elite group of nations including France, Britain, Russia, and the United States. India has been modernising her bases at Kawar, a strategically located naval facility in Karnataka. India is also strengthening her tri-services strategic command at the Andaman and Nicobar Islands. India is also considering deployment of Sukhois and building several airfields across the island groups. A total of 17 squadrons are planned to be deployed along India's borders with China and Pakistan and the south to survey the country's southern flank up to the Andaman and Nicobar Islands. Since the 2000s, the Indian Navy has been organising the Indian Naval symposium (IONS) with friendly navies and setting up think tanks to brainstorm various maritime issues. India has also established the National Maritime Foundation (NMF) as its primary think tank to provide important inputs and strategic vision with action plans for the future.

Indian policymakers have also taken note of the significance of the Andaman and Nicobar Islands. The islands assume much importance given their proximity to critical choke points, such as the Strait of Malacca. This view has been reiterated by several scholars who believe "India needs to strengthen its Andaman and Nicobar Command by stationing one or two large warships there on a permanent basis and by setting up Brahmos cruise missile silos on some of the larger islands." These islands will be a vital cog in case there is a naval clash between New Delhi and Beijing. Brewster (2010) opines that "The islands have also been described by certain Chinese analysts as a 'metal chain' which could lock China out of the Indian Ocean."

While there are significant developments in the expansion of the Indian Navy, one needs to acknowledge the fact that sustenance of a powerful naval force is directly linked to a sound industrial base. India continues to rely on other countries when it comes to naval hardware. Admiral Arun Prakash very rightly points out that "every piece of hardware that the Indian armed forces acquire from abroad places them at the mercy of the seller nation for the lifetime of the equipment."[34] Thus, there is an urgent need to augment India's industrial base to satisfy the increasing demands of an expanding navy. This is an area that has not shown enough development over the last few years.

At the diplomatic level, India needs to continue its engagement with the Indian Ocean littoral states through joint naval exercises, anti-piracy options, sea patrolling, sea visits, and fleet reviews. India will have to bank upon her image as a responsible power. New Delhi must rigorously focus her attention on maritime diplomacy in the Indian Ocean region. The current NDA government, under the dynamic leadership of Prime Minister Narendra Modi, appears to have realised the importance of maritime diplomacy in India's foreign policy. During his visit to the Seychelles, Mauritius, and Sri Lanka in March 2015, Modi enunciated his ambitious and proactive policy for the Indian Ocean. This policy has been given the acronym, "SAGAR"—Security and Growth for All in the Region. The main features of this policy are: first, India will do everything to safeguard its mainland and island territories; second, India will focus on enhancing security cooperation with regional partners in the Indian Ocean region; and third, India believes that it is only through collective action and cooperation that peace and security can be established in the region. This was also reflected in PM Modi's comments on the Indian flag whereby he had remarked that "the Blue Chakra of our national flag represents the potential of Blue Revolution for the Ocean Economy."

Recognising the central weakness in its foreign policy, India has launched 'Project MAUSAM'. This project is essentially a Ministry of Culture initiative, promoting the creation of cultural links with India's maritime neighbours. Pursued in tandem with the Archaeological Survey of India (ASI), the project's objective is two-fold. This project is considered to be the government's major foreign policy initiative designed to counter China.[35] The project is inspired by India's historical role as the focal point for trade in the Indian Ocean. Through Project Mausam, Indian strategic outreach to the Indian Ocean littoral states, thus, appears to be non-assertive and quite cooperative in nature. It tries to address maritime issues in a collaborative manner based on mutual respect and a respect for international law. The underlying belief is, thus, that maritime security could be best achieved through cooperative endeavour. India projects itself as a country seeking a climate of trust and transparency, respect for international maritime rules and norms by all countries. The purpose is to project India's image as a benign power.[36]

Viewing 'Project Mausam' with a limited viewpoint of countering China would be restrictive and counterproductive. The move needs to be understood in terms of the larger foreign policy picture of the Modi government, which has accorded high importance to civilisational ties while establishing multilateral and bilateral relations. It is an assertion of India's soft power that will be strategically utilised in relationship building. Indian soft power will thus be focused on building a capability to attract other states through its culture, political values, etc. In a holistic manner, Project Mausam, when effectively blended with programmes like SAGAR, could go a long way in strengthening India's strategic objectives.

With these strategic and other options at hand, India enjoys a geographical prominence in the Indian Ocean region. Perhaps, in the event of a clash in the Himalayan region, India will use its naval pre-eminence in the Indian Ocean region to restrict China. This view has been supported by a noted academician and an expert on India-China relations, John W. Garver, who says, "Perhaps in response to the defeat of Indian land forces in the Himalayan region, Indian leaders would opt to utilize their power in the area where it had a substantial superiority and where it could inflict crippling damage on China by severing

Chinese commerce in the Indian Ocean."[37] When the Doklam standoff took place, there were unconfirmed reports that the Indian PM deliberated with other stakeholders on sending India's sole boomer, Arihant, to the sea so as to caution the adversary of India's preparedness in case of any conflictual eventuality at the Himalayan juncture.[38]

Thus, the current assessment of India's position does not appear to be as vulnerable. The strategic and non-strategic moves and structural advantages would be utilised by the Indian state in case of any sign of aggression. Although these options may not appear as significant in comparison, yet the position of India is significantly strong for them to act as deterrents. In this unique situation, India may counter China in the Indian Ocean, thanks to its geography and current military capabilities. India does not pose any danger to China as an aggressor. This situation may be viewed as a situation of 'deterrence'.

Moreover, as far as the Indo-Pacific at large is concerned, the recent United States' declassified document, titled "US Strategic Framework for the Indo-Pacific", has indicated a larger role for India where its strategy aims to become New Delhi's preferred partner on security and in countering the burgeoning influence of China in the Indo-Pacific region (Karambelkar, 2021).

Conclusion

An overall assessment of the evolving security dynamics in the Indo-Pacific region reveals that China is trying to beef up its presence where earlier the US had enjoyed its military advantage and is now creating a vacuum for geopolitical competition between China and India. However, both the US and China are not in a position to unilaterally dominate the region. They still cannot assume the role which the US had once played in the region. This inability to dominate the region will result in a balance of power situation. This balance of power situation, however, is likely to be prolonged since the asymmetry in terms of naval capabilities between the two nations is still narrow. Since states are not 'mindless aggressors', this balance of power is likely to continue. However, New Delhi and the US should keep this asymmetry narrow enough so as to keep this equilibrium intact.

Coming from a neo-realist frame, this study finds substantial evidences of Chinese manoeuvres as 'offensive' as understood by Mearsheimer and the corresponding stance of the Indo-Pacific countries, especially the US and India, as more of a deterrence.

Theoretically, the two positions may give rise to a balance of power situation; however, whether this balance will give rise to an era of peace or will result in a power struggle leading to destabilisation in the region has contentious interpretations among scholars and analysts. This paper argues that there is a greater possibility of a 'geopolitical instability' in the region given the developments that have occurred despite the high stakes. There is visible evidence that the two states and their allies have taken sides, especially in the maritime domain.

Thus, Beijing will be aiming to gain maximum power in the Indo-Pacific so as to reach a position where it can exercise a dominant role in the region. This will be achieved by creating a Blue Water Navy. The evidence cited in the paper suggest that China is putting all its efforts into reaching such a position.

In this scenario, India's position would have become precarious if it had kept its hands off in its backyard. Evidence suggests that India has taken enough measures to counter China's aggression through peaceful means. As discussed in this paper, New Delhi is quite aware of Beijing's dependencies on the safety of the SLOCs and that all the available three solutions to the Malacca dilemma do not make Beijing safe enough. India, owing to its geographical advantage, will use the options to the best of its recently enhanced capabilities. These advantages will always keep a check on China in case of any eventuality. As mentioned earlier, India is working on its capabilities to an extent that has made its position formidable as a deterrent.

Moreover, some observers are of the opinion that a very straightforward approach of not getting regional and global powers engaged in violent confrontation would be where, on the one hand, the US could make room for China's primacy in East Asia, and on the other hand, China could acknowledge India's ascendency in the Indian Ocean. However, recently, China has affirmed that it seeks to use its hard power to safeguard overseas interests. In this backdrop, China has developed its stakes in the Indian Ocean and will not acknowledge this region as India's backyard or sphere of influence. In the realist understanding, war is considered as a legitimate means of exercising power. Building further on this thesis, it can be easily asserted that a situation of 'war to come' and its possible consequences, too, act like a preventive measure to a war. The case of US-China relations in the Indo-Pacific successfully demonstrates this situation, where, despite all the power manoeuvres, the two nations are not any closer to war than they were before. This 'balance of power' has resulted from the power positions of the two nations in a unique geopolitical site of the Indo-Pacific.

In the end, it can be inferred that the prevailing security dilemma, where the defensive measures by China have been enacted against the purported American threat, are not necessarily against the US but against the other countries in the region as well. Since the last few years, China is building up its military infrastructure and modernising its armed forces on the pretext of the American threat, but it would equally harm other countries and the prime target of its burgeoning military might would be primarily India, which might be followed by other smaller nations or nations in the Indo-Pacific.

Notes

1. John Mearsheimer, The tragedy of great power politics, 2001, p. 33.
2. OpCit.
3. C Raja Mohan, Samudra Mantah: Sino-Indian Rivalry in the Indo-Pacific, Carnegie Endowment for International Peace, James, Online web Access: https://doi.org/10.2307/j.ctt6wpjb4/, 28/11/2012.
4. Salman Khurshid, Putting out to sea a new vision, 2013.
5. Pant, 2015, pp. 47-69.
6. Medcalf,
7. Hornat, 2016, pp. 423-445.
8. Bell, 2007, p. 22.
9. Singh S. , 2011, pp. 235-248.
10. Garver J. W., 2001, p. 81.
11. Madhav, Indo-Pacific is the Power Axis of the 21st Century, 2021, p. 6.
12. Mohan R. , 2012, p. 41.
13. Prakash, China's Maritime Challenge in the Indian Ocean, 2011, pp. 1-16.
14. Lanteigne, 2008, pp. 143-161.
15. Kalha, 2011, pp. 338-340.
16. Macaes, Belt and Road: A Chinese World Order, 2019, p. 22.
17. Mearsheimer, The Tragedy of Great Power Politics, 2001.
18. Prakash, China's Maritime Challenge in the Indian Ocean, 2011, pp. 1-16.
19. Latagenie: 2008, You: 2007, Zhang; 2011.
20. Joshi, China and India: Awkward Ascents, 2011, Also See Prakash, China's Maritime Challenge in the Indian Ocean, 2011.

21. Mearsheimer, The tragedy of great power politics, 2001, p. 29.
22. Yoshimatsu, 2017, pp. 294-315.
23. Macaes, Nuts and Bolts, 2019, p. 71).
24. Lo, 2020.
25. Michael Martina, 2017.
26. Malik J. M., 2017, pp. 1-17.
27. Khurana, 2008.
28. Joshi, China and India: Awkward Ascents, 2011.
29. Pehrson, 2006, p. 169.
30. Medcalf, Chapter 8, Beneath the waves.
31. Mearsheimer, The Tragedy of Great Power Politics, 2001, p. 34.
32. Scott, 2006, p. 99.
33. Holslag, 2010, p. 129.
34. Prakash, Maritime Security of India Future Challenges, 2014, p. 68.
35. Pillalamarri, 2014.
36. Padmaja, 2015.
37. Garver J. , 2011.
38. Medcalf, Contest For The Indo-Pacific, 2020.

References

Das, U. (July 13, 2019), *What Is the Indo-Pacific?* Retrieved from *The Diplomat*: https://thediplomat.com/2019/07/what-is-the-indo-pacific/

Singh, A. (n.d.), *Vikrant Kumar Edara Asked: What does the term "Indo-Pacific" signifies, as distinct from Asia-Pacific?* Retrieved from Manohar Parrikar Institute for Defence Studies and Analyses : https://idsa.in/askanexpert/termIndoPacificsignifies

Ghosh, C. P. (2004), *Maritime Security Challenges in South Asia and the Indian Ocean: Response Strategies.* Honolulu, Hawaii : Center for Strategic and International Studies.

Salman Khurshid, J. B. (November 2, 2013), *Putting out to sea a new vision.* Retrieved from *The Hindu*: https://www.thehindu.com/opinion/op-ed/putting-out-to-sea-a-new-vision/article5305845.ece

Abraham, S. (2015), *China's Role in the Indian Ocean: Its Implications on India's National Security.* Delhi: VIJ Books (India) Pty Ltd.

Salman Khurshid, J. B. (November 2, 2013), *Putting out to sea a new vision.* Retrieved from *The Hindu*: https://www.thehindu.com/opinion/op-ed/putting-out-to-sea-a-new-vision/article5305845.ece

Medcalf, R. (Ibid.). Ibid. Ibid: Ibid.

Bell, C. (2007), *The End of the Vasco Da Gama Era: The Next Landscape of World Politics.* Sydney: Lowy Insitute. Retrieved from https://www.lowyinstitute.org/sites/default/files/pubfiles/LIP21_BellWEB_1.pdf

Pant, H. V. (2015), "The American "Pivot" and the Indian Navy", *Naval War College Review,* 68(1). Retrieved from https://digital-commons.usnwc.edu/cgi/viewcontent.cgi?article=1181&context=nwc-review

Hornat, J. (2016), "The power triangle in the Indian Ocean: China, India and the United States", *Cambridge Review of International Affairs, 29*(2). Retrieved from https://www.tandfonline.com/doi/abs/10.1080/09557571.2014.974507

Chellaney, B. (June 23, 2015), *China's Indian Ocean strategy.* Retrieved from *The Japan Times*: https://www.japantimes.co.jp/opinion/2015/06/23/commentary/world-commentary/chinas-indian-ocean-strategy/#.WmFoMudG3IU

Mearsheimer, J. (2001), *The tragedy of great power politics.* New York: W.W. Norton & Company.

Ibid. (n.d.). Ibid.

Mearsheimer, J. (2001), *The Tragedy of Great Power Politics.* New York: W.W. Norton & Company.

Medcalf, R. (Ibid). Ibid. Ibid: Ibid.

Macaes, B. (2019), *Belt and Road: A Chinese World Order.* Gurgaon: Penguin Random House India.

Macaes, B. (Ibid). Ibid. Ibid: Ibid.

Lo, K. (April 18, 2020), *Beijing moves to strengthen grip over disputed South China Sea.* Retrieved from *South China Morning Post*: https://www.scmp.com/news/china/diplomacy/article/3080559/beijing-moves-strengthen-grip-over-disputed-south-china-sea

Michael Martina, M. N. (November 3, 2017), *China says has agreement with Vietnam on managing S.China Sea dispute.* Retrieved from *Reuters*: https://www.reuters.com/article/southchinasea-china-vietnam/china-says-has-agreement-with-vietnam-on-managing-s-china-sea-dispute-idUKL4N1N91DS

Zeeshan, M. (January 21, 2021), *India and the US: Ideological Convergence No More?* Retrieved from *The Diplomat*: https://thediplomat.com/2021/01/india-and-the-us-ideological-convergence-no-more/

Madhav, R. (January 2021), Indo-Pacific is the Power Axis of the 21st Century. *India Foundation Journal, II*(1), p. 76. Retrieved from https://indiafoundation.in/wp-content/uploads/2021/01/January-February-2021-Issue-of-India-Foundation-Journal.pdf

Madhav, R. (n.d.). Ibid. Ibid.

Deudney, D. H. (n.d.), *Encyclopedia Britannica.* Retrieved from https://www.britannica.com/topic/geopolitics

Yoshimatsu, H. (2017), "China, Japan and the South China Sea Dispute: Pursuing Strategic Goals Through Economic and Institutional Means", *Journal of Asian Security and International Affairs.*

Macaes, B. (2019), "Nuts and Bolts". In B. Macaes, *Belt and Road: A Chinese World Order.* Gurgaon: Penguin Random House.

Kapila, S. (September 9, 2018), "China's Maritime Silk Road Strategically Impacts Indo-Pacifc Security—Analysis". Retrieved from *Eurasian Review*: https://www.eurasiareview.com/09092018-chinas-maritime-silk-road-strategically-impacts-indo-pacifc-security-analysis/

PIB (March 2, 2019), *Indo-Pacific Regional Dialogue – 2019.* Retrieved from https://pib.gov.in/Pressreleaseshare.aspx?PRID=1567131

Medcalf, R. (2020), *Contest For The Indo-Pacific.* Carlton, Australia: La Trobe University Press.

Karambelkar, A. (January 25, 2021), *De-classified US Strategy Document on the Indo-Pacific.* Retrieved from Vivekananda International Foundation: https://www.vifindia.org/2021/january/25/de-classified-us-strategy-document-on-the-indo-pacific

Mohan, C. R. (2012), *Samudra Manthan: Sino-Indian Rivalry in the Indo-Pacific.* Oxford University Press.

Singh, S. (2011), "China's forays into the Indian Ocean: strategic implications for India", *Journal of the Indian Ocean Region.*

Garver, J. W. (2001), *Protracted Contest: Sino-Indian Rivalry in the Twentieth Century.* University of Washington Press.

Ibid. (n.d.). Ibid.

Cheng, D. (2011), *Sea Power and the Chinese State: China's Maritime Ambitions.* The Heritage Foundation.

Ibid. (n.d.). Ibid.

Mohan, R. (2012), *Samudra Manthan: Sino-Indian Rivalry in the Indo-Pacific.* Brookings Institution Press.

Prakash, A. (2011), "China's Maritime Challenge in the Indian Ocean", *Maritime Affairs: Journal of the National Maritime Foundation of India.*

Lanteigne, M. (2008), "China's Maritime Security and the "Malacca Dilemma"", *Asian Security.*

Kalha, S. R. (2011), "The Straits of Malacca and China's Strategic Vulnerability", *USI.*

Mearsheimer, J. (2001), *The Tragedy of Great Power Politics.* WW Norton & Company.

Prakash, A. (2011), "China's Maritime Challenge in the Indian Ocean", *Maritime Affairs.*

Joshi, S. (2011), "China and India: Awkward Ascents", *Orbis.*

Malik, M. (2011). *China and India: Great Power Rivals.* First Forum Press.

Jae-Hyung, L. (2002), "China's Expanding Maritime Ambitions in the Western Pacific and the Indian Ocean", *Contemporary Southeast Asia.*

Prakash, A. (2011), "China's Maritime Challenge in the Indian Ocean", *Maritime Affairs.*

Mearsheimer, J. (2001), *The tragedy of great power politics.* WW Norton & Company.

Ibid. (n.d.). Ibid.

Malik, J. M. (2017), "Myanmar's Role in China's Maritime Silk Road Initiative", *Journal of Contemporary China.*

Khurana, G. (2008), "China's 'String of Pearls' in the Indian Ocean and Its Security Implications", *Strategic Analysis*, pp. 1-39.

Joshi, S. (2011), "China and India: Awkward Ascents", *Orbis*, pp. 558-576.

Pehrson, C. J. (2006), *String of Pearls: Meeting the challenge of china's rising power across the asian littoral.* Army War Coll Strategic Studies Inst Carlisle Barracks PA.

Len, C. (2015), "China's 21st Century Maritime Silk Road Initiative, Energy Security and SLOC Access", *Maritime Affairs*, pp.1-18.

Krishnan, A. (June 11, 2014), *Hasina seeks partnership with China.* Retrieved from *The Hindu*: https://www.thehindu.com/news/international/south-asia/hasina-seeks-partnership-with-china/article6105189.ece

Mearsheimer, J. (2001), *The Tragedy of Great Power Politics.* WW Norton & Company.

Scott, D. (2006), "India's "Grand Strategy" for the Indian Ocean: Mahanian Visions", *Asia-Pacific Review*, 97129.

Ibid. (n.d.). Ibid.

Ibid. (n.d.). Ibid.

Holslag, J. (2010), *China and India: Prospects for Peace.* Columbia University Press.

Navy, I. (2007), *Ensuring Secure Seas: Indian MARITIME Security Strategy.* Indian Navy. Retrieved from https://www.indiannavy.nic.in/sites/default/files/Indian_Maritime_Security_Strategy_Document_25Jan16.pdf

Opinion. (August 13, 2013), "A strategic milestone". Retrieved from *The Hindu*: https://www.thehindu.com/opinion/editorial/a-strategic-milestone/article5016330.ece

Brewster, D. (2010), "An Indian Sphere of Influence in the Indian Ocean?" *Security Challenges*, pp. 1-20.

Prakash, A. (2014), "Maritime Security of India Future Challenges", *Vayau Aerospace and Defence Review.*

Pillalamarri, A. (September 18, 2014), "Project Mausam: India's Answer to China's 'Maritime Silk Road'". Retrieved from *The Diplomat*: https://thediplomat.com/2014/09/project-mausam-indias-answer-to-chinas-maritime-silk-road/

Padmaja, G. (2015), "Modi's Maritime Diplomacy: A Strategic Opportunity", *Maritime Affairs*, pp. 25-42.

Garver, J. (2011), *Protracted contest: Sino-Indian rivalry in the twentieth century.* University of Washington Press.

6

The Zheng He Voyages: China's Encounters with the Sea-Faring Nations of the East and the Maritime Legacy

Anuraag Khaund

In the post-Cold War scenario, after a brief unipolar moment enjoyed by the US, the international political arena saw the rise of multilateral groupings with the emergence of countries such as India, Japan, China, the European Union (EU), and the Association of Southeast Asian Nations (ASEAN), and likewise. However, in recent times, China has emerged as a potential challenger to the hegemonic position of the US with several scholars characterising it as a 'New Cold War'. In this regard, the Belt and Road Initiative (BRI), launched under President Xi Jinping, has emerged as a major manifestation of China's outreach and assertion of its consolidated economic and military ambitions. At the same time, the BRI has been characterised by Chinese leaders, especially President Xi Jinping himself, as the legacy and revitalisation of the ancient Silk Road as well as the maritime voyages of the famous Ming era, especially those of Admiral Zheng He during the 15th century.[1] Xi Jinping has described Zheng He's voyages as "friendly emissaries leading ... sailing treasure-loaded ships who built a bridge for peace and East-West cooperation".[2]

However, a close look at the Ming era adventures in the maritime domain, led by Zheng He, or the land-based expansion into neighbouring Southeast Asian polities in the Yunnan province and Annam (present-day Vietnam) present a completely different picture, as diplomatic-military campaigns were often conducted under the garb of 'benign trade furthering missions'. It is, therefore, important to examine the underlying geopolitics behind Zheng He's voyages as well as the similarities between the historical and current Chinese geopolitical ambitions inherent in projects such as the BRI. This paper gives a brief description of the Zheng He voyages in the context of the Ming era followed by an examination of the diplomatic-military aspects of the latter and the similarities that one could draw with the present times.

The beginning of Ming Expansionism

The Zheng He expeditions or exploration took place during the reign of the second Ming Emperor, Yongle (1402-1424). Yongle was born as Prince Zhu Di and was the fourth son of Zhu Yuanzhang or Emperor Hongwu, who founded the Ming dynasty in 1368. However, the succession of the Ming throne from Hongwu to Yongle was not a smooth one. It involved Zhu Di's usurpation of the power of the chosen emperor, the latter's nephew, Jian-wen, in 1399. With his ascension, Zhu Di took the reign title of 'Yongle' or perpetual happiness.[3] Throughout this ordeal, Zhu Di or Yongle was supported in his efforts by the loyal Muslim palace eunuch, Zheng He, who later rose through the ranks to become the Admiral who would lead the Ming voyages in the coming years.[4] It was this usurpation act of Yongle which set the context for the Ming expansion into the southern polities of Yunnan and Annam, as well as the maritime Zheng He voyages. As per scholars, the earlier mentioned campaigns were launched by the Ming court to increase the legitimacy of the Yongle emperor by extending the outreach and domination of the latter beyond the borders of the empire. However, these missions, especially the Zheng He voyages, were also initiated with the ostentatious aim of capturing the erstwhile Jian-wen emperor, who is believed to have escaped and taken shelter in the lands beyond China.[5] The basis for such strategy on the part of

Yongle was the traditional 'tribute system', which encompassed the East Asian polities of Ming, Korea, and Japan, as well as the horse-riding communities like the Manchus and Mongols living beyond the Great Wall. Under this tribute system, China, under the Mings, was seen as the Middle Kingdom or the 'centre of civilization' whereby the Ming emperor legitimised the rulers or dynastic succession in other polities in return for tributes arriving at the Ming capital from these subservient rulers.[6] Hence, the Yongle emperor decided to strengthen his legitimacy by seeking to bring more such tributary states, near and far, under the Sinocentric tributary system.

The first of such expeditions under Yongle were the land-based expansion and military interactions with the southern polities of the Yuenan and Annam provinces. The invasion of Yuenan, during the time of Emperor Hongwu, was justified on the grounds that the region was an erstwhile province of China since the Han dynasty and hence, had to be recaptured. The annexation of Yuenan involved the deployment of 250,000 troops and the settlement of Chinese 'Han' military families in the region. In addition, native Yuenan polities that accepted the Ming overlordship in return for Chinese legitimation were subject to annual tribute demands. An example of the same was the polity of Tai Mao of Lu- chuan that was ordered to send 15,000 horses and 500 elephants, as well as a large amount of silver.[7] During the time of Yongle, the Ming control over Yunnan was further strengthened with the establishment of Chinese military battalions in the territories of the subservient polities and the appointment of Ming clerks and scholars to 'assist' the indigenous rulers in their administration as the native polities were also asked to provide manpower for labour as well as military campaigns.[8] However, the conquest and annexation of Dai Viet or Annam (modern-day Vietnam) was the most important aspect of Yongle's southern expedition. The immediate context to the invasion was provided by the killing of the Ming-backed local king, Tran Thien Binh, by the nobles of Dai Viet, which spurred clashes between Annam soldiers and Ming forces comprising 95,000 infantry, 10,000 cavalry, and 30,000 'native troops' conscripted from the Yuenan polities. As with the case of Yuenan, the Ming consolidated their control over Dai Viet (Annam) through the re-drawing of maps and administrative boundaries and establishment of tax offices, Confucian schools, and military offices and garrisons, which included both Chinese as well as Annam troops.[9]

The consolidation of Ming rule in Yuenan and the annexation and transformation of Annam into a Chinese province not only provided the Yongle emperor an opportunity to boost his legitimacy but also access to a steady supply of gold, silver, and other resources, such as troops, elephants, and horses, through the tributary missions from the native polities, which added to the wealth and military strength of the empire. In addition, the 'pacification' of these areas also thwarted any military challenge that could have been posed from the southern borders, and at the same time, Annam provided the Mings access to the maritime trade of the Indian Ocean region.[10]

The Zheng He Voyages—Maritime Consolidation and its Geopolitical Implications

The link between the Zheng He voyages and the aim of building legitimacy for the Yongle emperor can be established from the fact that the construction of the Treasure Fleet ships, warships, and ocean-going vessels was ordered by the emperor in the second year of his reign in 1403.[11] In addition, the underlying military nature of the apparently 'diplomatic friendly' voyages could be gauged from the scale of shipbuilding as well as the manpower involved in these missions. For instance, a typical mission or voyage comprised 100 eunuchs of various grades, 93 military captains, 104 lieutenants, 103 sub-lieutenants, and various related staff members, as well as astrologers. Most importantly, the mission also comprised 20,000 military men, including crack troops and irregular troops carrying advanced fire and projectile weapons of the period, out of the total of 27,000 to 30,000 crew members.[12] The Treasure Fleets of Zheng He consisted of around 300-400 ocean-going vessels, including the prized 'Treasure Ships', which were the largest in the fleet, measuring around 426 feet, with innovations, such as compartmentalised hulls, waterproof bulkheads, and mechanical steering devices[13], as well as five-masted *fuchuan* warships of 165 feet armed with cannons and the latest projectile devices.[14] Hence, the prominent and over-arching military component of the expedition was to subdue the nearby kingdoms by the use of force with a clear aim to seek tributary from the subservient kingdoms in the distant regions of the Indian Ocean to bolster Yongle's legitimacy. At the same time, the Treasure Fleet voyages also represented Yongle's overturning of the earlier isolationist policy and trade restrictions of the preceding Emperor Hongwu by claiming that 'Now all within the four seas were one family' and the imperial decree that promoted trade in order 'to supply the country's needs and to encourage distant people to come'.[15] However, instead of equal and free trade exchanges, the Ming court attempted to monopolise commercial activities in the Indian Ocean region through the control of maritime traffic as well as the oceanic routes of connection.[16] Such control over maritime trade would allow Ming China to emerge as the centre of global commerce and further bolster the image of the Yongle emperor. Both these objectives—creation of legitimacy and maritime control—were to be achieved by a demonstration of power and might under the Treasure Fleets of Admiral Zheng He.

With the objective of establishing Ming hegemony, the Zheng He voyages were involved in numerous military conflicts and skirmishes in the regions discovered by the Treasure fleet. The first such action was in the port city of Palembang in modern-day Indonesia, which was populated by merchant Chinese communities who had established chieftainships during the 14th century. Here, Zheng He, upon hearing about the atrocities and piracy committed by the chieftain Chen Zuyi, engaged in a military conflict with the latter in which around 5000 pirates lost their lives and Chen was sent as a prisoner to the Ming court and beheaded. Afterwards, the Ming emperor appointed and legitimised the Chinese merchant, Shi Jinqing, as the new chieftain of Palembang, which became a tributary to the Ming empire, and the latter's control over the port city allowed it access to the trade routes emanating from Southeast Asia.[17] At times, the Ming naval forces, under Zheng He, would also intervene in local conflicts between polities, supporting the demands of one faction against another. For instance, in 1408, when the polity of the island of Brunei (Chinese—*Boni*) wanted to be free from the demand of sending tributes to the *Majapahit* polity of Java kingdom, the Ming court, which had established its rule over the Majapahit through Zheng He, ordered the Java kingdom to cease such demands. In turn, the Brunei kingdom was to send tributary missions to the Ming capital in Beijing and become a subsidiary kingdom under the Yongle emperor.[18] However, the most important method of achieving Ming hegemony over the oceanic realm was the control of strategic choke points and the creation of alternative nodes in the Indian oceanic trade. This was evident in Zheng He's interactions with the polity in the Malacca Strait, which was ruled by a chieftain and had to pay tributary to the powerful neighbouring kingdom of Siam. In 1405, the chieftain, Parameswara, expressed his desire for the emergence of Malacca as an independent kingdom under the overlordship of the Ming emperor, and following this, the third expedition of Zheng He in 1409 was tasked with the gifting of an Imperial Seal of Yongle in Malacca, thereby enfeoffing the latter as an independent kingdom or polity equal in stature with that of the kingdoms of Siam and Java. The prime reason behind the Ming interest in Malacca was its function as an entrepot for maritime trade goods, such as Indian spices, nutmeg, cloves, textiles, pearls, and bird plumes. Hence, with the enfeoffment of Malacca as a Ming tributary, Zheng He also established a *guanchang* (government depot) including granaries and warehouses, which were guarded by a large Ming military garrison.[19] The establishment of the military garrison and the depot was indicative of the Chinese attempt to not just establish trade relations but also militarily control the routes of exchange.

Such control of nodes and the establishment of alternative hubs was also evident in the Treasure Fleet's interactions in South Asia with the polities of Calicut and Cochin on the Malabar Coast. By the late 13th century, regions around the Malabar coast had emerged as an important source of spices, such as pepper, and were the transit point for Chinese trading ships heading for the Persian Gulf.[20] Among the port- kingdoms along the coast, Calicut had emerged as the most important port for Chinese traffic given its status as the leading exporter of pepper and its proximity to Sinhala or Sri Lanka (Chinese *Sengjiala*).[21] Although Calicut and the ruling polity of King Zamorin (*Samoothiri*) had accepted the overlordship of the Ming empire and sent tributary missions to China in 1407 along with Zheng He, yet the domination of Arab Muslim middlemen in the trade as well as administration may have prevented the extension and entrenchment of Ming influence in the Court. Hence, the Ming search for alternative sources of pepper other than Calicut led to Zheng He's interaction with the polity of Cochin, which sold pepper at a cheaper rate, and the absence of any middlemen allowed the Ming empire to establish a base from which to control the maritime trade and further explore the Western Ocean region. This resulted in Yongle granting special status to the polity of Cochin headed by King Keyili in 1416.[22] However, this enfeoffment and granting of special status to the rival port of Cochin became the point of conflict between the Ming empire and Calicut because of which the tribute missions from the latter declined by 1433. In addition, the conflict also took on a military colour involving Zheng He, whereby the latter took part in a local conflict between Calicut and Cochin in 1433 and led a retaliatory violent campaign against Zamorin for aiding in the massacre of the Chinese merchants in Malabar. The military nature of Zheng He's campaign in Calicut can be gleaned from a later description of the same by the Jewish merchant, Joseph of Cranganore, according to whom the Chinese 'inflicted no small slaughter on the people of Calicut, and after that returned no more.'[23]

Perhaps the most glaring evidence of the military nature of the Zheng He voyages was the Ming conflict with the local polities of Sri Lanka during the third voyage of the Treasure Fleet in 1411. As per the Chinese text, *Taizongshilu,* the local king of Sri Lanka, *Ya-lie Ku-nai-er*, acted in an 'insulting and disrespectful manner' with the Ming envoys led by Zheng He and even went to the extent of demanding 'gold, silver and precious objects' as tribute for landing on the shores of his kingdom. The text further adds that the local king also planned to rob the Ming Treasure Fleets by deploying 50,000 Sri Lankan troops and also cut down trees on the way between the royal palace and the shores in order to block the Ming emissaries from rendering any assistance to the crew in the ships. However, Zheng He got wind of this conspiracy and sent two messengers through an alternative route to warn the crew and soldiers of the ships of the impending attack. Finding the capital city and the royal palace vulnerable, Zheng He led 2,000 troops and took the king and members of the royal family captive. At the same time, the local troops sent to attack the Ming ships returned and laid siege to the capital, trapping Zheng He and his soldiers inside. Zheng He and his forces managed to move from the capital city back to their ships by keeping the royal family hostage and cutting through the felled trees blocking the path. The *Taizong* adds that the king and the entire royal family were presented before the Ming Court for sentencing and punishment. However, it is said that Yongle pardoned the 'stupidity and ignorance' of the captured king and instead, selected a 'worthy member of the family' named *Ye-bai-nai-na*, who was enfeoffed as the new king and invested as a tributary monarch under Yongle's overlordship.[24] As per Sri Lankan sources of the same conflict, such as the *Saddharmaratnakaraya* and *Alakesvarayayuddhaya,* the local king, Ya-lie Ku-nai-er, was identified as Alakeshvara or Alagokkonara, who, as per some other sources, was not the king but a high official or regent with the title of 'Prabhuraja'[25] in the Kotte kingdom. The Ming-enfeoffed monarch was identified as Parakramabahu Apana (Ye-bai-nai-na), who, as per scholar GPV Somaratne, was murdered the same day of his return to the kingdom in 1414. Somaratne holds the opinion that given the name of Kotte's reigning monarch being Parakramabahu as well, the Ming sources mistook the two individuals with the same name and Alakeshvara himself utilised this confusion and sent regular tributes to the Ming court.[26] In addition, the Sri Lankan sources put the blame for the violence not on Akakeshvara but the 'Chinese stratagems' and 'craftiness' of the *Dos Raja* (Yongle/Zheng He) who carried away the king, killing four of his younger brothers.[27] Despite the confusion and distortions present in both Ming and Sri Lankan sources, the episode in Sri Lanka highlights the violent and military aspect of the Zheng He voyages, which brought about a regime change or forced foreign rulers, by show of force, to accept the overlordship of Yongle. The establishment of Ming influence and hegemony over the Kotte kingdom was in line with the strategy of controlling the choke points of maritime trade similar to Malacca, given Sri Lanka's strategic position in the Indian Ocean region as a transit point for ships sailing to the Persian Gulf and as an entrepot of goods and traffic.[28]

The above strategy of Zheng He, involving regime-change, acquiring submission of polities, and the creation of alternative nodes as well as exercising control over choke points, have been characterised by scholar Geoff Wade as 'maritime colonialism' or proto-colonialism. According to Wade, the Zheng He voyages did not involve large-scale Ming expansion or colonisation of other polities, which marked the colonialism practised by early modern Western European powers. Rather, the Mings exercised political and military control over the sea lanes and maritime traffic by exercising overlordship or indirect rule over port-polities, such as Palembang, Malacca, Cochin, and Sri Lanka, for reaping political and economic benefits.[29] As stated above, the political goal of furthering the legitimacy of the Yongle emperor through the acquisition of subservient overseas polities was fulfilled with the arrival of tributary missions from the rulers of Palembang, Malacca, Calicut, and Sri Lanka to the Ming Court—the physical presence of such missions at the time of a new emperor's ascendancy justified and legitimised the reign of the latter.[30] At the same time, economic benefits to the Ming capital accrued in the form of bolstering of trade. David C. Kang elaborates on how trade in the Ming era involved primarily tribute trade or the exchange of gifts and precious materials between the envoys of the subservient polities and the Ming court; and official trade or trade conducted by the tributary envoys in the Ming capital in personal capacity. However, there were different rules of tributary and official trade for different kingdoms, depending on the stature and proximity of the subservient polities, where some, such as the Choson kingdom of Korea, were allowed certain privileges in terms of permissible volume and time period as compared to others.[31]

Such trade brought magnificent prosperity to the Ming empire, allowing the Yongle emperor to construct an extravagant porcelain pagoda in honour of his late mother, Empress Ma[32], thereby showing filial piety and further adding to his legitimacy. However, one must keep in mind the use of coercion in the Zheng He voyages despite the lack of any large-scale sign of occupation and establishment of overseas colonies. As seen above, this was evident in the events which took place in Palembang, Calicut, and Sri Lanka. Even the threat of force was quite frequent to bring polities to heel, as in the case of Brunei and Malacca where the sheer size of the Treasure Fleet and threatening messages from Yongle prevented the earlier present polities of Java and Siam from harassing these newly established polities.[33]

One of the major geopolitical implications of the Zheng He voyages was the creation of 'an era of pax Ming'.[34] The pax Ming era allowed for apparently uninterrupted maritime trade and traffic, which was monopolised and controlled towards the political and economic advantage of the Ming court, especially the Yongle emperor. Another geopolitical implication was the support or creation of port-based polities, such as Palembang, Malacca, Cochin, and Sri Lanka, which were subservient to the Mings and in extension, provided the latter with access to nodes, entrepots, and choke points for the policing and monopolisation of maritime traffic. Such subservience achieved through cultural and economic appeal as well as military coercion prevented any threat of invasion on the part of the entrenched polities, such as Siam and Java, given that, in the words of Roderich Ptak, "maritime countries' ground troops probably would have outnumbered the Chinese marine troops in the battle field, but foreign navies were definitely inferior to the Ming fleets, both in terms of quality and quantity".[35] At the same time, polities such as

Malacca, which lacked natural resources of their own and relied on maritime trade for survival[36], became increasingly dependent on the tributary relations and maritime hegemony offered by the Mings. In addition, the appearance of and increased awareness of Ming naval superiority also led to increasing competition among polities to seek Ming alliance or overlordship[37], often for their own existence and stability. This was seen in the case of the Bengal Sultanate where the Sultan, in 1420, sought Yongle's aid in warding off attacks from the neighbouring Sharqi Sultanate of Jaunpur. This request from the Bengal Sultan was followed by the visit of the Ming envoy, Hou Xian, with Imperial orders asking both the polities to 'cultivate good relations with their neighbours and each would protect their own territory'.[38] However, the edicts of Yongle were also backed by the presence and stationing of a Ming military contingent in Bengal to ward off any second thoughts on the part of the Sharqi Sultan. At the same time, Bengal developed a tributary relationship with the Ming court (for strengthening diplomatic-military ties), sending eight missions, and the Mings, in turn, were able to benefit from the maritime commerce that existed between Bengal and China.[39]

Conclusion

The geopolitical implications of the maritime proto-colonialism practised by the Ming empire through the Treasure Fleet voyages led by Zheng He are clearly stated above. Although these voyages are currently portrayed by the modern Chinese state as well as in popular memory as peaceful diplomatic exchanges, yet the military episodes, especially during the regime-change in Sri Lanka, highlight their underlying coercive and violent motivations and nature. The maritime proto-colonialism, along with the Ming colonisation of Yuenan and Annam, not only allowed political benefits in the form of increasing legitimacy for the Yongle emperor and subservient tributary polities but also brought economic benefits in the form of monopolisation of maritime commerce and bolstering of trade, thereby increasing China's prosperity. Later, the Zheng He voyages or similar oceanic adventures were discontinued by the Ming Court for various reasons, such as the demise of the Yongle emperor as well as the increasing costs of such ventures, which were seen by later emperors and their supporters as wasteful.[40] However, the Ming precedent was soon taken up and further developed with the arrival of new maritime powers, such as the Portuguese, who practised and achieved domination in the Indian Ocean through the display and threat of superior naval force—the Portuguese collected a kind of protection fee from other ships in exchange for issuing *cartaz* or pass allowing safe passage through maritime routes to ships from the Malabar Coast as well as Sri Lanka.[41]

The legacy of the Zheng He and the Ming maritime colonialism can be easily gauged in the current situation of Chinese assertion. The link between Zheng He and current Chinese politics is quite evident in Xi Jinping's flagship BRI, where the admiral has been promoted as the poster boy of the project who 'built a bridge of peace and East-West co-operation' in Xi's opening speech at the Belt and Road Forum (BRF) summit in 2017.[42] At the same, a closer inspection would reveal far greater similarities between the Ming proto-colonialism and current Chinese assertion. The BRI, just like the Treasure Fleet, is motivated by both political and economic reasons. The aim of the BRI, as stated in official circles and the public sphere, is economic prosperity for both China and other member nations of the project—more so for China's western provinces, such as Xinjiang, where linkages with Central and South Asia are expected to bring much needed investment and development—and on a general level, arrest the gradual slowing down of the Chinese economy. However, at the same time, the BRI is also being seen as an attempt to bolster the legitimacy of Xi Jinping (similar to Yongle), given the latter's background and his rise marked first by the anti-corruption drive within the top echelons of the Communist Party of China (CPC) in 2012-13 and then, tightening control over the limited freedoms offered by the earlier leaderships. In the same vein, many scholars have compared the BRI to America's Apollo Mission in the 1960s—large-scale projects designed to secure the stability of regimes by diverting the attention of the public away from internal problems or satisfying the general expectations of the populace by presenting a better image of their country to the outside world.[43]

The imprint of Zheng He becomes more pronounced when considering the military and strategic aspects of the BRI. A major link was the inauguration of the first Chinese overseas naval base in Djibouti as part of the Maritime Silk Route (MSR) where the Chinese navy ships destined for the Horn of Africa set sail on July 2017, coinciding with the demeanour of the beginning of the Zheng He voyages. The military characteristics of Djibouti have been further underlined with the stated aims of the base as aiding 'escorting, peace-keeping and providing humanitarian aid to Africa and West Asia' along with 'military cooperation, joint exercises, evacuating and protecting overseas Chinese as well as jointly maintaining security of international strategic seaways'[44]—similar to protecting and policing maritime routes of Indian Ocean trade by the Mings. However, the most striking resemblance with the Zheng He voyages can be best described under the 'String of Pearls theory', as Chinese strategists worldwide often like to name it. It refers to the building of naval bases in strategic locations of the Indian Ocean, such as Gwadar in Pakistan, Hambantota in Sri Lanka, Kyaukpyu in Myanmar, Chittagong in Bangladesh, and Marao Atoll in the Maldives, in a bid to exercise hegemony in the Indian Ocean region and encircle India to buttress the land-based China Pakistan Economic Corridor (CPEC).[45] Although being touted by the Chinese state as commercial port facilities, yet the location and frequent visits by Chinese submarines to ports such as the Gwadar often betray the military-strategic nature of these ventures. In addition, the development of these facilities, such as Hambantota and Gwadar, have allowed China to be a decisive factor in the domestic political and economic spheres of both Sri Lanka and Pakistan, given the latters' debt from Beijing as part of the BRI investments.[46] This dependence on and Chinese presence in Sri Lanka and Pakistan can be compared to the Ming influence over the erstwhile port polities, such as Malacca, Cochin, and the Sri Lankan kingdom of Kotte, which also witnessed the establishment of Chinese bases and military garrisons by Zheng He, similar to the ports mentioned above. Finally, the shift in China's maritime strategy from a largely coastal-defence navy to a blue water navy, with plans to extend from Japan to Australia by 2050, as per Admiral Liu Huaqing's 'three island chain' approach[47], which were first encapsulated in 1988, and the current focus of the MSR can be compared with the ship-building project undertaken by Yongle in 1403 as part of the Treasure Fleet voyages.

Given the converges between the two events separated by more than 600 years in history, it is not easy to predict which legacy of Zheng He—'friendly emissaries' (peaceful and mutual beneficial trade) or 'conquerors with warships, guns or swords' (maritime proto-colonialism)[48]—comes to define Chinese ambitions in the maritime domain in the 21st century.

Notes

1. Daniel Nexon & Paul Musgrave, 'Zheng He's Voyages and the Symbolism Behind Xi Jinping's Belt and Road Initiative', *The Diplomat,* 22 December, 2017.
2. Nexon & Musgrave, 'Zheng He's Voyages and the Symbolism Behind Xi Jinping's Belt and Road Initiative'.
3. Geoff Wade, 'The Zheng He Voyages: A Reassessment', *Journal of the Malaysian Branch of the Royal Asiatic Society,* vol. 78, no. 1 (288), 2005, pp. 37-58, see p. 39.
4. Wade, 'The Zheng He Voyages: A Reassessment', p. 39.
5. Louise Levathes, *When China Ruled the Seas- the Treasure Fleet of the Dragon Throne (1405-1433),* New York: Simon & Schuster, 1994, p. 73.
6. David C. Kang, *East Asia Before the West- Five Centuries of Trade and Tribute*', New York: Columbia University Press, 2012, p. 2.
7. Wade, 'The Zheng He Voyages: A Reassessment', p. 41.
8. Wade, 'The Zheng He Voyages: A Reassessment', pp. 41-42.
9. Ibid., pp. 42-43.
10. Wade, 'The Zheng He Voyages: A Reassessment', p. 43.
11. Levathes, *When China Ruled the Seas- the Treasure Fleet of the Dragon Throne (1405-1433),* p. 73.
12. Wade, 'The Zheng He Voyages: A Reassessment', p. 45.
13. Jeremiah Jenne, 'Belt and Whip', *China Channel- Los Angeles Review of Books,* October 19, 2018.
14. Levathes, *When China Ruled the Seas- the Treasure Fleet of the Dragon Throne (1405-1433),* p. 82.
15. Ibid., p. 88.
16. Tansen Sen, *India, China and the World- A Connected History,* New York: Rowman & Littlefield, 2017, p. 200.
17. Sen, *India, China and the World—A Connected History,* pp. 204-205.
18. Ibid., p. 206.
19. Levathes, *When China Ruled the Seas—The Treasure Fleet of the Dragon Throne (1405-1433),* pp. 107-110.
20. Tansen Sen, 'Zheng He's Military Interventions in South Asia, 1405-1433, *Brill China & Asia,* vol.1, 2019, pp. 158-191, see p.161.
21. Sen, 'Zheng He's Military Interventions in South Asia, 1405-1433, p. 162.
22. Ibid., pp. 163-164.
23. Ibid., pp. 167-168.
24. Ibid., pp. 169-170.
25. Ibid., pp. 171-172.
26. Ibid., pp. 173-174.
27. Ibid., pp.171-172.
28. Ibid., p. 175.

29. Wade, 'The Zheng He Voyages: A Reassessment', p. 51.
30. Sen, 'Zheng He's Military Interventions in South Asia, 1405-1433, p. 164.
31. Kang, *East Asia Before the West- Five Centuries of Trade and Tribute'*, p. 109.
32. Levathes, *When China Ruled the Seas- the Treasure Fleet of the Dragon Throne (1405-1433),* p. 121.
33. Levathes, *When China Ruled the Seas- the Treasure Fleet of the Dragon Throne (1405-1433),* p. 107.
34. Wade, 'The Zheng He Voyages: A Reassessment', p.55.
35. Sen, *India, China and the World- A Connected History,* p. 200.
36. Levathes, *When China Ruled the Seas- the Treasure Fleet of the Dragon Throne (1405-1433),* p. 108.
37. Sen, *India, China and the World- A Connected History,* p. 202.
38. Sen, 'Zheng He's Military Interventions in South Asia, 1405-1433, pp. 182-183.
39. Ibid., pp. 183-184.
40. Wade, 'The Zheng He Voyages: A Reassessment', p. 52.
41. Ibid.
42. 'Full text of President Xi's speech at opening of Belt and Road forum', *Xinhua NET,* 14 May, 2017.
43. Nexon & Musgrave, 'Zheng He's Voyages and the Symbolism Behind Xi Jinping's Belt and Road Initiative'.
44. Gideon Elazar, 'China in the Red Sea: The Djibouti Naval Base and the Return of Admiral Zheng He', *Begin-Sadat Centre for Strategic Studies,* 2017.
45. 'Here is All You Should Know About 'String of Pearls', China's Policy to Encircle India', *India Times,* June 23, 2017.
46. Nexon & Musgrave, 'Zheng He's Voyages and the Symbolism Behind Xi Jinping's Belt and Road Initiative'.
47. Balaji Chandramohan, 'China's maritime strategy', *New Zealand International Review,* vol.39, no.3, May/June 2014, pp. 22-24, see pp. 23-24.
48. 'Full text of President Xi's speech at opening of Belt and Road forum'.

Reference

Chandramohan, Balaji, "China's maritime strategy", *New Zealand International Review,* vol. 39, no. 3, May/June 2014, pp. 22-24.

Elazar, Gideon, "China in the Red Sea: The Djibouti Naval Base and the Return of Admiral Zheng He", Begin-Sadat Centre for Strategic Studies, 2017.

'Full text of President Xi's speech at opening of Belt and Road forum', *Xinhua NET,* May 14, 2017, http://www.xinhuanet.com/english/2017-05/14/c_136282982.htm.

"Here is All You Should Know About 'String of Pearls', China's Policy to Encircle India", *India Times,* June 23, 2017, https://www.indiatimes.com/news/india/here-is-all-you-should-know-about-string-of-pearls-china-s-policy-to-encircle-india-324315.html.

Jenne, Jeremiah, "Belt and Whip", *China Channel- Los Angeles Review of Books,* October 19, 2018, https://chinachannel.org/2018/10/19/zheng-ze/.

Kang, David C, *East Asia Before the West- Five Centuries of Trade and Tribute*, New York: Columbia University Press, 2012.

Levathes, Louise, *When China Ruled the Seas- the Treasure Fleet of the Dragon Throne (1405-1433),* New York: Simon & Schuster, 1994.

Nexon, Daniel & Musgrave, Paul, "Zheng He's Voyages and the Symbolism Behind Xi Jinping's Belt and Road Initiative", *The Diplomat,* December 22, 2017, https://thediplomat.com/2017/12/zheng-hes-voyages-and-the-symbolism-behind-xi-jinpings-belt-and-road-initiative/.

Sen, Tansen, *India, China and the World- A Connected History,* New York: Rowman & Littlefield, 2017.

Sen, Tansen, "Zheng He's Military Interventions in South Asia, 1405-1433", *Brill China & Asia,* vol. 1, 2019, pp. 158-191.

Wade, Geoff, "The Zheng He Voyages: A Reassessment", *Journal of the Malaysian Branch of the Royal Asiatic Society,* vol. 78, no. 1 (288), 2005, pp. 37-58.

7

US-China Geopolitical Competition: A Showdown between the Indo-Pacific and the BRI

Raymond Kwun-Sun Lau

Introduction

Speaking at the Asia-Pacific Economic Cooperation (APEC) leaders summit in Vietnam during his marathon tour in Asia in November 2017, the then US President, Donald Trump, announced a new initiative—the 'Indo-Pacific dream'—as the centerpiece of his administration's strategy towards the region.[1] This vision for a free and open Indo-Pacific, according to President Trump, is 'a place where sovereign and independent nations, with diverse cultures and many different dreams, can all prosper side-by-side, and thrive in freedom and in peace'.[2] Trump's vision echoed then US Secretary of State Rex Tillerson's remarks on US-India relations in Washington, DC in October that year: "the United States and India should be partners to further a 'free and open Indo-Pacific' because democratic India has been rising as a responsible power, upholding the rule of law and freedom of navigation, while China has not".[3]

Trump's vision of the 'Indo-Pacific', however, stands in sharp contrast to Chinese President Xi Jinping's advocacy of 'Asia-Pacific Century'.[4] During the APEC CEO Summit in Peru in November 2016, the Chinese President outlined a four-pronged economic development plan, including: (i) promotion of an open and integrated economy in the form of a Free Trade Area of the Asia-Pacific (FTAAP); (ii) enhancement of connectivity for achieving interconnected development in the context of the Belt and Road Initiative (BRI); (iii) strengthening of reforms and innovation on the basis of the G20 Blueprint on Innovative Growth adapted by the 2016 G20 Hangzhou Summit; and (iv) promotion of win-win cooperation for forging stronger Asia-Pacific partnership.[5]

With both the American and the Chinese leaders sharing their visions for the region, it is worth noting that behind the demonstration of their divergent 'worldview' is a more serious message: both Washington and Beijing seek to counterbalance each other's influence in Asia (whether it is named as the Asia-Pacific or Indo-Pacific). Particularly important, from Beijing's perspective, is the continuous effort made by the US to counterbalance China's advocacy of the BRI through the advancement of its 'Free and Open Indo-Pacific Strategy'.[6] This seemed to reinforce the views shared by many Chinese observers that the strategic competition between the US and China would become more intense because of the potential shift in US-China relations since the 2008 global financial crisis.[7] In this sense, the intensifying strategic competition between Washington and Beijing is poised to exacerbate the mutual distrust of long-term intentions, or what is known as 'strategic distrust', between the two major powers.[8]

The crux of the matter, amidst this growing strategic distrust between the US and China, is that Washington, from Beijing's perspective, intends to consolidate its strategic supremacy through working closely with regional allies and security partners, such as India. Beijing, from Washington's viewpoint, aims to play a leadership role in regional economic development and inter-connectivity, thereby dominating the Asia-Pacific through naval build-up and economic initiatives, such as the BRI.[9] Therefore, the emergence of the two distinctive geographical concepts, the 'Indo-Pacific' and the 'Asia-Pacific', needs to be understood in the context of the deepening strategic distrust between the US and China.

While the issue of strategic distrust has gradually become a central concern in US-China relations,[10] the role of assertive nationalism in Chinese foreign policy-making in creating an atmosphere of tension and misunderstanding between Beijing and Washington has been largely overlooked. This chapter, therefore, seeks to understand the emerging prominence of assertive nationalism in China as a result of China's seemingly inexorable rise, its ramifications for the country's foreign policy, and its relations with the US. It offers a comparative analysis of the US-led Indo-Pacific strategy and China's BRI in the context of the US-China strategic competition.

Against the background of China's growing ambitions and assertiveness,[11] the overarching driver of China's foreign policy is to demonstrate its system, self-confidence, and belief that China can offer a Chinese model of economic development—the path of socialism with Chinese characteristics as an alternative to the Western model for the world.[12] Yet, this chapter also argues that the offensives initiated by the Chinese government (especially by the Chinese diplomats) to defend Beijing's national interests in a confrontational manner, which are driven by assertive Chinese nationalism and often termed by many observers as the 'wolf-warrior diplomacy',[13] has exacerbated the strategic distrust between Beijing and Washington. In this context, the resurgence of an increasingly confident China under President Xi and his efforts to make China an assertive player in the region, particularly via the launch of the BRI, has indicated Beijing's unwillingness to comply with (if not explicitly challenge) the 'rules-based international order' upheld/ depended upon by Washington.[14]

This chapter begins by addressing China's rise and the growth of assertive nationalism in the country's foreign policy-making, with a particular focus on the emergence of wolf-warrior diplomacy in recent years. It then examines China's pursuit of political, ideological, and economic interests in the region via the launch of the Belt and Road Initiative by President Xi Jinping since 2013. It also attempts to make an analysis of the US-led Indo-Pacific strategy and the establishment of the Quadrilateral Security Dialogue (Quad), which comprises the United States, Australia, India, and Japan, in the region. The next section elaborates the nature of this intensifying US-China strategic competition and their growing mutual strategic distrust. The chapter concludes with a discussion of the implications of the interplay between Beijing's BRI and Washington's Indo-Pacific strategy on US-China relations in the post Covid-19 world.

An increasingly confident China under Xi: The growth of Assertive Nationalism

To begin with, it is apparently clear that China's foreign policy-making has witnessed a fundamental transformation since President Xi Jinping came into power in 2013. The three-decade logic of 'keeping a low profile' under former leader Deng Xiaoping has been replaced by the strategy of 'striving for achievement' since 2013.[15] In the eyes of President Xi, China 'has achieved a tremendous transformation, as the country 'has stood up, grown rich and is becoming strong'.[16] As such, there is no reason why China has to shy away from world leadership, but instead, as the new Chinese leader argued, 'it is time for us to take centre stage in the world and to make a greater contribution to humankind'.[17]

Xi Jinping and his 'China Dream'

What has prompted Beijing to adopt a more proactive approach in world affairs by abandoning Deng Xiaoping's 'Hide your strength, bide your time'[18] philosophy? The simple and straightforward answer is Xi Jinping's strong belief in his country's 'national rejuvenation'. Being perhaps one of Xi's most important ideological campaigns, the notion of 'China Dream'—with 'national rejuvenation' being the core concept—has constantly been promoted as the vision for the country's development since his coming into office in 2013. The essence of the 'China Dream', in President Xi's own words, is 'a rich and powerful country, revitalizing the nation and enhancing the well-being of the people', and that it constitutes 'the inner meaning of upholding and developing socialism with Chinese characteristics'.[19]

In terms of policy implementation, this great rejuvenation of the Chinese nation can materialise through realising the two centennial goals, that is, to establish a 'moderate well-off society by 2021 and a rich and strong country by 2049'.[20] Accordingly, the China Dream can only be implemented through the path of 'socialism with Chinese characteristics', and, perhaps most importantly, the leadership of the Chinese Communist Party (CCP) in leading the national revival of the Chinese nation, because 'only the CCP can rejuvenate China'.[21]

Xi Jinping and his 'four confidences' doctrine

Underlying this path of 'socialism with Chinese characteristics' is, first and foremost, the assumption of Beijing's growing self-confidence of China's economic achievements and its model of development during the past four decades. Indeed, the fact remains that an average 10 per cent annual GDP growth that China has experienced since it began to open up and reform its economy in 1978 has transformed the country from a centrally planned to a 'socialist-market' economy. As a result of the significant improvements in access to health, education, and other services over the same period, more than 800 million people have been lifted out of poverty.[22]

It is against this backdrop that President Xi has placed the emphasis on China's road of unique development. Along with the above-mentioned 'China Dream', Xi's emphasis on China's road of unique development, as shaped by socialism with Chinese characteristics, is evidenced by his advocacy of 'four confidences' in his inaugural speech at the closing meeting of the 13th National People's Congress (NPC) in March 2018: that is, confidence in the path, theory, system, and culture of socialism with Chinese characteristics.[23] According to Beijing's official interpretation, these are being referred to as 'four matters of confidence':

"Confidence in the path" is confidence in the direction of socialism with Chinese characteristics and confidence in its future; "confidence in the theory" is confidence in the scientific, true, and authentic nature of the theory of socialism with Chinese characteristics; "confidence in the system" is confidence in the advanced and superior nature of the system of Chinese socialism; and "confidence in culture" is a full affirmation of the value of China's culture and a faith in its vitality.[24]

While these 'four matters of confidence' have been added to the Party Constitution in 2017, Beijing's leaders' growing confidence in the country's capacity to manage social and economic affairs, however, can be traced back to its success in weathering the 2008 global financial crisis. The contrast between China's high growth rate and the weakening economy of OECD countries has made the Chinese President believe that a rejuvenated Chinese nation, as Xi himself put it, is able to offer 'Chinese wisdom and a Chinese approach' as 'a new option for other countries and nations who want to speed up their development'.[25] In many ways, the launch of the Belt and Road Initiative in

2013 can be seen as a demonstration of China's confidence and capacity of being a leading force among emerging market economies.

Yet, perhaps most fundamentally, Beijing's growing self-confidence amidst the 2008 global financial crisis has encouraged China to act more assertively.[26] One prominent example of this growing sense of assertiveness is President Xi's call for a 'new model of major-country relationship' during his talks with the US President, Barack Obama, in Beijing in November 2014, as the Chinese President outlined 'no conflict, no confrontation', 'mutual respect', and 'win-win cooperation' as the three principal elements of the construction of this new model of major-country relationship between the two countries.[27]

Although academic discussion in mainland China over the concept of a 'new type of great power relations' can be traced back to the late 1990s, it is important to note that President Xi's effort to push the international community to build what he called a 'new type of international relations with win-win cooperation at the core' is an attempt to recast China-US relations on more equal terms.[28] In other words, China, because of its self-perceived shrinking power gap with the United States, wants to be regarded as a great power, certainly to be coequal with the US.[29]

Beijing's attempt to assert its Great Power status on the world stage, from Washington's perspective, suggested that the pursuit of economic development/ modernisation is no longer Beijing's primary objective. Instead, 'the Americans are alarmed at China's expanded global influence, exemplified by the Belt and Road Initiative, and its reinforcement of the role of the state in economy and society, as well as the consolidation of the Communist Party leadership and its ideology'.[30] Therefore, as rightfully predicted by many Chinese scholars, the 2008 global financial crisis did constitute a turning point in the history of US-China relations because it set down the simmering competition between the two countries in a global context, thereby exacerbating the strategic mistrust with each other.[31]

Yet, while the Chinese government seemed to have placed heavy emphasis in pursuing domestic economic growth for the past four decades, what is equally important is the efforts of the CCP to cultivate nationalism as a replacement for the class struggle—the Party's basic line—during Mao Zedong's rule.[32] Therefore, before digging deep into the strategic distrust as a result of the simmering competition between the US and China, it is necessary to address the internal impact and external influence of China's seemingly inexorable rise: the growth of assertive nationalism and the emergence of wolf-warrior diplomacy

Safeguarding core interests at all costs: Assertive nationalism in China's foreign policy-making

Among other things, the most important driving force of Chinese foreign policy-making is to enhance the domestic political legitimacy of the Chinese Communist Party and the head of state in order to keep the regime in power.[33] Particularly important is the decisive leadership provided by the CCP to ensure the country to step out of the shadow cast by what the CCP described as the 'Century of shame and humiliation'.[34] According to this logic, the legitimacy of the CCP is built on its success in restoring the territorial integrity and sovereignty and the international dignity of China. One of the most popular communist propaganda songs in the People's Republic of China—'Without the Communist Party, there would be no new China'—actually describes how the CCP has delivered the country out of its plundered, humiliated, and divided past (caused by the Western imperialists and Japanese 'devils') and into its prosperous present and brighter future.[35]

The CCP's claim to political legitimacy by restoring China's dignity, according to David Shambaugh, can be understood as a combination of defensive nationalism and retributive nationalism: China, on the one hand, is 'defensive' in the face of foreign demands, while China, on the other, seeks retribution and compensation from foreigners for perceived past wrongs.[36] In this sense, President Xi's notion of the above-mentioned 'China Dream'—with 'national rejuvenation' being the core concept—is not about promoting the idea of pushing China to become a superpower. Instead, from the Chinese perspective, the rationale behind this project of 'national rejuvenation' is to correct the 'historical mistake' of China's decline by regaining international prestige and restoring fairness,[37] thereby ending the above-mentioned 'Century of shame and humiliation'.

Yet, along with the sentiments of defensive and retributive nationalism, it has become noticeable that Chinese leaders have increasingly signalled their resolve in China's rising power aspirations by reorienting the country's foreign policy in a more assertive direction since 2008. This increasingly 'muscular' foreign policy behaviour of China is characterised by Beijing's willingness to defend China's self-proclaimed core (national) interests. The issues relating to China's core interests, as mentioned in the Chinese government's official document, *China's Peaceful Development*, involve state sovereignty, national security, territorial integrity, and national reunification.[38] While these issues refer almost exclusively to Taiwan, Tibet, and Xinjiang, there has been a tendency for the Chinese government to expand the self-proclaimed core interest issues by including the territorial claims in the South China Sea and East China Sea. Also, perhaps most fundamentally, China's core interests, including important national interests, from Beijing's perspective, are essentially non-negotiable, and the use of military force to defend specific core interests cannot be ruled out.[39]

This growing assertiveness of China's foreign policy-making and Beijing leaders' increased confidence to forcefully safeguard China's core interests since 2008 is increasingly at odds with Allen Whiting's observation in his seminal work, *Assertive Nationalism in Chinese Foreign Policy* (1983), that Beijing's action was well-calculated to ensure that Chinese nationalism would not worsen the country's relationship with great powers.[40] Instead, after four decades of high-speed economic growth and the coming into power of Xi Jinping, China has seen a strident turn to assertive nationalism as the government has become more willing to confront the Western powers and its neighbours. To further complicate China's foreign relations, Beijing's reckless pursuit of its self-proclaimed core interests, as a result of 'the convergence of the Chinese state nationalism and popular nationalism'[41], has started arousing alarm in the US and other countries in Asia, as proclaimed by Suisheng Zhao.

The emergence and development of 'wolf-warrior diplomacy'

This increasingly assertive style of foreign policy-making adopted by Beijing in recent years is referred to as 'wolf-warrior diplomacy', which is named after the production of two domestic blockbuster movies, *Wolf Warrior* (2015) and *Wolf Warrior II* (2017). These two Chinese action blockbusters, which highlight life-risking missions carried out by Chinese special operation forces in war-torn African countries, are known to the locals as 'the Chinese Rambo'.[42] Yet, while patriotic movies were nothing new in China, what is noteworthy about the chest-thumping patriotism on show in *Wolf Warrior II* in particular is that it was 'definitely a product of Xi's reign and the idea of the rejuvenation'.[43] 'It's the mentality that the 100 years of oppression from foreign powers is over and we are now in a phase where China can stand on its own feet and defend itself and its citizens', as stated by one film critic.[44]

The wild success of *Wolf Warrior II*, the highest-grossing film ever in China's box office,[45] has popularised the use of the term 'wolf-warrior diplomacy', as mentioned above. In many respects, this new approach is a fundamental transformation of Chinese diplomacy 'from conservative, passive, and low-key to assertive, proactive, and high-profile'.[46] In examining why Beijing has resorted to 'wolf-warrior diplomacy' and whether this aggressive foreign policy-making style has become a new norm, Zhiqun Zhu has highlighted three factors: soaring nationalism in China, including the continuous promotion of Xi's 'four confidences' doctrine (as mentioned above); a growing tendency of the Chinese government to 'tell the [true] China story' by responding to biased Western media portrayal of China; and an increasing diversity of the Chinese foreign policy establishment.[47]

Indeed, in the context of the Chinese Communist Party's active promotion of 'four matters of confidence', the Chinese diplomats, especially the foreign ministry spokespersons such as Hua Chunying and Zhao Lijian, have pursued increasingly assertive tactics to shape how China is perceived online through hitting back at criticism by Western powers over China's handling of the Covid-19 outbreak via Twitter.[48] Zhao, on another occasion, tweeted a cartoon graphic of an Australian soldier holding a knife to the throat of an Afghan child in November 2020. This implicit criticism by the Chinese foreign ministry spokesperson of Australian soldiers serving in Afghanistan and their involvement in unlawful killings has triggered a sharp escalation of tensions between Canberra and Beijing.[49]

Beijing's confrontational way of defending China's core interests and rebuking external criticism, however, is not only confined to the use of abrasive language. For instance, the Chinese government has increased its efforts to artificial island building and infrastructure construction, after making expansive sovereignty claims in the South China Sea (SCS) in recent years. Along with the construction of ports, military installations, and airstrips in the Paracel and Spratly Islands, China has also begun its deployment of fighter jets, cruise missiles, and a radar system in Woody

Island, one of China's largest possessions in the SCS.[50] In responding to what many critics called 'the militarization of the South China Sea',[51] the Chinese foreign ministry spokesperson repeatedly cited China's indisputable sovereignty over the area as a justification to its land reclamation work on relevant islands and reefs.[52]

To be sure, from Beijing's perspective, this assertive and often abrasive stance adopted by its diplomats is purely a 'justified defence' to protect China's core interests against the offensive and aggressive Western diplomacy. While Deng Xiaoping's 'keeping a low profile' policy of the early 1990s was well-suited for the early phases of China's economic modernisation, the fact that China's international status has undergone a fundamental change, as suggested by Yan Xuetong of Tsinghua University, means 'China should take charge as a great, responsible power' because [c]ontinuing low-profile type policies will bring more harm than benefit to China'.[53]

Yet, perhaps the most crucial implication of this growing acceptance of 'wolf-warrior diplomacy' among China's foreign policy officials and scholars is that it represents the irreversible process of Beijing's growing self-confidence on the world stage. In other words, the fact that China managed to escape the 2008 global financial crisis (GFC) relatively unscathed (while the US was the epicentre of the GFC) and overtook Japan as the world's second largest economy two years later has reinforced Beijing's confidence in China's model of economic development and the country's status on the world stage. The launch of the Belt and Road Initiative (BRI) is the most obvious manifestation of China's self- confidence in its system and, as mentioned above, President Xi's determination to offer 'Chinese wisdom and a Chinese approach as a new option for other countries and nations who want to speed up their development'.[54]

An increasingly confident China under Xi: The launch of the Belt and Road Initiative

Along with his advocacy of 'China Dream' within the country, the Belt and Road Initiative (BRI) is arguably the most eye-catching initiative and visionary idea put forward by President Xi on the world stage. It was during his visit to Kazakhstan in September 2013 and to Indonesia in the same year that the new Chinese leader proposed the building of the New Silk Road Economic

Belt and the 21st century Maritime Silk Road.[55] Initially termed as One Belt One Road (OBOR), this vision of the Silk Road Economic Belt is aimed at connecting China and Europe through countries across central Eurasia, while the 21st century Maritime Silk Road envisions China's connection with Southeast Asia, Africa, and Europe through the South China Sea and the Indian Ocean.

Shortly after the official endorsement of the OBOR at the Third Plenary Session of the 18th Central Committee of the Communist Party of China in November 2013, the National Development and Reform Commission (NDRC) issued the official founding document for OBOR, 'Vision and Actions on Jointly Building Silk Road Economic Belt and 21st century Maritime Silk Road' (Visions and Actions, for short) in March 2015.[56] According to Vision and Actions, the BRI is aimed at enhancing connectivity across the Asian, European, and African continents through 'promoting orderly and free flow of economic factors, highly efficient allocation of resources and deep integration of markets'. And China, as the document reads, has since promoted key cooperation projects in the fields of infrastructure connectivity, industrial investment, resource development, economic and trade cooperation, financial cooperation, cultural exchanges, ecological protection, and maritime cooperation.

This signature foreign policy vision advocated by President Xi seemed to be gaining momentum after the 1st and the 2nd Belt and Road Forum for International Cooperation took place in Beijing in 2017 and 2019 respectively. According to the Green Belt and Road Initiative Center (Green BRI Center), some 140 countries have joined the Belt and Road Initiative by signing a Memorandum of Understanding (MoU) with China (as of January 2021), and China's investments in the BRI countries between 2013 and 2020 in sectors such as energy and transport is estimated to comprise a total volume of USD 770 bn.[57]

Beijing's advocacy of the BRI, in the words of President Xi, is meant to foster a 'new type of international relations' featuring 'win-win cooperation' with Belt and Road countries. This foreign policy vision, according to the Chinese President, has nothing to do with 'outdated geopolitical maneuvering' as China has 'no intention to interfere in other countries' internal affairs, export our own social system and model of development, or impose our own will on others'. Instead, what China hopes to achieve is 'a new model of win-win cooperation' as the country is 'ready to share practices of development with other countries'.[58]

On the surface, Xi's advocacy of the BRI is Beijing's effort to present a global framework for common development through promoting economic and trade cooperation between Asia, Europe, and Africa. Yet, it is important to note that this initiative is an integral part of China's 13th Five-Year Plan (2016–2020), which guides the national investment strategy throughout that period.[59] Above all, the BRI is, therefore, a top-level design for connecting the Chinese economy to regional and global raw material suppliers and markets through the construction of a coherent infrastructure of transportation networks.[60] Economically speaking, this is a significant shift in China's strategy on development, which involves economic upgrading, rebalancing, and further opening, a process that Jia Qingguo of Peking University called 'new wave of opening': 'Unlike in the past when China opened itself up to attract foreign investment, technology, and management skills, China is now reversing its role by opening outwards to help push through its domestic reforms'.[61]

Therefore, it is important to note that this changing development strategy of China, with its focus on connectivity and infrastructure construction across Eurasia and Oceania, is logically connected with President Xi's notion of 'China Dream' and his emphasis on the great rejuvenation of the Chinese nation, as mentioned above. With the BRI encompassing 4.4 billion people, at least 65 countries (most of them developing economies), and a combined economic output of USD 21 trillion (29 per cent of global GDP), this foreign policy vision can reasonably be understood as a long-standing deeply held belief by President Xi that a rejuvenated Chinese nation, as Xi himself put it, is able to offer 'Chinese wisdom and a Chinese approach as a new option for other countries and nations who want to speed up their development'.[62] Kerry Brown, one of the most influential Western thinkers about Chinese politics, has rightly depicted the Chinese leaders' mentality on the BRI:

> 'The rationale here is that after four decades of rapid industrialization and construction, China is in a position than before to show others how to undertake urbanization and build high speed railways and motorways,

> among other things. China … has usually been figured in ways which place it as a student, and the outside world—Europe, America and the developed world in particular—as its teachers.' Now this situation has changed. No other country has lifted so many from poverty and built so much hard infrastructure in such a short period of time. It is now, therefore, the era of China the teacher, not China the student. The Belt and Road Initiative is one way that this is unfolding.[63]

Political, ideological, and economic Interests in China's Belt and Road Initiative

In this sense, the introduction of the BRI to the world after Xi Jinping's coming into power is premised on Xi's belief that the China model of development, which could simply be understood as a mixture of a state capitalist economy (mainly through spending money and building large-scale infrastructure projects) and an authoritarian state, can potentially be promoted to develop and improve the infrastructure and financing system of the world's impoverished areas. This explains why President Xi, in his landmark speeches during his 2013 visit to Kazakhstan and Indonesia, placed emphasis on the shared 'strategic goals' of achieving national rejuvenation and strength through the pursuit of economic development between China and countries in Central Asia and Southeast Asia. Clearly, Xi's use of language regarding 'common development' is a deliberate design to appeal to the developing country audiences in the Global South.[64]

As such, notwithstanding the rhetoric about the 'common development' between China and other countries, China has been instrumental in not only defending but also advancing its core national interests via the launch of the BRI. It is, therefore, one thing to understand China's BRI as a reflection of new-found assertiveness in Chinese foreign policy but quite another to identify China's national interest in its advocacy of the BRI. Here, Beijing's attempt to advance its national interests through the pursuit of the BRI can be identified in three dimensions: political, ideological, and economic.

Politically, the Chinese government has ratcheted up efforts to project itself as the de facto leader of the developing world, since the theme of 'common development' has consistently been included in Xi's speeches to developing country audiences since 2013.[65] Particularly important was Xi's deliberate attempt to characterise his developmentalist worldview as 'open and inclusive' (in a vision which he called a 'community of common destiny'). This implies that China, while pursuing its economic growth and development, will be more beneficial to developing countries because Beijing would be 'shouldering greater responsibilities for regional and world peace and development, as opposed to seeking greater monopoly over regional and world affairs'.[66] In this sense, securing the support of developing countries as potential economic partners is of immense importance politically in the Global South. The launch of the BRI is also of immense importance ideologically for China's pursuit of core interests. In arguing that 'there is no one-size-fits-all development model in the world', President Xi has been trying hard to champion the Chinese development model—socialism with Chinese characteristics—as a 'new path' to modernisation for 'all developing countries'.[67] Beijing's subtle promotion of its own brand of state capitalism, however, is not entirely unanticipated because, as suggested by Ian Taylor, it has long been one of China's major foreign policy goals: 'By portraying itself as an advocate for the developing world and emphasizing the rhetoric of the South-South cooperation, China has arguably sought to offer itself up as an alternative model to Western dominance'.[68] Therefore, China's ideological interest is manifested in Beijing's efforts to spread and popularise China's successful development model, where a capitalist economy is married to an authoritarian state.[69]

Economically, with its growing demand for energy driven by four decades of high-speed economic growth, China has become the world's largest oil consumer and importer since 2017, surpassing the US.[70] According to one estimate, approximately 70 per cent of China's oil requirements were fulfilled through imports in 2018, and this proportion is expected to increase to 80 per cent by 2040.[71] With the growth of domestic crude oil production being constrained by the COVID-19 pandemic, China's oil demand maintained an upward trend. In the face of China's continuing dependency on foreign crude oil, 'the 80-per cent oil import dependence plus the 80 per cent of that coming through the sea lanes will have pretty profound strategic implications for China'.[72]

Indeed, the fact that some 80 per cent of China's oil has to pass through the Strait of Malacca, a narrow stretch of water between the Indonesian island of Sumatra and the Malay Peninsula, has made the country's oil dependency become a strategic vulnerability. By publicly calling attention to what is being known later as the 'Malacca Dilemma', the then President, Hu Jintao, suggested new strategies must be adopted to mitigate the perceived vulnerability.[73] From Beijing's perspective, it is important to prevent the country's oil imports from being choked off because oil supply disruptions could potentially derail China's economic achievements and rise. Therefore, ensuring free and safe maritime routes/sea lines of communication (SLOCs) in the Pacific and Indian Oceans is of utmost importance because a secure and sustained supply of energy is crucial to safeguarding China's national security.[74]

In this sense, despite the benign nature of the BRI being constantly emphasized by the Chinese leadership, China's political, ideological, and economic interests in its pursuit of Xi's foreign policy vision are clearly visible. Graham Allison, in his 2017 book, *Destined For War: Can America and China Escape Thucydides's Trap?*, argued that the rise of China as 'the biggest player in the history of the world' has heralded a new balance of power known as geoeconomics: 'the use of economic instruments (from trade and investment policy to sanctions, cyber attacks, and foreign aid) to achieve geopolitical goals'.[75]

The conduction of Chinese foreign policy through economics, however, has inevitably exacerbated strategic distrust between Beijing and Washington. From Beijing's perspective, the fundamental reason why the country is faced with this so-called 'Malacca Dilemma' is because, in the words of then President Hu Jintao, 'certain major powers' were bent on controlling the strait.[76] In the view of Beijing's leaders, the US maritime policy is aimed at blocking main choke points along regional SLOCs, through working closely with regional allies and security partners, in order to consolidate its strategic supremacy and intimidate China.[77] In the eyes of Washington, however, China's move to make itself a proactive player in the region to advocate stronger infrastructure connectivity through economic initiatives such as the BRI is designed to assert its Great Power status by transforming its economic power into regional and global influence.[78] Against this backdrop, the United States finds it imperative to counterbalance China's seeming unwillingness to comply with the rules-based international order upheld/defended by Washington.

An increasingly vigilant America since Trump: The gradual emergence of the Indo-Pacific strategy

In important respects, China's growing assertiveness in its foreign policy-making and its geoeconomic offensive via the BRI has shaken the very foundation of the United States as a hegemonic power in the Asia-Pacific in the past four decades. The US government, since the Barack Obama administration, has noted the strategic importance of the Asia-Pacific region and paid increasing attention to the growing challenge of China's ambition. For instance, in her article, "America's Pacific Century", written for *Foreign Policy* in October 2011, the then US Secretary of State, Hillary Clinton, argued for the geoeconomic, geostrategic, and geopolitical importance of the Asia-Pacific: 'the future of politics will be decided in Asia, not Afghanistan or Iraq, and the United States will be right at the center of the action'.[79]

It is against this background that President Obama put in place the policy of strategic rebalancing to Asia by shifting the focus of US foreign policy from the Middle East, particularly its military counter-insurgency campaigns in Iraq and Afghanistan, to the Asia- Pacific.[80] The underlying goal of Obama's shift in his government's foreign policy is to prevent China from becoming the dominant power in the Asia–Pacific region.[81] As a result, the Obama administration put a lot of effort into enhancing Washington's economic and strategic partnership with countries in the Asia-Pacific region. The signing of the Trans-Pacific Partnership (TPP), one of the world's biggest multinational trade deals, between the US and 11 other Pacific Rim countries[82] and the joint military exercises among the US, Japan, South Korea, Australia, and some ASEAN countries are two cases in point.

This so-called 'US pivot to Asia' policy, according to some observers, 'signified America's leadership in Asia and power to counter-balance China's pervasive regional influence'.[83] Yet, with President Obama suggesting that 'the United States welcomes the rise of a China that is peaceful, stable, prosperous, and a responsible player in global affairs',[84] it suggests that the principle of engagement was still regarded as the guiding force underpinning US policy towards China under Obama: 'integrating China into the US-led international system to serve US strategic and economic interests by shaping the direction of China's development toward market economy, political democratization and the supporter of the US leadership in international affairs'.[85]

However, this principle of a 'qualified American welcome to the rise of China', which has guided the US policy towards China through eight presidencies and four decades,[86] has undergone a significant change since President Donald Trump took office in January 2017. On 18 December that year, the Trump administration released its first National Security Strategy (NSS).[87] Along with highlighting the United States as engaged in a global power struggle for economic and military dominance, the document, in particular, identifies China as a strategic 'competitor' and 'revisionist' power trying to 'shape a world antithetical to US values and interests'.[88] In the face of the deliberate undermining of the 'international rules-based order' by an increasingly powerful China, the Trump administration, in contrast to the Obama administration, no longer held the view that China would liberalise as it developed and became integrated into the post-war international order.[89]

Particularly important is the Trump administration's effort to enshrine in the NSS the Indo-Pacific as a geopolitical and geo-economic construct. By highlighting the danger of 'a geopolitical competition between free and repressive visions of world order' in the Indo-Pacific region, the NSS, for the first time, singles out the 'Indo-Pacific', which stretches from the west coast of India to the western shores of the US, as a distinctive region for the advancement of US national interests. This is completely in line with President Trump's push of an 'Indo-Pacific dream' during the 2017 APEC leaders' summit in Vietnam, as his government sees the US foreign and economic policy battleground with China lies in the 'Indo-Pacific region'.[90]

In an attempt to defend the global interests of the US, the document outlines three priority actions for implementing Washington's Indo-Pacific strategy:[91] first, to redouble US commitment to established alliances and expand relationships with new partners that share respect for sovereignty, fair and reciprocal trade, and the rule of law; second, to maintain free and open seaways, transparent infrastructure financing practices, unimpeded commerce, and the peaceful resolution of disputes through regional economic cooperation; and third, to maintain a forward military presence capable of deterring and, if necessary, defeating any adversary, and strengthen a defence network with US allies and partners including Japan, South Korea, Taiwan, India, the Philippines, Thailand, Singapore, Vietnam, Indonesia, and Malaysia.

On January 19, 2018, the Department of Defense (DoD) issued the National Defense Strategy (NDS). The reemergence of long-term, strategic competition with revisionist powers like China was identified in the NDS as the central challenge to the US (economic) prosperity and (military) security.[92] China, as the document states, 'is leveraging military modernization, influence operations, and predatory economics to coerce neighbouring countries to reorder the Indo-Pacific region to their advantage'. Beijing's ultimate goal, from Washington's point of view, is, therefore, to seek Indo-Pacific regional hegemony in the near-term and displacement of the US to achieve global preeminence in the future.[93]

In the face of Beijing's growing ambitions and assertiveness, the DoD document highlights the importance of strengthening US alliances and partnerships in the Indo-Pacific to a 'networked security architecture'.[94] Given that enduring coalitions and long-term security partnerships are crucial in preserving the free and open international system, these Indo-Pacific alliances and partnerships have to be 'capable of deterring aggression, maintaining stability, and ensuring free access to common domains'.[95]

In further elaborating the US vision of a 'free and open Indo-Pacific', the DoD published the second key document, *Indo-Pacific Strategy Report: Preparedness, Partnerships and Promoting a Networked Region,* in June 2019.[96] By highlighting the Indo-Pacific as 'the single most consequential region for America's future', the report envisions a free Indo-Pacific in which all states enjoy freedom to exercise their sovereignty without coercive interference by other countries. Domestically speaking, this refers to good governance and the fundamental protection of human rights and civil liberties. An open Indo-Pacific, as envisioned in the report, on the other hand, is one where all countries 'enjoy access to international waters, airways, and cyber and space domains, and are able to pursue peaceful resolution of territorial and maritime disputes'.[97] Economically speaking, this corresponds to 'fair and reciprocal trade, open investment environments, and transparent agreements between nations'.[98]

Shortly after the *Indo-Pacific Strategy Report* was published, the Department of State released the third key document, *Free and Open Indo-Pacific: Advancing a Shared Vision,* in November 2019.[99] 'Ensuring that the future of the Indo-Pacific is one of freedom and openness rather than coercion and corruption', as the document points out, fully conforms to the fundamental interests of the US. While emphasising the importance of engaging partners, the report particularly singles out India, 'a fellow democracy of 1.3 billion people that shares our vision for the Indo-Pacific', as a 'strategic partner' of the US to 'address shared challenges and advance a shared vision', because 'a strong U.S.-India partnership is vital to the U.S. Indo-Pacific vision'.[100]

Also worth noting in the State Department's Report is its call for a stronger role for the US in developing 'physically secure, financially viable, economically sustainable, and socially responsible' infrastructure for the Indo-Pacific region. Through these new infrastructures, the US not only promotes investment, innovation, and market-based growth in the region but also provides a strong alternative to state-directed initiatives (i.e., Chinese).[101]

As such, a closer look at these three above-mentioned fundamental documents issued by the White House, the Department of Defense, and the State Department suggests that the US vision of 'Indo-Pacific' has become a 'whole-of-government' approach on account of the continuous use of the term in official US strategy papers since 2017.[102] This is evidenced by the change in name from the US Pacific Command to the US Indo-Pacific Command (INDOPACOM) in May 2018.[103] Indeed, the importance of this 'whole-of-government' effort to support a free and open Indo-Pacific is threefold. First, this US-led 'Indo-Pacific' is directed primarily at responding to China's BRI.[104] Second, the term acknowledges the new reality that new partnerships must be formed in an expansive two-ocean region where economic ties and strategic competition coexist.[105] Third, in the context of the US-China strategic competition, 'a strong India, in cooperation with like-minded countries, would act as a counterbalance to China'.[106] Therefore, this use of the term 'Indo-Pacific', as Rory Medcalf at Australian National University correctly points out, 'is no mere wordplay':

> 'It reflects something real: a changing approach by many nations to security, economics and diplomacy. Far from being an obscure account of words and maps, the narrative of the Indo-Pacific helps nations face one of the great international dilemmas of the 21st century: how can other countries respond to a strong and often coercive China without resorting to capitulation or conflict?'[107]

An increasingly vigilant America since Trump: The Quad's revival

The most obvious manifestation of this changing approach is the Quadrilateral Security Dialogue (which is also known as 'the Quad'). At its simplest, the Quad is a loose grouping of states comprising the US, India, Japan, and Australia whose origin can be traced back to the Boxing Day tsunami in the Indian Ocean in 2004. In the wake of the worst-ever humanitarian catastrophe in decades, the then US President, George W. Bush, announced the establishment of what was known as the Tsunami Core Group for coordinating international relief efforts.[108] Although a short-lived policy measure, this US-led Humanitarian Assistance and Disaster Relief (HADR), joined by India, Japan, and Australia, not only provided essential logistical support for the humanitarian effort but also illustrated 'the critical importance of diplomatic cooperation and operational coordination when the US works with its treaty allies and strategic partners'.[109]

In hindsight, the year 2007 proved to be a turning point for the gradual revival of the Quad. This four-nation tsunami team held its inaugural meeting in Manila at the level of senior officials on the sidelines of the ASEAN Regional Forum in May that year. The meeting, which was characterised as an 'informal grouping' like the tsunami core group in 2004, was preceded by the first-ever trilateral exercises among the US, Japanese, and Indian navies in April the same year. This, somewhat interestingly, coincided with the visit of the then Chinese Premier, Wen Jiabao, to Japan.[110]

Yet, however, it was the then Japanese Prime Minister, Shinzo Abe, who unveiled a new vision of regional connectivity. In his address to the Parliament during his visit to India in August 2007, Abe suggested that a 'new "broader Asia" takes shape at the confluence of the two seas of the Indian and Pacific Oceans'.[111] By proposing the idea of linking the Pacific with the Indian Ocean, Prime Minister Abe's advocacy of an 'arc of prosperity and freedom' helped bring the Quad countries closer together since the disbanding of the core group in early 2005, thereby laying an important foundation for the emergence of 'the Indo-Pacific region' as a new geopolitical concept replacing the 'Asia-Pacific'.[112]

Since then, this new geopolitical concept has been employed and (somewhat) institutionalised across the Quad countries. The Australian government, in its Defence White Paper released in 2016, identified three

Strategic Defence Interests, which are of fundamental significance for strategic defence planning: a secure, resilient Australia; the support of the security of maritime South East Asia and the South Pacific; and a stable Indo-Pacific region and rules-based global order.[113] The US government renamed its Pacific Command as Indo-Pacific Command (USINDOPACOM) in May 2018, as mentioned earlier. The Japanese government, in its Diplomatic Bluebook 2019, highlighted three pillars of Tokyo's efforts to realise a free and open Indo-Pacific.[114] The Indian government set up a new Indo-Pacific division within the Ministry of External Affairs, thereby adopting the umbrella approach to the Indo-Pacific region as one strategic continuum.[115] Various countries embraced the Indo-Pacific as a new geopolitical concept at different times. The nature of the Quad as a loose grouping of states is revealed in the divergent priorities and interests of the Quad states (at least in the early years): Japan tends to emphasise the democratic nature of the Quad partnership,[116] while India and Australia tend to pay more attention to functional cooperation by downplaying the significance of the Quad partnership as a formal alliance.

While there may be concerns about 'Whose "Indo- Pacific"?' exactly, and what the concept refers to,[117] it is important to note that these diverging national perspectives have not stopped the Quad's evolution from a loose grouping of states focusing on humanitarian assistance/disaster relief operations to one 'with a strategic outlook centered on the rising concerns over free and open seas and a rules-based order'.[118] Particularly important is the Trump administration's effort to revitalise the Quad by resuming formal dialogue in late 2017. After a 10-year hiatus, the Quad has, since, met twice a year, with the dialogue being upgraded to the level of foreign minister/secretary of state in 2019. The global pandemic of Covid-19 has further driven the creation of Quad Plus, adding New Zealand, South Korea, and Vietnam as new Quad partners, for coordinating actions on the Covid-19, repatriating citizens, and opening up trade and economic activity within the region.[119]

Notably, the unifying elements among the Quad partnership are twofold: the democratic set-up of the four countries in the Indo-Pacific region and their shared concern over China's growing assertiveness, regionally and internationally. Conceptually speaking, the Quad is founded on the concept of democratic peace where established democracies rarely go to war with each other. Tokyo's active efforts to promote the democratic nature of the Quad via Abe's advocacy of Asia's democratic security diamond, and Canberra's search for a values-based security and foreign policy[120] have laid an important foundation for making the Quad 'an inharmonious concert of democracies'.[121] As such, the coming together of US-Japan-India-Australia as four Indo-Pacific democracies through interlinked strategic partnerships could help 'advance political cooperation and stability founded on a community of values'.[122]

Along with the normative origin, another unifying element among the Quad countries is the convergence of interests in addressing China's seemingly inexorable rise. In other words, even though the Quad is not acknowledged (even among the four Indo-Pacific democracies) as a formal anti-China alliance, it is hard to dispute the impact of the China factor in (re)shaping the dynamics of the quadrilateral grouping. The attendees at the second Quad Foreign Ministers' Meeting held in October 2020 in Tokyo, for instance, vowed to take stronger action to realize a free and open Indo-Pacific and tackle, what Washington called, China's 'exploitation, corruption, and coercion' of smaller states in the region.[123]

This signals the birth of a revitalized Quad, and China, in Ramesh Thakur's terms, can be considered as 'the godfather of Quad 2.0'.[124] Indeed, the divergent perspectives among the Quad countries about the regional order of the Indo-Pacific have been overcome by their shared awareness of the risks posed by an increasingly confident China and its foreign policy driven by assertive nationalism.[125] For Japan, the issue at stake, as clearly depicted in its 2019 Defence White Paper, is China's expansive defence capabilities in space, cyberspace, and electromagnetic spectrum, as well as increased land reclamation activities and militarisation of islands in the East China Sea and the South China Sea.[126] Australia is concerned with its trade dependency on China and Beijing's projection of sharp power and its growing presence in the South Pacific. India's strategic concern is China's rising influence in India's primary area of maritime interest—South Asia and the Indian Ocean Region (IOR)—as well as the 'all- weather friendship' between China and Pakistan.[127] The US, in perceiving itself as being engaged in a continuous strategic competition with China, is determined to maintain its strategic primacy in the Indo-Pacific region and prevent China from challenging the rules-based international order and dissolving America's alliances and partnerships.[128]

Perhaps not surprisingly, this revitalised Quad or Quad 2.0, from Beijing's perspective, is nothing more than 'an exclusive clique rallying countries to work against China'.[129] This US-led Indo-Pacific strategy, in the words of Chinese Foreign Minister Wang Yi, is a 'big underlying security risk', whose objective is 'to trumpet the old-fashioned Cold War mentality and to stir up confrontation among different groups and blocs and to stoke geopolitical competition'.[130] This, therefore, explains Beijing's outright rejection of the 'Indo-Pacific' concept (not to mention the term 'Free and Open Indo-Pacific'), since this shift from the Asia-Pacific to the Indo-Pacific, in Beijing's eyes, represents a containment strategy directed against China.

When a confident China meets a vigilant America: An irreversible confrontation amidst worsening strategic distrust

It has become clear that the growing acceptance of the Indo-Pacific concept, in particular the US-led 'Free and Open Indo-Pacific Strategy', and the revitalisation of the Quad since 2017 have been increasingly at odds with China's BRI and Xi's advocacy of 'Asia-Pacific Century'. Beijing is not convinced with Washington's claim that 'the free and open Indo-Pacific Strategy is not just about China',[131] as this strategy is, in Beijing's eyes, nothing more than 'the most recent US response to China's rise'.[132] In this context, Beijing's outright rejection of the 'Indo-Pacific' concept is evidenced in the continuous use of the term 'Asia-Pacific region' by the Chinese foreign ministry spokespersons.

Then, what explains this growing sense of hostility between the United States and China? A simple and straightforward answer to this question would be the worsening strategic distrust between an increasingly confident China and an increasingly vigilant America. China's strategic distrust of the United States, according to some observers, is induced by four fundamental structural changes in the international system since 2008:[133] (1) China's strong sense of self-worth about its ascendance as a first class global power; (2) China's assessment of America's relative decline since the 2008 global financial crisis; (3) the emergence of the BRICS countries and their willingness to challenge Western dominance; and (4) the growing acceptance of China's development model as an alternative to Western democracy and free market economy for developing countries to learn from.

America's strategic distrust of China, on the other hand, is mainly driven by China's growing confidence in asserting itself on the world stage politically, economically, and militarily. Factors include: 1) China's one- party authoritarian political system and Beijing's rebuttal of Western- style liberal democracy; 2). China's attempt to export (albeit indirectly) its path of economic development as an alternative development model for the developing countries (as a way of implementing its system); and 3). China's military modernisation and the People's Liberation Army (PLA)'s aspirations for dominance in the region as a potential challenge for American freedom of access and action in international waters.

The inevitable consequence of the growing mutual distrust between Washington and Beijing is the intensifying US-China strategic competition. In other words, the BRI, launched by an increasingly confident China, and the 'Free and Open Indo-Pacific Strategy', advocated by an increasingly vigilant America, are on a collision course. To put it more accurately, the nature of the clash between China's BRI and US-led 'Free and Open Indo-Pacific Strategy' is twofold. First, as Yan Xuetong notes, 'China has gone through the stages of *standing up* and *getting rich* and is now advancing to the stage of *becoming strong*'.[134] This suggests that China's success in narrowing the gap in power with the US has resulted in what many Chinese scholars called 'structural contradictions' between the hegemon and the rising power.[135] These 'structural contradictions', as a result of China's self-perceived shrinking power gap with the world's only superpower, have resulted in fundamental changes in the style and substance of Chinese foreign policy making: The emergence of the wolf-warrior diplomacy, as mentioned earlier, is indicative of Beijing's unwillingness to avoid confrontation with Washington (style), and the launch of the BRI is a reflection of Beijing's enthusiasm to lay out a distinctive path of an economic development model (which is uniquely Chinese and different from the Western model) on the world stage (substance).

However, in the eyes of US policymakers, China's strengthening position relative to the US and its desperate desire to be treated as a coequal major power have highlighted the failure of long-standing US efforts to integrate China peacefully into the US-led international system. In this sense, Trump's 'Indo-Pacific dream' and the US government's formulation of the 'Free and Open Indo-Pacific Strategy' as an interdepartmental response to Xi's advocacy of 'Asia-Pacific Century' and China's BRI suggested the end of grand consensus or the convergence of fundamental US-China strategic interests: China wanting to be integrated and the US wanting to integrate China.[136]

Second, despite China's insistence on rising peacefully and fostering win-win cooperation and a peaceful coexistence with the US, the growing strength of assertive nationalism in China has cultivated a stronger sense of self-confidence and, therefore, generated a deeper sense of hostility among its leaders and people that the United States is an inevitable enemy of China as a stronger and more influential power. As a result, even though Beijing has vowed never to seek hegemony, the interplay between China's BRI and US-led Indo-Pacific Strategy does reflect a strategic competition over international leadership and prestige between Beijing and Washington. China's quest for greater international prestige, from Beijing's perspective, is totally justifiable and desirable because 'China believes that its rise to great-power status entitles it to a new role in world affairs—one that cannot be reconciled with unquestioned US dominance'.[137]

Conclusion

The launch of the BRI, along with President Xi's advocacy of 'Asia-Pacific Century' is, according to Beijing's official rhetoric, meant to benefit people across the world by achieving economic integration and interconnected development. Yet, in the eyes of US policymakers, China's desperate desire for 'striving for achievement' under Xi Jinping and cultivating a 'New Model of Major Power Relations' with the US represents a divergence (and even a clash) of fundamental strategic interests between Beijing and Washington: China no longer wants to be integrated into the US-led international order and the US no longer sees integrating China as possible or desirable.

This fundamental shift of China's foreign policy from 'keeping a low profile' to 'striving for achievement' is primarily driven by the growing strength of assertive nationalism in China. This is revealed in Beijing's willingness to defend China's self-proclaimed core (national) interests assertively (thereby weakening its 'peaceful rise' narrative) and its growing sense of confidence in projecting China's path of economic development as an alternative development model on the world stage. Beijing's strong sense of self-confidence, as characterised by Xi Jinping's advocacy of 'four matters of confidence', was clearly shown in an article published by the *People's Daily*, the CCP's flagship newspaper, in January 2018:

> 'The world needs China...[as] China was at a historic period for the cause of socialism with Chinese characteristics to leap forward, for the system of socialism with Chinese characteristics to mature and for the world pattern to reshape.'[138]

In this context, the Covid-19 pandemic has given Beijing the historic opportunity to subtly promote the 'Chinese experience' and 'Chinese solution' of treating Covid-19, especially the use of traditional Chinese medicine (TCM).[139] Although the Chinese government has rejected claims that Beijing is using its vaccine assistance to engage in 'vaccine diplomacy',[140] the coronavirus pandemic further intensified the strategic competition between the US and China. Beijing will see the global vaccine shortage as an opportunity to boost China's image in vaccine-recipient countries and to position itself as a global health leader through the promotion of the so-called 'Health Silk Road'.[141]

With this in consideration, the showdown between China's BRI and the US-led 'Free and Open Indo-Pacific Strategy' will remain a key characteristic of the long-term strategic competition between Washington and Beijing. China continues to see its wolf-warrior diplomacy as useful, perhaps even necessary, to further its self-proclaimed core national interests and counter foreign interference. The US, on the other hand, is more convinced that working with its partners and allies to advance a 'free and open' Indo-Pacific region through a revitalised Quad is crucial for US success in counterbalancing China's quest for greater prestige and coequality as a great power. This fundamental clash of strategic interests between the United States and China, therefore, has become more sharpened in the post Covid-19 world. A long-term US-China strategic competition, as a result, is predictable but irreversible.

Notes

1. 'Remarks by President Trump at APEC CEO Summit | Da Nang, Vietnam', US Mission to ASEAN, 10 November 2017, https://asean.usmission.gov/remarks-president-trump-apec-ceo-summit-da-nang-vietnam/. Accessed on July 11, 2021.

2. Ibid.
3. Alyssa Ayres, 'Tillerson on India: Partners in a "Free and Open Indo-Pacific"', Council on Foreign Relations', 18 October 2017, https://www.cfr.org/blog/tillerson-india-partners-free-and-open-indo-pacific. Accessed on July 11, 2021.
4. 'Keynote speech by Chinese President Xi Jinping at the APEC CEO Summit', *Global Times,* 20 November 2016, https://www.globaltimes.cn/content/1019023.shtml. Accessed on July 11, 2021.
5. Ibid.
6. Minghao Zhao, 'Is a New Cold War Inevitable? Chinese Perspectives on US-China Strategic Competition', *The Chinese Journal of International Politics,* Vol. 12, Issue 3, Autumn 2019, p. 372.
7. Ibid., pp. 372-373.
8. Kenneth Lieberthal and Wang Jisi, 'Addressing US-China Strategic Distrust', JohnL. Thornton China Center Monograph Series, no. 4, (Washington, DC: Brookings Institution, March 2012).
9. Muhammad Saeed, 'From the Asia-Pacific to the Indo-Pacific: Expanding Sino-U.S. Strategic Competition', *China Quarterly of International Strategic Studies*, Vol. 3, No. 4, p. 501.
10. See Kenneth Lieberthal and Wang Jisi, 'Addressing US-China Strategic Distrust', John L. Thornton China Center Monograph Series, no. 4, (Washington, DC: Brookings Institution, March 2012).
11. 'Beijing's ambitions and assertiveness will grow', Oxford Analytica Expert Briefing, 24 September 2020, https://www.emerald.com/insight/content/doi/10.1108/OXAN-DB256448/full/html. Accessed on July 28, 2021.
12. 'China Focus: Socialism with Chinese Characteristics: 10 Ideas to Share with World', *Xinhua*, 8 October 2017, http://www.xinhuanet.com/english/2017-10/08/c_136665156.htm. Assessed on July 29, 2021.
13. Zhiqun Zhu, 'Interpreting China's 'Wolf-Warrior Diplomacy'', *The Diplomat,* 15 May 2020, https://thediplomat.com/2020/05/interpreting-chinas-wolf-warrior-diplomacy/. Assessed on August 1, 2021.
14. Zaini Majeed, 'Blinken Blasts China, Says It 'disturbs' Rules-based Order Which US 'strongly Defends', *RepublicWorld,* 9 June 2021, https://www.republicworld.com/world-news/us-news/blinken-blasts-china-says-it-disturbs-rules-based-order-which-us-strongly-defends.html. Accessed on August 1, 2021.
15. Xuetong Yan, 'From Keeping a Low Profile to Striving for Achievement', *The Chinese Journal of International Politics,* Vol. 7, Issue 2 (Summer 2014), pp. 153-184.
16. Xi Jinping, *Secure a decisive victory in building a moderately prosperous society in all respects and strive for the great success of socialism with Chinese characteristics for a new era,* report delivered at 19th National Congress of the GCP, Beijing, 18

October 2017. Available at http://www.xinhuanet.com/english/download/Xi_Jinping's_report_at_19th_CPC_National_Congress.pdf. Accessed on August 2, 2021.

17. 'Xi Jinping: 'Time for China to take centre stage', BBC News, 18 October 2017, https://www.bbc.com/news/world-asia-china-41647872. Assessed on August 2, 2021.
18. Richard Javad Heydarian, 'Hide your strength, bide your time', *Al Jazeera*, 21 November 2014, https://www.aljazeera.com/opinions/2014/11/21/hide-your-strength-bide-your-time. Assessed on August 2, 2021.
19. Quoted in Peter Ferdinand, 'Westward ho—The China Dream and "One Belt, One Road": Chinese Foreign Policy Under Xi Jinping', *International Affairs,* Volume 92, Issue 4, July 2016, p. 946.
20. 'CPC Q&A: What are China's two centennial goals and why do they matter?', *Xinhua*, 17 October, 2017, http://www.xinhuanet.com/english/2017-10/17/c_136686770.htm. Accessed on August 2, 2021.
21. Camilla T.N. Sørensen, 'The Significance of Xi Jinping's "Chinese Dream" for Chinese Foreign Policy: From "Tao Guang Yang Hui" to "Fen Fa You Wei"', *Journal of China International Relations,* Vol. 3, No. 1 (2015), pp. 53-73.
22. 'China Overview: Development news, research, data', *World Bank*, 29 March 2021, https://www.worldbank.org/en/country/china/overview. Accessed on August 2, 2021.
23. 'Speech delivered by President Xi at the NPC closing meeting', *China Daily*, 22 March 2018, http://www.chinadaily.com.cn/hkedition/2018-03/22/content_35894512.htm. Accessed on August 2, 2021.
24. 'July 1, 2016 Four matters of confidence', *China Internet Information Center*, 1 July 2016, http://www.china.org.cn/china/2021-06/01/content_77231327.htm. Accessed on August 2, 2021.
25. 'Full Text of Xi Jinping's Report at 19th CPC National Congress', *China Daily*, 4 November 2017, https://www.chinadaily.com.cn/china/19thcpcnationalcongress/2017-11/04/content_34115212.htm. Accessed on August 2, 2021.
26. Alastair Iain Johnston, 'How New and Assertive is China's New Assertiveness?', *International Security*, Vol. 37, No. 4 (2013), pp. 7-48.
27. 'Xi Jinping Holds Talks with President Barack Obama of the US, Stressing Promoting Construction of New Model of Major-Country Relationship Between China and the US in Six Key Directions and Putting into Practice Principles of No Conflict, No Confrontation, Mutual Respect, and Win-Win Cooperation', *Ministry of Foreign Affairs of the People's Republic of China*, 12 November 2014, https://www.fmprc.gov.cn/mfa_eng/topics_665678/ytjhzzdrsrcldrfzshyjxghd/t1211022.shtml. Accessed on August 3, 2021.

28. 'Xi Jinping Calls for the Building of New Type of International Relations with Win-Win Cooperation at the Core in a Speech at the Moscow State Institute of International Relations', Ministry of Foreign Affairs of the People's Republic of China, 23 March 2013, https://www.fmprc.gov.cn/mfa_eng/topics_665678/xjpcf1_665694/t1024781.shtml. Accessed on August 4, 2021; Timothy Doyle and Dennis Rumley, *The Rise and Return of the Indo-Pacific* (Oxford: Oxford University Press, 2019), pp. 147-148.
29. Christian Shepherd, 'China says it wants to resolve differences with U.S. 'on equal footing', *Reuters*, 3 August 2018, https://www.reuters.com/article/us-asean-singapore-china-usa-idUSKBN1KO12M. Accessed on August 4, 2021.
30. Wang Jisi, 'America and China: Destined for Conflict or Cooperation? We Asked 14 of the World's Most Renowned Experts', *National Interest*, 30 July 2018, https://nationalinterest.org/feature/america-and-china-destined-conflict-or-cooperation-we-asked-14-worlds-most-renowned-experts. Accessed on August 4, 2021.
31. Minghao Zhao,'Is a New Cold War Inevitable? Chinese Perspectives on US-China Strategic Competition', p. 374.
32. Barry Buzan, 'China's rise in English school perspective', *International Relations of the Asia-Pacific*, Vol. 18, No. 3 (2018), p. 458.
33. David Shambaugh, *China Goes Global: The Partial Power* (Oxford: Oxford University Press, 2013), p. 56.
34. Matt Schiavenz, 'How Humiliation Drove Modern Chinese History', *The Atlantic*, 26 October 2013, https://www.theatlantic.com/china/archive/2013/10/how-humiliation-drove-modern-chinese-history/280878/. Accessed on August 5, 2021.
35. David Shambaugh, *China Goes Global: The Partial Power*, p. 56.
36. Ibid., p. 56 (*Italics* original).
37. Timothy Doyle and Dennis Rumley, *The Rise and Return of the Indo-Pacific*, pp. 146-147.
38. The State Council of The People's Republic of China, 'White Paper: China's Peaceful Development', 6 September 2011. Available at http://english.www.gov.cn/archive/white_paper/2014/09/09/content_281474986284646.htm. Accessed on August 5, 2021.
39. Michael D. Swaine, 'China's Assertive Behavior—Part One: On "Core Interests"', China Leadership Monitor No. 34 (22 February 2011), https://carnegieendowment.org/files/CLM34MS_FINAL.pdf. Accessed on August 5, 2021).
40. Allen S. Whiting, 'Assertive Nationalism in Chinese Foreign Policy', *Asian Survey* Vol. 23, No. 8 (1983), pp. 913–933.

41. Suisheng Zhao, 'Foreign Policy Implications of Chinese Nationalism Revisited: the strident turn', *Journal of Contemporary China,* Volume 22, Issue 82 (July 2013), pp. 546-549.
42. Wilson VornDick, 'Analysts Take Note: Wolf Warrior Is the New Chinese Rambo', *The Diplomat*, 20 September 2017, https://thediplomat.com/2017/09/analysts-take-note-wolf-warrior-is-the-new-chinese-rambo/. Accessed on August 10, 2021.
43. Tom Phillips, 'China finds its own Top Gun and Rambo in wave of patriotic movies', *The Guardian,* 24 September 2017, https://www.theguardian.com/world/2017/sep/23/china-finds-its-own-top-gun-and-rambo-in-wave-of-patriotic-movies. Accessed on August 10, 2021.
44. Ibid.
45. Gaochao Zhang, 'Wolf Warrior 2' becomes China's highest-grossing film of all time', *Los Angeles Times*, 15 August 2017, https://www.latimes.com/business/hollywood/la-fi-ct-china-box-office-wolf-warrior2-story.html. Accessed on August 13, 2021.
46. Zhiqun Zhu, 'Interpreting China's "Wolf-Warrior Diplomacy"', *The Diplomat*, 15 May 2020, https://thediplomat.com/2020/05/interpreting-chinas-wolf-warrior-diplomacy/. Accessed on August 13, 2021.
47. Ibid.
48. Jessica Brandt and Bret Schafer, 'How China's 'wolf warrior' diplomats use and abuse Twitter', Brookings Institutions, 28 October 2020, https://www.brookings.edu/techstream/how-chinas-wolf-warrior-diplomats-use-and-abuse-twitter/. Accessed on August 15, 2021.
49. Julia Hollingsworth, 'Australia demands apology after Chinese official tweets 'falsified image' of soldier threatening child', *CNN*, 30 November 2020, https://edition.cnn.com/2020/11/30/australia/australia-china-twitter-intl-hnk/index.html. Accessed on August 15, 2021.
50. Victor Robert Lee, 'South China Sea: China's Unprecedented Spratlys Building Program', *The Diplomat,* 25 April 2015, https://thediplomat.com/2015/04/south-china-sea-chinas-unprecedented-spratlys-building-program/. Accessed on August 15, 2021.
51. Amruta Karambelkar, 'China's Militarisation of South China Sea', *Vivekananda International Foundation*, 15 September 2020, https://www.vifindia.org/2020/september/15/china-s-militarisation-of-south-china-sea. Accessed August on 15, 2021.
52. 'China says South China Sea land reclamation 'justified", *BBC News*, 10 September 2014, https://www.bbc.com/news/world-asia-china-29139125. Accessed on August 15, 2021.
53. Quoted in David Shambaugh, *China Goes Global: The Partial Power* (Oxford: Oxford University Press, 2013), p. 20.

54. 'Full Text of Xi Jinping's Report at 19th CPC National Congress', *China Daily*, 4 November 2017, https://www.chinadaily.com.cn/china/19thcpcnationalcongress/2017-11/04/content_34115212.htm. Accessed on August 2, 2021.
55. 'President Xi Jinping Delivers Important Speech and Proposes to Build a Silk Road Economic Belt with Central Asian Countries', *Ministry of Foreign Affairs of the People's Republic of China*, 7 September 2013, https://www.fmprc.gov.cn/mfa_eng/topics_665678/xjpfwzysiesgjtfhshzzfh_665686/t1076334.shtml. Accessed August on 15, 2021.
56. 'Full text of the Vision for Maritime Cooperation under the Belt and Road Initiative', *The State Council, The People's Republic of China*, 20 June 2017, http://english.www.gov.cn/archive/publications/2017/06/20/content_281475691873460.htm. Accessed on August 16, 2021.
57. Christoph Nedopil, 'Investments in the Belt and Road Initiative', Beijing, IIGF Green BRI Center, 2021, https://green-bri.org/investments-in-the-belt-and-road-initiative-bri/. Accessed on August 17, 2021.
58. 'Full text of President Xi's speech at opening of Belt and Road forum', *Xinhua*, 14 May 2017, http://www.xinhuanet.com//english/2017-05/14/c_136282982.htm. Accessed on August 15, 2021.
59. Xugang Yu and Cristiano Rizzi, 'China and the "Belt and Road" Initiative: What Is It All About?', in Yu Xugang (*et. al.*), *China's Belt and Road: The Initiative and Its Financial Focus*. (Singapore: World Scientific, 2018), pp. 55-88.
60. Nele Noesselt, 'One Belt, One Road: A New Roadmap for a Sinocentric World?', *The Asan Forum*, 20 October 2016, https://theasanforum.org/one-belt-one-road-a-new-roadmap-for-a-sinocentric-world/. Accessed on August 16, 2021.
61. Quoted in Zhao Hong, *China's One Belt One Road: An Overview of the Debate*. Trends in Southeast Asia No. 6 (Singapore: ISEAS Yusof Ishak Institute, 2016), p. 11.
62. 'Full text of Xi Jinping's report at 19th CPC National Congress', *China Daily*, 4 November 2017, https://www.chinadaily.com.cn/china/19thcpcnationalcongress/2017-11/04/content_34115212.htm. Accessed on August 16, 2021.
63. Kerry Brown, 'Five Years On: The significance of the Belt and Road Initiative extends beyond roads and railways', *Beijing Review*, No. 38, 20 September 2018, http://www.bjreview.com/Opinion/201809/t20180917_800141589.html. Accessed on August 16, 2021.
64. Rosemary Foot and Amy King, 'China's world view in the Xi Jinping Era: Where do Japan, Russia and the USA fit?', *The British Journal of Politics and International Relations*, Vol. 23, Issue 2 (May 2021), p. 214.

65. Ibid., p. 214.
66. Quoted in ibid, p. 214.
67. 'Wang Yi Talks about the Essence of Major Country Diplomacy with Chinese Characteristics: To Promote More Countries' Understanding and Recognition of Socialism Path with Chinese Characteristics', *Ministry of Foreign Affairs of the People's Republic of China*, 19 October 2017, https://www.fmprc.gov.cn/mfa_eng/zxxx_662805/t1503756.shtml. Accessed on August 17, 2021.
68. Ian Taylor, *The International Relations of Sub-Saharan Africa* (London: The Continuum International Publishing Group, 2011), p. 33.
69. Suisheng Zhao, 'The China Model: An Authoritarian State-Led Modernization', in Carla P. Freeman (ed.), *Handbook on China and Developing Countries* (Cheltenham, UK and Northampton, MA: Edward Elgar Publishing, 2015), pp. 21-50.
70. 'China surpassed the United States as the world's largest crude oil importer in 2017', *US Energy Information Administration*, 31 December 2018, https://www.eia.gov/todayinenergy/detail.php?id=37821, Accessed on August 17, 2021.
71. Michael Lelyveld, 'China's Oil Import Dependence Climbs as Output Falls', *Radio Free Asia*, 4 December 2017, https://www.rfa.org/english/commentaries/energy_watch/chinas-oil-import-dependence-climbs-as-output-falls-12042017102429.html. Accessed on August 17, 2021.
72. Quoted in ibid.
73. Marc Lanteigne, 'China's Maritime Security and the "Malacca Dilemma"', *Asian Security*, (Vol. 4, Issue 2, 2008), pp. 143-161.
74. Muhammad Saeed, 'From the Asia-Pacific to the Indo-Pacific: Expanding Sino-US Strategic Competition', *China Quarterly of International Strategic Studies*, Vol. 3, No. 4 (2017), p. 501; Jatswan S. Sidhu and Roy Anthony Rogers, 'China's Strategic Ambitions in the Indian Ocean Region, India's Anxiety and the United States' Concerns'. *Malaysian Journal of International Relations*, Vol. 3, No. 1 (2015), p. 88.
75. Graham Allison, *Destined For War: Can America and China Escape Thucydides's Trap?* (London and Melbourne: Scribe Publications, 2017), p. 20.
76. Quoted in Patrick Mendis and Joey Wang, 'Unveiling China's Grand Plan', *Harvard International Review*, Vol. 40, No. 3 (Summer 2019), pp. 36-39.
77. Muhammad Saeed, 'From the Asia-Pacific to the Indo-Pacific: Expanding Sino-U.S. Strategic Competition', p. 501.
78. Jinghan Zeng and Shaun Breslin, 'China's "new type of Great Power relations": a G2 with Chinese characteristics?, *International Affairs* Volume 92, Issue 4 (July 2016), pp. 773-794.
79. Hillary Clinton, 'America's Pacific Century', *Foreign Policy*, Vol. 189, No. 1 (2011), pp. 56-63.

80. White House, 'FACT SHEET: Advancing the Rebalance to Asia and the Pacific', Office of the Press Secretary, 16 November 2015, https://obamawhitehouse.archives.gov/the-press-office/2015/11/16/fact-sheet-advancing-rebalance-asia-and-pacific. Accessed on August 18, 2021.
81. Renato Cruz De Castro, 'The Obama Administration's Strategic Rebalancing to Asia: Quo Vadis in 2017?', *Pacific Focus*, Vol. 33, Issue 2 (August 2018), pp. 179-208.
82. Rebecca Howard, 'Trans-Pacific Partnership trade deal signed, but years of negotiations still to come', *Reuters*, 4 February 2016, https://www.reuters.com/article/us-trade-tpp-idUSKCN0VD08S. Accessed on August 18, 2021.
83. Martin S. Indyk, Kenneth G. Lieberthal, and Michael E. O'Hanlon, 'Scoring Obama's Foreign Policy: A Progressive Pragmatist Tries to Bend History', *Foreign Affairs*, Vol. 91, No. 3 (May/June 2012), p. 33.
84. White House, Remarks by President Obama and President Xi of the People's Republic of China in Joint Press Conference', Office of the Press Secretary, 25 September 2015, https://obamawhitehouse.archives.gov/the-press-office/2015/09/25/remarks-president-obama-and-president-xi-peoples-republic-china-joint, Accessed on August 18, 2021; Stephanie Condon, 'Obama: "We Welcome China's Rise"', *CBS News*, 20 January 2011, https://www.cbsnews.com/news/obama-we-welcome-chinas-rise/, Accessed on August 18, 2021.
85. Suisheng Zhao, 'American Reflections on the Engagement with China and Responses to President Xi's New Model of Major Power Relations', *Journal of Contemporary China*, Vol. 26, No. 106 (2017), p. 494.
86. Carrie Gracie, 'Collision course? Rise of China a stress for the US', *BBC News*, 26 September 2015, https://www.bbc.com/news/world-asia-china-34368249, Accessed on August 18, 2021.
87. Jim Garamone, 'Trump Announces New Whole-of-Government National Security Strategy', *DoD News*, 18 December 2017. Available at https://www.defense.gov/Explore/News/Article/Article/1399392/trump-announces-new-whole-of-government-national-security-strategy/. Accessed on August 18, 2021.
88. Demetri Sevastopulo, 'Trump labels China a strategic 'competitor'', *Financial Times*, 19 December 2017, https://www.ft.com/content/215cf8fa-e3cb-11e7-8b99-0191e45377ec. Accessed on August 19, 2021.
89. White House, *The National Security Strategy of the United States of America.* (Washington, DC: Government of the United States of America, 2017), p. 25, https://trumpwhitehouse.archives.gov/wp-content/uploads/2017/12/NSS-Final-12-18-2017-0905.pdf. Accessed on August 19, 2021.
90. Felix Heiduk and Gudrun Wacker, 'From Asia-Pacific to Indo-Pacific: Significance, Implementation and Challenges', SWP Research Paper 9, July

2020. (Berlin: German Institute for International and Security Affairs, 2020), p. 11, https://www.swp-berlin.org/fileadmin/contents/products/research_papers/2020RP09_IndoPacific.pdf. Accessed on August 18, 2021.

91. White House, *The National Security Strategy of the United States of America.* (Washington, DC: Government of the United States of America, 2017), pp. 46-47, https://trumpwhitehouse.archives.gov/wp-content/uploads/2017/12/NSS-Final-12-18-2017-0905.pdf. Accessed on August 19, 2021.
92. US Department of Defense, *Summary of the 2018 National Defense Strategy of the United States of America: Sharpening the American Military's Competitive Edge* (Washington DC: the Department of Defense, 2018), p. 2 (*italic* original), https://dod.defense.gov/Portals/1/Documents/pubs/2018-National-Defense-Strategy-Summary.pdf. Accessed on August 18, 2021.
93. Ibid., p. 2.
94. Ibid., p. 9.
95. Ibid., p. 9.
96. US Department of Defense, *Indo-Pacific Strategy Report: Preparedness, Partnerships and Promoting a Networked Region,* 1 June 2019, (Washington DC: the Department of Defense, 2019), https://media.defense.gov/2019/Jul/01/2002152311/-1/-1/1/DEPARTMENT-OF-DEFENSE-INDO-PACIFIC-STRATEGY-REPORT-2019.PDF. Accessed on August 18, 2021.
97. Ibid., p. 4 (*italics* original).
98. Ibid., p. 4.
99. US Department of State, *Free and Open Indo-Pacific: Advancing a Shared Vision* (Washington DC: the Department of State, 2019), https://www.state.gov/a-free-and-open-indo-pacific-advancing-a-shared-vision/. Accessed on August 19, 2021.
100. Ibid., pp. 4, 9.
101. Ibid., p. 15.
102. 'Indo-Pacific Strategy: Implications for the Region', *The Daily Star*, 20 March 2019, https://www.thedailystar.net/round-tables/news/indo-pacific-strategy-implications-the-region-1717426. Accessed on August 19, 2021.
103. Idree Ali, 'In symbolic nod to India, U.S. Pacific Command changes name', *Reuters*, 31 May 2018, https://www.reuters.com/article/us-usa-defense-india-idUSKCN1IV2Q2. Accessed on August 19, 2021.
104. Felix Heiduk and Gudrun Wacker, 'From Asia-Pacific to Indo-Pacific: Significance, Implementation and Challenges', SWP Research Paper 9, July 2020. (Berlin: German Institute for International and Security Affairs, 2020), p. 15, https://www.swp-berlin.org/fileadmin/contents/products/research_papers/2020RP09_IndoPacific.pdf. Accessed on August 18, 2021.
105. Rory Medcalf, *Contest for the Indo-Pacific: Why China Won't Map the Future* (Melbourne: La Trobe University Press, 2020), p. 4.

106. White House, 'U.S. Strategic Framework for the Indo-Pacific', (Washington, DC: Government of the United States of America, 2021), p. 2, https://trumpwhitehouse.archives.gov/wp-content/uploads/2021/01/IPS-Final-Declass.pdf. Accessed on August 19, 2021.
107. Rory Medcalf, *Contest for the Indo-Pacific: Why China Won't Map the Future,* p. 3.
108. 'Bush announces tsunami aid coalition', *CNN*, 29 December 2004, http://edition.cnn.com/2004/US/12/29/bush.quake/. Accessed on August 19, 2021.
109. Nilanthi Samaranayake, 'Cooperation of consequence: Lessons from the 2004 tsunami response in the era of COVID-19', Observer Research Foundation (ORF) report, 1 May 2020, https://www.orfonline.org/expert-speak/cooperation-of-consequence-65491/. Accessed on August 20, 2021; Marc Grossman, 'The Tsunami Core Group: A Step toward a Transformed Diplomacy in Asia and Beyond', *Security Challenges,* Vol. 1, No. 1 (2005), pp. 11-14
110. Rajeev Sharma, 'Asia's New Strategic Baby: The Quadrilateral Forum', *DW* News, 15 June 2007, https://www.dw.com/en/asias-new-strategic-baby-the-quadrilateral-forum/a-5212697. Accessed on August 21, 2021.
111 Ministry of Foreign Affairs, Government of Japan, "Confluence of the Two Seas" Speech by H.E.Mr. Shinzo Abe, Prime Minister of Japan at the Parliament of the Republic of India, 22 August 2007, https://www.mofa.go.jp/region/asia-paci/pmv0708/speech-2.html. Accessed on August 21, 2021.
112. Gurpreet S. Khurana, 'What is the Indo-Pacific? The New Geopolitics of the Asia-Centred Rim Land', in Axel Berkofsky and Sergio Miracola (eds.), *Geopolitics by Other Means: The Indo-Pacific Reality* (Milan: Ledizioni LediPublishing, 2019), p. 7.
113. Department of Defence, Government of Australia, '2016 Defence White Paper', p. 17, https://www1.defence.gov.au/about/publications/2016-defence-white-paper. Accessed on August 21, 2021.
114. Ministry of Foreign Affairs, Government of Japan, 'Towards a Free and Open Pacific', November 2019, https://www.mofa.go.jp/files/000407643.pdf. Accessed on August 22, 2021.
115. Eshwar Ranjana, 'India Sets Up New Indo-Pacific Desk, Experts Laud 'Strategic Move'', *The Quint*, 15 April 2019, https://www.thequint.com/news/india/india-sets-up-new-indo-pacific-desk-experts-laud-strategic-move. Accessed on August 22, 2021.
116. In December 2012, Japanese Prime Minister Shinzo Abe, in his op-ed written for Project Syndicate, advocated the establishment of Asia's 'democratic security diamond' (DSD) for the sake of preserving peace, stability, and freedom of navigation in the Pacific and Indian Ocean. See Shinzo Abe, 'Asia's Democratic Security Diamond', *Project Syndicate*, 27 December 2012, https://www.project-syndicate.org/onpoint/a-strategic-alliance-for-japan-and-india-by-shinzo-abe. Accessed on August 24, 2021.

117. Thomas S. Wilkins, 'Whose "Indo Pacific"? competing visions of regional order', The Japan Institute of International Affairs Policy Brief, 12 November 2020, https://www.jiia-jic.jp/en/news/policy-briefwhose-indo-pacific-competing-visions-of-regional-order.html. Accessed on August 24, 2021.
118. Amrita Jash, 'The Quad Factor in the Indo-Pacific and the Role of India', *The Journal of Indo-Pacific Affairs*, Vol. 4, Issue 2 (Spring 2021), pp. 78-85.
119. Indrani Bagchi, 'New alliances, grouping being created in response to Covid-19', *The Times of India*, 14 May 2020, https://timesofindia.indiatimes.com/india/new-alliances-grouping-being-created-in-response-to-covid-19/articleshow/75745739.cms. Accessed on August 25, 2021.
120. Benjamin Reilly, 'The return of values in Australian foreign policy', *Australian Journal of International Affairs*, Vol. 74, 2020-Issue 2, pp. 116-123.
121. Brahma Chellaney, 'Quad Initiative': an inharmonious concert of democracies', *The Japan Times*, 19 July 2007, https://www.japantimes.co.jp/opinion/2007/07/19/commentary/quad-initiative-an-inharmonious-concert-of-democracies/. Accessed on August 25, 2021.
122. Ibid.
123. '"Quad" nations vow to step up coordination for free and open Indo-Pacific', *The Japan Times*, 6 October 2020, https://www.japantimes.co.jp/news/2020/10/06/national/politics-diplomacy/quad-free-open-indo-pacific-china/. Accessed on August 25, 2021.
124. Ramesh Thakur, 'China as the godfather of Quad 2.0', *The Strategist,* 20 July 2020, https://www.aspistrategist.org.au/china-as-the-godfather-of-quad-2-0/. Accessed on August 25, 2021.
125. For a comprehensive analysis of the China factor and the Quad's revival, see Jyotsna Mehra, 'The Australia-India-Japan-US Quadrilateral: Dissecting the China Factor', *ORF Occasional Paper No. 264*, August 2020, Observer Research Foundation.
126. Ministry of Defense, Government of Japan, 'Defense of Japan: Defence White Paper 2019', September 2019, https://www.mod.go.jp/en/publ/w_paper/wp_2019.html. Accessed on August 25, 2021.
127. Gurpreet Khurana, 'China's "String of Pearls" in the Indian Ocean and Its Security Implications', *Strategic Analysis* Vol. 32, No. 1, January 2008, pp. 1-39; Andrew Small, *The China–Pakistan Axis: Asia's New Geopolitics* (Oxford: Oxford University Press, 2015).
128. White House, 'U.S. Strategic Framework for the Indo-Pacific', (Washington, DC: Government of the United States of America, 2021), pp. 1-2, https://trumpwhitehouse.archives.gov/wp-content/uploads/2021/01/IPS-Final-Declass.pdf. Accessed on August 19, 2021.
129. 'Quad an exclusive 'clique', working against China: Foreign ministry', *Hindustan Times*, 12 May 2021, https://www.hindustantimes.com/world-news/quad-an-

exclusive-clique-working-against-china-foreign-ministry-101620821263120.html. Accessed on August 25, 2021.

130. 'Wang Yi: U.S. "Indo-Pacific Strategy" Undermines Peace and Development Prospects in East Asia', *Ministry of Foreign Affairs of the People's Republic of China*, 13 October 2020, https://www.fmprc.gov.cn/mfa_eng/zxxx_662805/t1824140.shtml. Accessed on August 26, 2021.
131. US Department of State, 'Briefing on the Indo-Pacific Strategy', Alex N. Wong, deputy assistant secretary, Bureau of East Asian and Pacific Affairs, Washington DC, 2 April 2018.
132. Feng Liu, 'The recalibration of Chinese assertiveness: China's responses to the Indo-Pacific challenge', *International Affairs*, Vol. 96, No. 1 (2020), p. 16.
133. Kenneth Lieberthal and Wang Jisi, 'Addressing US-China Strategic Distrust', John L. Thornton China Center Monograph Series, no. 4, (Washington, DC: Brookings Institution, March 2012), p. vii.
134. Yan Xuetong, 'Becoming Strong: The New Chinese Foreign Policy', *Foreign Affairs*, Vol. 100, No. 4 July/August 2021, p. 40-47 (*italic* added).
135. See, for instance, Yuan Peng, 'Contradictions and Strategic Anxieties in China-US Relations', 9 October 2011, *China-US Focus,* https://www.chinausfocus.com/peace-security/strategic-reassurance-bidens-post-afghanistan-challenge-in-southeast-asia. Accessed on August 26, 2021.
136. Suisheng Zhao, 'American Reflections on the Engagement with China and Responses to President Xi's New Model of Major Power Relations', *Journal of Contemporary China*, Vol. 26, No. 106 (2017), pp. 489-503.
137. Yan Xuetong, 'Becoming Strong: The New Chinese Foreign Policy', *Foreign Affairs*, Vol. 100, No. 4 July/August 2021, p. 40.
138. 'CPC newspaper says China should "grasp historic opportunity"', *Xinhua*, 15 January 2018, http://www.china.org.cn/china/2018-01/15/content_50228877.htm. Accessed on August 27, 2021.
139. Pratik Jakhar, 'Covid-19: China pushes traditional remedies amid outbreak', *BBC News*, 29 June 2020, https://www.bbc.com/news/world-asia-53094603. Accessed on August 27, 2021.
140. 'Foreign Ministry Spokesperson Zhao Lijian's Regular Press Conference on July 29, 2021', *Ministry of Foreign Affairs of the People's Republic of China*, 29 July 2021, https://www.fmprc.gov.cn/mfa_eng/xwfw_665399/s2510_665401/t1896083.shtml. Accessed on August 27, 2021.
141. Jacob Mardell, 'China's "Health Silk Road": Adapting the BRI to a pandemic-era world', *MERICS Short Analysis*, 25 November 2020, https://merics.org/en/short-analysis/chinas-health-silk-road-adapting-bri-pandemic-era-world. Accessed on August 27, 2021.

References

Abe, Shinzo (2012), "Asia's Democratic Security Diamond", *Project Syndicate*, 27 December, https://www.project-syndicate.org/onpoint/a-strategic-alliance-for-japan-and-india-by-shinzo-abe. Accessed on August 24, 2021.

Ali, Idree (2018), "In symbolic nod to India, U.S. Pacific Command changes name", *Reuters*, 31 May, https://www.reuters.com/article/us-usa-defense-india-idUSKCN1IV2Q2. Accessed on August 19, 2021.

Allison, Graham (2017), *Destined For War: Can America and China Escape Thucydides's Trap?* London and Melbourne: Scribe Publications.

Ayres, Alyssa (2017), "Tillerson on India: Partners in a "Free and Open Indo-Pacific"", Council on Foreign Relations, 18 October, https://www.cfr.org/blog/tillerson-india-partners-free-and-open-indo-pacific. Accessed on July 11, 2021.

Bagchi, Indrani (2020), "New alliances, grouping being created in response to Covid-19", *The Times of India*, 14 May, https://timesofindia.indiatimes.com/india/new-alliances-grouping-being-created-in-response-to-covid-19/articleshow/75745739.cms. Accessed on August 25, 2021.

BBC News, 2017, "Xi Jinping: 'Time for China to take centre stage'", *BBC News*, 18 October, https://www.bbc.com/news/world-asia-china-41647872. Assessed on August 2, 2021.

BBC News, 2014, "China says South China Sea land reclamation 'justified'", 10 September, https://www.bbc.com/news/world-asia-china-29139125. Accessed August on 15, 2021.

Brandt, Jessica and Bret Schafer (2020), "How China's 'wolf warrior' diplomats use and abuse Twitter", Brookings Institutions, 28 October, https://www.brookings.edu/techstream/how-chinas-wolf-warrior-diplomats-use-and-abuse-twitter/. Accessed on August 15, 2021.

Brown, Kerry (2018), "Five Years On: The significance of the Belt and Road Initiative extends beyond roads and railways", *Beijing Review*, NO. 38, 20 September, http://www.bjreview.com/Opinion/201809/t20180917_800141589.html. Accessed on August 16, 2021.

Buzan, Barry (2018), "China's rise in English school perspective", *International Relations of the Asia-Pacific*, Vol. 18, No. 3, pp. 449-476.

Chellaney, Brahma (2007), "Quad Initiative: an inharmonious concert of democracies", *The Japan 'Times*, 19 July, https://www.japantimes.co.jp/opinion/2007/07/19/commentary/quad-initiative-an-inharmonious-concert-of-democracies/. Accessed on August 25, 2021.

China Daily, 2018, 'Speech delivered by President Xi at the NPC closing meeting', 22 March, http://www.chinadaily.com.cn/hkedition/2018-03/22/content_35894512.htm. Accessed on August 2, 2021.

China Daily, 2017, 'Full text of Xi Jinping's report at 19th CPC National Congress', 4 November, https://www.chinadaily.com.cn/china/19thcpcnationalcongress/2017-11/04/content_34115212.htm. Accessed on August 16, 2021.

China Internet Information Center, 2016, 'July 1, 2016 Four matters of confidence', 1 July, http://www.china.org.cn/china/2021-06/01/content_77231327.htm. Accessed on August 2, 2021.

Clinton, Hillary (2011), "America's Pacific Century", *Foreign Policy*, Vol. 189, No. 1 (2011), pp. 56-63.

CNN, 2004, 'Bush announces tsunami aid coalition', 29 December, http://edition.cnn.com/2004/US/12/29/bush.quake/. Accessed on August 19, 2021.

Condon, Stephanie (2011), "Obama: "We Welcome China's Rise"", *CBS News*, 20 January, https://www.cbsnews.com/news/obama-we-welcome-chinas-rise/. Accessed on August 18, 2021.

De Castro, Renato Cruz (2018), "The Obama Administration's Strategic Rebalancing to Asia: Quo Vadis in 2017?", *Pacific Focus*, Volume 33, Issue 2 (August), pp. 179-208.

Department of Defence, Government of Australia, 2016, '2016 Defence White Paper', https://www1.defence.gov.au/about/publications/2016-defence-white-paper. Accessed on August 21, 2021.

Doyle, Timothy and Dennis Rumley (2019), *The Rise and Return of the Indo-Pacific*. Oxford: Oxford University Press.

Ferdinand, Peter (2016), "Westward ho—The China Dream and "One Belt, One Road": Chinese Foreign Policy Under Xi Jinping", *International Affairs*, Volume 92, Issue 4 (July), pp. 941-957.

Foot, Rosemary and Amy King (2021), "China's world view in the Xi Jinping Era: Where do Japan, Russia and the USA fit?", *The British Journal of Politics and International Relations*, Volume 23, Issue 2, (May), pp. 210-227.

Garamone, Jim (2017), "Trump Announces New Whole-of-Government National Security Strategy", *DoD News*, 18 December, https://www.defense.gov/Explore/News/Article/Article/1399392/trump-announces-new-whole-of-government-national-security-strategy/. Accessed on August 18, 2021.

Global Times, 2016, 'Keynote speech by Chinese President Xi Jinping at the APEC CEO Summit', 20 November, https://www.globaltimes.cn/content/1019023.shtml. Accessed on July 11, 2021.

Gracie, Carrie (2015), "Collision course? Rise of China a stress for the US", *BBC News*, 26 September, https://www.bbc.com/news/world-asia-china-34368249. Accessed on August 18, 2021.

Grossman, Marc (2005), "The Tsunami Core Group: A Step toward a Transformed Diplomacy in Asia and Beyond", *Security Challenges*, Vol. 1, No. 1, pp. 11-14.

Heiduk, Felix and Gudrun Wacker (2020), "From Asia-Pacific to Indo-Pacific: Significance, Implementation and Challenges", *SWP Research Paper* 9, July.

Berlin: German Institute for International and Security Affairs, https://www.swp-berlin.org/fileadmin/contents/products/research_papers/2020RP09_IndoPacific.pdf. Accessed on August 18, 2021.

Heydarian, Richard Javad (2014), "Hide your strength, bide your time", *Al Jazeera*, 21 November, https://www.aljazeera.com/opinions/2014/11/21/hide-your-strength-bide-your-time. Assessed on August 2, 2021.

Hindustan Times, 2021, "Quad an exclusive 'clique', working against China: Foreign ministry", 12 May, https://www.hindustantimes.com/world-news/quad-an-exclusive-clique-working-against-china-foreign-ministry-101620821263120.html. Accessed on August 25, 2021.

Hollingsworth, Julia (2020), "Australia demands apology after Chinese official tweets 'falsified image' of soldier threatening child", *CNN*, 30 November, https://edition.cnn.com/2020/11/30/australia/australia-china-twitter-intl-hnk/index.html. Accessed on August 15, 2021.

Hong, Zhao (2016), *China's One Belt One Road: An Overview of the Debate*. Trends in Southeast Asia No. 6. Singapore: ISEAS Yusof Ishak Institute.

Howard, Rebecca (2016), "Trans-Pacific Partnership trade deal signed, but years of negotiations still to come", *Reuters*, 4 February, https://www.reuters.com/article/us-trade-tpp-idUSKCN0VD08S. Accessed on August 18, 2021.

Indyk, Martin S., Kenneth G. Lieberthal, and Michael E. O'Hanlon (2012), "Scoring Obama's Foreign Policy: A Progressive Pragmatist Tries to Bend History", *Foreign Affairs*, Vol. 91, No. 3 (May/June 2012), pp. 29-43.

Jakhar, Pratik (2020), "Covid-19: China pushes traditional remedies amid outbreak", *BBC News*, 29 June, https://www.bbc.com/news/world-asia-53094603. Accessed on August 27, 2021.

Japan Times, 2020, '"Quad" nations vow to step up coordination for free and open Indo-Pacific', 6 October, https://www.japantimes.co.jp/news/2020/10/06/national/politics-diplomacy/quad-free-open-indo-pacific-china/. Accessed on August 25, 2021.

Johnston, Alastair Iain (2013), "How New and Assertive is China's New Assertiveness?", *International Security*, Vol. 37, No. 4, pp. 7-48.

Karambelkar, Amruta (2020), "China's Militarisation of South China Sea", Vivekananda International Foundation, 15 September, https://www.vifindia.org/2020/september/15/china-s-militarisation-of-south-china-sea. Accessed on August 15, 2021.

Khurana, Gurpreet S. (2019), "What is the Indo-Pacific? The New Geopolitics of the Asia-Centred Rim Land", in Axel Berkofsky and Sergio Miracola (eds.), *Geopolitics by Other Means: The Indo-Pacific Reality*. Milan: Ledizioni Ledi Publishing, pp. 13-32.

Khurana, Gurpreet (2008), "China's "String of Pearls" in the Indian Ocean and Its Security Implications", *Strategic Analysis,* Vol. 32, No. 1, January, pp. 1-39.

Lanteigne, Marc (2008), 'China's Maritime Security and the "Malacca Dilemma"', *Asian Security*, Vol. 4, Issue 2, pp. 143-161.

Lee, Victor Robert (2015), "South China Sea: China's Unprecedented Spratlys Building Program", *The Diplomat*, 25 April, https://thediplomat.com/2015/04/south-china-sea-chinas-unprecedented-spratlys-building-program/. Accessed on August 15, 2021.

Lelyveld, Michael (2017), "China's Oil Import Dependence Climbs as Output Falls", *Radio Free Asia*, 4 December, https://www.rfa.org/english/commentaries/energy_watch/chinas-oil-import-dependence-climbs-as-output-falls-12042017102429.html. Accessed on August 17, 2021.

Lieberthal, Kenneth and Wang Jisi (2012), "Addressing US-China Strategic Distrust", John L. Thornton China Center Monograph Series, No. 4 (Washington, DC: Brookings Institution, March).

Liu, Feng (2020), "The recalibration of Chinese assertiveness: China's responses to the Indo-Pacific challenge", *International Affairs*, Vol. 96, No. 1, pp. 9-27.

Majeed, Zaini (2021), "Blinken Blasts China, Says It 'disturbs' Rules-based Order Which US 'strongly Defends'", *Republic World*, 9 June, https://www.republicworld.com/world-news/us-news/blinken-blasts-china-says-it-disturbs-rules-based-order-which-us-strongly-defends.html. Accessed on August 1, 2021.

Mardell, Jacob (2020), "China's "Health Silk Road": Adapting the BRI to a pandemic-era world", *MERICS Short Analysis*, 25 November, https://merics.org/en/short-analysis/chinas-health-silk-road-adapting-bri-pandemic-era-world. Accessed on August 27, 2021.

Medcalf, Rory (2020), *Contest for the Indo-Pacific: Why China Won't Map the Future*. Melbourne: La Trobe University Press.

Mehra, Jyotsna (2020), "The Australia-India-Japan-US Quadrilateral: Dissecting the China Factor", *ORF Occasional Paper No. 264*, August. Observer Research Foundation.

Mendis, Patrick and Joey Wang (2019), "Unveiling China's Grand Plan", *Harvard International Review*, Vol. 40, No. 3 (Summer), pp. 36-39.

Ministry of Defense, Government of Japan, 2019, "Defense of Japan: Defence White Paper 2019", September, https://www.mod.go.jp/en/publ/w_paper/wp_2019.html. Accessed on August 25, 2021.

Ministry of Foreign Affairs, Government of Japan, 2019, "Towards a Free and Open Pacific", November, https://www.mofa.go.jp/files/000407643.pdf. Accessed on August 22, 2021.

Ministry of Foreign Affairs, Government of Japan, 2007, "Confluence of the Two Seas" Speech by H.E. Shinzo Abe, Prime Minister of Japan at the Parliament of the Republic of India, 22 August, https://www.mofa.go.jp/region/asia-paci/pmv0708/speech-2.html. Accessed on August 21, 2021.

Ministry of Foreign Affairs of the People's Republic of China, 2021, "Foreign Ministry Spokesperson Zhao Lijian's Regular Press Conference on July 29, 2021", 29 July 2021, https://www.fmprc.gov.cn/mfa_eng/xwfw_665399/s2510_665401/t1896083.shtml. Accessed on August 27, 2021.

Ministry of Foreign Affairs of the People's Republic of China, 2020, "Wang Yi: U.S. "Indo-Pacific Strategy" Undermines Peace and Development Prospects in East Asia", 13 October, https://www.fmprc.gov.cn/mfa_eng/zxxx_662805/t1824140.shtml. Accessed on August 26, 2021.

Ministry of Foreign Affairs of the People's Republic of China, 2017, "Wang Yi Talks about the Essence of Major Country Diplomacy with Chinese Characteristics: To Promote More Countries' Understanding and Recognition of Socialism Path with Chinese Characteristics", 19 October, https://www.fmprc.gov.cn/mfa_eng/zxxx_662805/t1503756.shtml. Accessed on August 17, 2021.

Ministry of Foreign Affairs of the People's Republic of China, 2014, "Xi Jinping Holds Talks with President Barack Obama of the US, Stressing Promoting Construction of New Model of Major-Country Relationship Between China and the US in Six Key Directions and Putting into Practice Principles of No Conflict, No Confrontation, Mutual Respect, and Win-Win Cooperation", 12 November, https://www.fmprc.gov.cn/mfa_eng/topics_665678/ytjhzzdrsrcldrfzshyjxghd/t1211022.shtml. Accessed on August 3, 2021.

Ministry of Foreign Affairs of the People's Republic of China, 2013a, "President Xi Jinping Delivers Important Speech and Proposes to Build a Silk Road Economic Belt with Central Asian Countries", 7 September, https://www.fmprc.gov.cn/mfa_eng/topics_665678/xjpfwzysiesgjtfhshzzfh_665686/t1076334.shtml. Accessed on August 15, 2021.

Ministry of Foreign Affairs of the People's Republic of China, 2013b, "Xi Jinping Calls for the Building of New Type of International Relations with Win-Win Cooperation at the Core in a Speech at the Moscow State Institute of International Relations", 23 March, https://www.fmprc.gov.cn/mfa_eng/topics_665678/xjpcf1_665694/t1024781.shtml. Accessed on August 4, 2021.

Nedopil, Christoph (2021), "Investments in the Belt and Road Initiative", Beijing, IIGF Green BRI Center, https://green-bri.org/investments-in-the-belt-and-road-initiative-bri/. Accessed on August 17, 2021.

Noesselt, Nele (2016), "One Belt, One Road: A New Roadmap for a Sinocentric World?", *The Asan Forum*, 20 October, https://theasanforum.org/one-belt-one-road-a-new-roadmap-for-a-sinocentric-world/. Accessed on August 16, 2021.

Oxford Analytica Expert Briefing, 2020, "Beijing's ambitions and assertiveness will grow", 24 September, https://www.emerald.com/insight/content/doi/10.1108/OXAN-DB256448/full/html. Accessed on July 28, 2021.

Peng, Yuan (2011), "Contradictions and Strategic Anxieties in China-US Relations", 9 October, *China-US Focus*, https://www.chinausfocus.com/peace-security/strategic-reassurance-bidens-post-afghanistan-challenge-in-southeast-asia. Accessed on August 26, 2021.

Phillips, Tom (2017), "China finds its own Top Gun and Rambo in wave of patriotic movies", *The Guardian*, 24 September, https://www.theguardian.com/world/2017/sep/23/china-finds-its-own-top-gun-and-rambo-in-wave-of-patriotic-movies. Accessed on August 10, 2021.

Ranjana, Eshwar (2019), "India Sets Up New Indo-Pacific Desk, Experts Laud 'Strategic Move'", *The Quint*, 15 April, https://www.thequint.com/news/india/india-sets-up-new-indo-pacific-desk-experts-laud-strategic-move. Accessed on August 22, 2021.

Reilly, Benjamin (2020), "The return of values in Australian foreign policy", *Australian Journal of International Affairs,* Vol. 74, Issue 2, pp. 116-123.

Rajeev Sharma (2007), "Asia's New Strategic Baby: The Quadrilateral Forum", *DW News*, 15 June, https://www.dw.com/en/asias-new-strategic-baby-the-quadrilateral-forum/a-5212697. Accessed on August 21, 2021.

Saeed, Muhammad (2017), "From the Asia-Pacific to the Indo-Pacific: Expanding Sino-US Strategic Competition", *China Quarterly of International Strategic Studies*, Vol. 3, No. 4, pp. 499-512.

Samaranayake, Nilanthi (2020), "Cooperation of consequence: Lessons from the 2004 tsunami response in the era of COVID19", Observer Research Foundation (ORF) report, 1 May, https://www.orfonline.org/expert-speak/cooperation-of-consequence-65491/. Accessed on August 20, 2021.

Schiavenz, Matt (2013), "How Humiliation Drove Modern Chinese History", *The Atlantic*, 26 October, https://www.theatlantic.com/china/archive/2013/10/how-humiliation-drove-modern-chinese-history/280878/. Accessed on August 5, 2021.

Sevastopulo, Demetri (2017), "Trump labels China a strategic 'competitor'", *Financial Times*, 19 December, https://www.ft.com/content/215cf8fa-e3cb-11e7-8b99-0191e45377ec. Accessed on August 19, 2021.

Shambaugh, David (2013), *China Goes Global: The Partial Power*, Oxford: Oxford University Press.

Shepherd, Christian (2018), "China says it wants to resolve differences with U.S. 'on equal footing'", *Reuters*, 3 August, https://www.reuters.com/article/us-asean-singapore-china-usa-idUSKBN1KO12M. Accessed on August 4, 2021.

Sidhu, Jatswan S. and Roy Anthony Rogers (2015), "China's Strategic Ambitions in the Indian Ocean Region, India's Anxiety and the United States' Concerns". *Malaysian Journal of International Relations*, Vol. 3, No. 1, pp. 75-104.

Small, Andrew (2015), *The China–Pakistan Axis: Asia's New Geopolitics*. Oxford: Oxford University Press.

Sørensen, Camilla T.N. (2015), "The Significance of Xi Jinping's 'Chinese Dream' for Chinese Foreign Policy: From 'Tao Guang Yang Hui' to 'Fen Fa You Wei'", *Journal of China International Relations*, Vol. 3, No. 1 (2015), pp. 53-73.

Swaine, Michael D. (2011), "China's Assertive Behavior—Part One: On 'Core Interests'", *China Leadership Monitor No. 34* (22 February), https://carnegieendowment.org/files/CLM34MS_FINAL.pdf. Accessed on August 5, 2021.

Taylor, Ian (2011), *The International Relations of Sub-Saharan Africa.* London: The Continuum International Publishing Group.

Thakur, Ramesh (2020), "China as the godfather of Quad 2.0", *The Strategist*, 20 July, https://www.aspistrategist.org.au/china-as-the-godfather-of-quad-2-0/. Accessed on August 25, 2021.

The Daily Star, 2019, 'Indo-Pacific Strategy: Implications for the Region', 20 March, https://www.thedailystar.net/round-tables/news/indo-pacific-strategy-implications-the-region-1717426. Accessed on August 19, 2021.

The State Council, The People's Republic of China, 2017, 'Full text of the Vision for Maritime Cooperation under the Belt and Road Initiative', 20 June, http://english.www.gov.cn/archive/publications/2017/06/20/content_281475691873460.htm. Accessed on August 16, 2021.

The State Council of The People's Republic of China, 2011, 'White Paper: China's Peaceful Development', 6 September, http://english.www.gov.cn/archive/white_paper/2014/09/09/content_281474986284646.htm. Accessed on August 5, 2021.

US Department of Defense, 2019, *Indo-Pacific Strategy Report: Preparedness, Partnerships and Promoting a Networked Region,* 1 June.Washington DC: the Department of Defense, https://media.defense.gov/2019/Jul/01/2002152311/-1/-1/1/DEPARTMENT-OF-DEFENSE-INDO-PACIFIC-STRATEGY-REPORT-2019.PDF. Accessed on August 18, 2021.

US Department of Defense, 2018, *Summary of the 2018 National Defense Strategy of the United States of America: Sharpening the American Military's Competitive Edge.* Washington DC: the Department of Defense, 2018, https://dod.defense.gov/Portals/1/Documents/pubs/2018-National-Defense-Strategy-Summary.pdf. Accessed on August 18, 2021.

US Department of State, 2019, *Free and Open Indo-Pacific: Advancing a Shared Vision.* Washington DC: the Department of State, https://www.state.gov/a-free-and-open-indo-pacific-advancing-a-shared-vision/. Accessed on August 19, 2021.

US Department of State, 2018, 'Briefing on the Indo-Pacific Strategy', Alex N. Wong, deputy assistant secretary, Bureau of East Asian and Pacific Affairs, Washington DC, 2 April.

US Energy Information Administration, 2018, 'China surpassed the United States as the world's largest crude oil importer in 2017', 31 December, https://www.eia.gov/todayinenergy/detail.php?id=37821. Accessed on August 17, 2021.

US Mission to ASEAN, 2017, 'Remarks by President Trump at APEC CEO Summit | Da Nang, Vietnam', 10 November, https://asean.usmission.gov/remarks-president-trump-apec-ceo-summit-da-nang-vietnam/. Accessed on July 11, 2021.

VornDick, Wilson (2017), "Analysts Take Note: Wolf Warrior Is the New Chinese Rambo", *The Diplomat*, 20 September, https://thediplomat.com/2017/09/analysts-take-note-wolf-warrior-is-the-new-chinese-rambo/. Accessed on August 10, 2021.

Wang Jisi (2018), "America and China: Destined for Conflict or Cooperation? We Asked 14 of the World's Most Renowned Experts", *National Interest*, 30 July, https://nationalinterest.org/feature/america-and-china-destined-conflict-or-cooperation-we-asked-14-worlds-most-renowned-experts. Accessed on August 4, 2021.

White House, 2021, 'U.S. Strategic Framework for the Indo-Pacific'. Washington, DC: Government of the United States of America, https://trumpwhitehouse.archives.gov/wp-content/uploads/2021/01/IPS-Final-Declass.pdf. Accessed on August 19, 2021.

White House, 2017, *The National Security Strategy of the United States of America*. Washington, DC: Government of the United States of America, https://trumpwhitehouse.archives.gov/wp-content/uploads/2017/12/NSS-Final-12-18-2017-0905.pdf. Accessed on August 19, 2021.

White House, 2015, 'Fact Sheet: Advancing the Rebalance to Asia and the Pacific', Office of the Press Secretary, 16 November, https://obamawhitehouse.archives.gov/the-press-office/2015/11/16/fact-sheet-advancing-rebalance-asia-and-pacific. Accessed on August 18, 2021.

White House, 2015, 'Remarks by President Obama and President Xi of the People's Republic of China in Joint Press Conference', Office of the Press Secretary, 25 September, https://obamawhitehouse.archives.gov/the-press-office/2015/09/25/remarks-president-obama-and-president-xi-peoples-republic-china-joint. Accessed on August 18, 2021.

Whiting, Allen S. (1983), "Assertive Nationalism in Chinese Foreign Policy", *Asian Survey* Vol. 23, No. 8, pp. 913-933.

Wilkins,Thomas S. (2020), "Whose "Indo Pacific"? Competing visions of regional order", *The Japan Institute of International Affairs Policy Brief*, 12 November, https://www.jiia-jic.jp/en/news/policy-briefwhose-indo-pacific-competing-visions-of-regional-order.html. Accessed on August 24, 2021.

World Bank, 2021, 'China Overview: Development news, research, data', 29 March, https://www.worldbank.org/en/country/china/overview. Accessed on August 2, 2021.

Xi, Jinping (2017), 'Secure a decisive victory in building a moderately prosperous society in all respects and strive for the great success of socialism with Chinese characteristics for a new era', report delivered at 19th National Congress of the CCP, Beijing, 18 October, http://www.xinhuanet.com/english/download/Xi_Jinping's_report_at_19th_CPC_National_Congress.pdf. Accessed on August 2, 2021.

Xinhua (2018), "CPC newspaper says China should "grasp historic opportunity"", 15 January, http://www.china.org.cn/china/2018-01/15/content_50228877.htm. Accessed on August 27, 2021.

Xinhua (2017a), "CPC Q&A: What are China's two centennial goals and why do they matter?", 17 October, http://www.xinhuanet.com/english/2017-10/17/c_136686770.htm. Accessed on August 2, 2021.

Xinhua (2017b), "China Focus: Socialism with Chinese Characteristics: 10 Ideas to Share with World", 8 October, http://www.xinhuanet.com/english/2017-10/08/c_136665156.htm. Assessed on July 29, 2021.

Xinhua (2017c), 'Full text of President Xi's speech at opening of Belt and Road forum', 14 May, http://www.xinhuanet.com//english/2017-05/14/c_136282982.htm. Accessed on August 15, 2021.

Yan, Xuetong (2021), "Becoming Strong: The New Chinese Foreign Policy", *Foreign Affairs*, Vol. 100, No. 4 July/August, pp. 40-48.

Yan, Xuetong (2014), "From Keeping a Low Profile to Striving for Achievement", *The Chinese Journal of International Politics*, Vol. 7, Issue 2 (Summer), pp. 153-184.

Yu, Xugang and Cristiano Rizzi (2018), "China and the "Belt and Road" Initiative: What Is It All About?", in Yu Xugang et al., *China's Belt and Road: The Initiative and Its Financial Focus*. Singapore: World Scientific, pp. 55-88.

Zeng, Jinghan and Shaun Breslin (2016), "China's "new type of Great Power relations": a G2 with Chinese characteristics?", *International Affairs* Vol. 92, Issue 4 (July), pp. 773-794.

Zhang, Gaochao (2017), "'Wolf Warrior 2' becomes China's highest-grossing film of all time", *Los Angeles Times*, 15 August, https://www.latimes.com/business/hollywood/la-fi-ct-china-box-office-wolf-warrior2-story.html. Accessed on August 13, 2021.

Zhao, Suisheng (2017), "American Reflections on the Engagement with China and Responses to President Xi's New Model of Major Power Relations", *Journal of Contemporary China*, Vol. 26, No. 106, pp. 489-503.

Zhao, Suisheng (2015), "The China Model: An Authoritarian State-Led Modernization", in Carla P. Freeman (ed.), *Handbook on China and Developing*

Countries. Cheltenham, UK and Northampton, MA: Edward Elgar Publishing, pp. 21-50.

Zhao, Suisheng (2013), "Foreign Policy Implications of Chinese Nationalism Revisited: the strident turn", *Journal of Contemporary China*, Vol. 22, Issue 82 (July), pp. 535-553.

Zhao, Minghao (2019), "Is a New Cold War Inevitable? Chinese Perspectives on US-China Strategic Competition", *The Chinese Journal of International Politics*, Vol. 12, Issue 3 (Autumn), pp. 371-394.

Zhu, Zhiqun (2020), "Interpreting China's 'Wolf-Warrior Diplomacy'", *The Diplomat*, 15 May, https://thediplomat.com/2020/05/interpreting-chinas-wolf-warrior-diplomacy/. Accessed on August 13, 2021.

8

BRI: The Dragon's Great Eurasian Sphere of Influence

Jayadev Parida

> "To fight and conquer in all our battles is not supreme excellence; supreme excellence consists in breaking the enemy's resistance without fighting."
>
> (*The Art of War*, Sun Tzu)

Tracing the Transformation of a Lion into a Dragon

Around 500-400 BC, Plato and Heraclitus had set a philosophical discourse to understand the nature of identity—the Ship of Theseus. In the 21st century, through the BRI, China is taking political, economic, and technological strides to revive the traditional glory of 'Silk Routes and the Middle Kingdom'. Russia, the EU, and to some extent, the US, are keeping an eagle eye on the progress of the work, while marking observations on the unfolding maritime domain. The Dragon is able to project two identical ships (win-win situation) for the regional actors by connecting the entire Eurasian region through different corridors. Who owns both the ships is the concern of future geopolitics. However, the basic premise of this chapter is that Beijing is settling to win the war without fighting—if the rest get busy in the maritime domain, land will fall under the influence of the Dragon. This paper attempts to examine the above-stated belief.

Napoleon's metaphorical lion or the present day Dragon was once ignored, underestimated, and unrecognised amidst the bloc politics. The duo, Nixon and Kissinger, on the verge of détente, were able to provide the much needed blood to the lion. Since then, there was no holding back for the rise of China and expansion of its sphere of influence. From Sir Halford John Mackinder to Zbigniew Brzezinski, there were/are many statesmen and researchers who have investigated the significance of the Eurasian region. At present, China has realised that it needs to revive the old glory of both territorial and maritime silk routes and connect them to the digital highways for better connectivity and trade with the outside world.

China witnessed a period of growth and reform when Deng Xiaoping was able to gather and revitalise the country's political economy in the late 1970s. It is significant to mention that the "24- Character Strategy" by Deng Xiaoping came in the wake of the brutal 1989 Tiananmen Square crackdown that played a pivotal role in the demise of the socialist camp at large. The strategy was seen by many scholars as a guiding principle on how China should act to protect its national interest, while increasing its interaction with the world. At that time, the helmsmen at the top believed that the country was not strong enough and the time was not yet ripe to assume global leadership. Deng, as a statesman as well as a keen observer of history, knew that "the path to global hegemony runs through economic development and prosperity that could be only achieved by transforming grass root level infrastructure, achieving economic developments, and rolling out new reforms." But the domestic circumstances were not conducive for such disruptive changes. To shift this Hobbesian milieu, Deng adopted the strategy which was used by Mao long ago—the psycho-political strategy, viz., instrumentalising nationalistic feelings to achieve 'the Chinese Dream'. Eventually, he succeeded in transforming China and set it on the path of stability and growth.

The onset of the 21st century witnessed a major change in the US foreign policy towards non-state actors and unilateralism, gradually shifting to multilateralism. This paved the way for China to engage formidably in multilateral forums, gradually assuming the core position, both in regional and global governance. China, as of now, is the opposite of what it has traditionally been for years. Does this beckon the resurgence or the rise of China? What does China's rise mean for the world (Menon 2016)—there have been significant debates floating around in global politics on this issue. Chinese President Hu Jintao, succeeded by Xi Jinping, have made considerable amendments to Deng Xiaoping's original idea and have envisioned a 'new era' to put forward a 'global Chinese century' akin to the Middle Kingdom that dominated the world in history.

Since Xi Jinping has assumed power as the head of the Chinese Communist Party, and more so with the recent elevation of his role by amending the constitution, he has sent a clear message to both China's enemies and friends about his vision and intention for China in the foreseeable future. In addition to his power politics, he has brought the ideas of his forefather to the forefront, building a strong amalgamation of Mao Zedong, Zhou Enlai, and Deng Xiaoping's ideological influences and moulding them according to the necessities of the current times. A certain play of destiny cannot be completely ruled out, as undoubtedly, the national conditions have worked out favourably for him; who would have thought that a country, which, three decades back, was way below the economic league of great powers has now, by orders of magnitude, risen to challenge their status and aspires to lead the world under Xi Jinping's leadership.

President Xi has directed most of his energy towards proving to the world that this century belongs to China, and to achieve this mission, he is working along three lines of development of China. The first is to end poverty within China by the year 2020[1] through working at grassroots level (though this is now overstretched – in 2024); the second is to ensure that China rises to a level of becoming a tech supergiant; and the third is to place China at the core of the world through the ambitious Belt and Road Initiative. All these are, in a way, interconnected to each other. According to the original proposal, the Belt and Road Initiative aspires to connect the regions of Asia to those of Europe and Africa via networks of land and maritime routes along these six different corridors: "The New Eurasian Land bridge Corridor (NELB); China-Mongolia-Russia Economic Corridor (CMREC); China-Central Asia- West Asia Economic Corridor (CCWAEC); China-Pakistan Economic Corridor (CPEC), The China-Indochina Peninsula Economic Corridor (CICPEC); Bangladesh-China-India-Myanmar Economic Corridor (BCIMEC)" (Gill, Lall and Lebrand, 2019). These corridors have been envisioned to meet China's needs of energy security, labour migration, economic interdependence, and technology transfer. Except for speculation, not much is known about what opportunities and repercussions this consensus would bring for both the regional and global order, but one aspect is evident that through the BRI, the Chinese will definitely bring their dominance initially at the door of Eurasian geopolitics, later spilling over to other parts of the world. It is apparent now that the lion that was sleeping peacefully over so many years was actually a wyrmling, which is now turning into a full grown Dragon.

Corridors of Dominance

The proposed corridors will cover global maritime checkpoints, highlighted by Alfred Thayer Mahan, to support China's rise in a world which will be defined by post-US and European politics. The rise and fall of the territorial "Silk Routes" were the reason for the European renaissance, subsequently leading them to become the global epicentre of power and dominate global affairs for centuries. The Chinese believe that the 21st century certainly needs a different set of rules of international engagement and that the BRI is a suitable fit to create a robust interdependent structure to manage the existing complex of interconnected interdependencies among nations and geographies.

The BRI aims to enhance trade by improving regional integration and stimulating the economic growth of countries beyond China. One of the famous anecdotes about Xi Jinping suggested that the years spent by him in rural Shaanxi province gave rise to his fascination for ancient Chinese history and the concept of the ancient Silk Road, which was a trade route during the ancient Han dynasty, connecting China to the Mediterranean region for years together (Tiezzi 2013, Grammaticas 2013). From the point of view of the political narrative, the intention of the Chinese Communist Party (CCP) is to enforce its authority on the people and maintain absolute power in every sense. It also aims to create a better social contract among the party, the leader, and the ordinary Chinese citizen through constant economic growth, employment, and reduction of poverty. Since there was also a need to guarantee a stable growth pattern internationally and re-stimulate stagnant economies, the BRI emerged as a flagship initiative whereby China could come centrestage and control international trade in the absence of a hegemon.

However, to re-emphasise, the BRI initiative is not just the sole idea of Xi Jinping, rather it is an amalgamation of his predecessors' thoughts, rebuilding of the national economy through understanding history, reconnecting entire China by addressing critical domestic issues, and then stepping into global politics. In other words, it is a culmination of a Chinese version of the Marshall Plan or a policy of the 'March West'[2] (Sun, 2013), which talks about mutual connectivity openly. This idea of mutual connectivity came during Wen Jiabao's speech in 2008 at the Opening Ceremony of the 4th Ministerial Conference of the Forum on China-Africa Cooperation. The prime idea was to deepen mutual connectivity and augment sustainable development. Furthermore, he presented the idea that "the path to trade and economic development runs through infrastructure development which would generate employment for "Chinese" local population and keep the economic flow moving." Undeniably, for greater economic integration, one needs proper connectivity.

The concept of the "Chinese Marshall Plan" (Lv, 2018) was developed by Xu Shanda, an economist and a member of the Chinese People's Political Consultative Conference, during the time of Hu Jintao. Xu Shanda's proposal was that China should learn from the US initiatives of post-World War II and create a long-term strategy to support its neighbours through loans and foreign aid and enhance their cooperation in the region. The idea gained strength because China, at that time, had significant amounts of foreign reserves in the People's Bank of China. Following the modern industrial revolution in China, the BRI is now a big step towards rebalancing and dominating the neo-liberal world order. This rebalancing act has been based internally on addressing the regional and economic disparities between the provinces, viz., the port cities of Shanghai, Shenzhen, and Beijing and deprived cities like Xinjiang, Kunming, Sichuan, Shaanxi, and others. The first stage of the BRI has taken shape through a set of both domestic and international measures, for instance, build-up of a paraphernalia of paradiplomacy and keeping a check on domestic separatist movements, attaining sustainable growth, and international engagements. In popular culture, filmmakers like Jia Zhangke, with his film "Ash is Purest White", have focused on depicting how the government is rewriting the social contract with depopulation of major cities and relocating the population, aggressively promoting the BRI via the medium of digital media. Xi's ambition through this project is extremely optimistic as he wants the underperforming regions in the country to gain importance and aims to make overseas investments and exert his soft power policy both at the national and international level.

"Marching West", which is the amalgamation of responses to the normative influence of the European Union in the west and the US maritime supremacy in the east, is a primary tool used by China in its aspiration to be inclusive with this part of the world. This idea was primarily adopted (proposed by Wang Jisi) as it carefully considered the traditional geopolitical competitions between eastern and western powers and wanted to ensure safe maritime routes along disputed regions where many countries, including the US, had geoeconomic stakes. This policy was stealthily put into effect to create a peaceful and benign image of China as the Chinese were aware that the 'March Westward' policy had huge potential for Chinese dominance. In other words, it was a way to promote strategic rebalancing as China began looking for new resource- rich regions in Central Asia, Europe, and the larger South Asian region. The Chinese also believed that this strategy would help to prevent any direct clash with the US in the maritime Asian region. The US has also been very keenly observing Chinese foreign policy moves in the post-Cold war period. From the pivot to Asia policy, the Shangrila Dialogue to the recent trade war, it shows that both are keeping a strategic distance while engaging at policy level.

The US is now proactively and strategically blocking China's rise through strengthened military alliances with India and Japan in the Indo-Pacific region and treading cautiously with the ASEAN group. These soft alliances are meant to push back China's economic integration process with Greater Asia and East Asia in particular. In view of this power matrix in the region, it is evident that countries like Japan are allowing the US to temporarily interfere in the region to keep a check on China. Put in perspective, these scenarios are actually creating a situation which is commonly referred to as the "Thucydides Trap"—metaphorically speaking—where the rise of Athens (China) instils a fear in the minds of Sparta (Japan and others), which could eventually led to a war (strategic blockage) between the two.

Guided by Mao Zedong's thought where he talked about "where the enemy advances, we retreat. Where the enemy retreats, we pursue", Xi Jinping is convinced that he wants to avoid war and create a situation by using the BRI to firstly, engage in the region which is resource- rich and less influenced by the US presence and second, ensure the presence of a formidable ally to support its vision. At this moment, Central Asia and the Middle Eastern region seem to be the most appropriate partners that could fit into China's designs along with Russia in the northern sphere, and this project could also easily become a stepping stone for China to make inroads in the European region. On the other hand, it could also fill up the vacuum of power created by US' retreat in the Middle Eastern region, which China now wants to exploit for its diversification of energy supplies. Also, after disengaging from war, Beijing is looking for convergence in relations with the US and be able to have a greater say in conflict resolution and global governance. Afghanistan is a perfect example of this. The US desperately wants to save its taxpayers' money and American lives, and the China-Pakistan nexus for peace talks in the Afghanistan region could help it fill the void, allowing it to withdraw peacefully. China also has plans to carry out developmental projects and extend the CPEC to Afghanistan post a peace deal to tackle both India and the US in the region. The apparent vacuum created in different regions by the absence of US presence creates a good occasion for China to step into new shoes of primacy and dominance as China, under President Xi, adopts a more assertive and determined stance on the global stage. More so, it is a 'personal' effort to strengthen Xi's vision, his power, and his legitimacy on the domestic front. It can also be seen as Xi Jinping's way to inscribe his personal legacy, not only within the country but also beyond its borders, in the pages of history. Moreover, gauging from a futuristic point of view, in post-modern global history, these corridors would come to define Chinese dominance in the greater Eurasian region.

Re-emergençe of the Greater Eurasian Geopolitics

Eurasia is indeed a complicated region, an area for collaboration and competition among global powers. It was overlooked for many years due to the dominance of the superpower politics/bipolar world politics, in addition to the unsettled conflicts of the erstwhile Soviet Union. However, around the end of the first decade of the 21st century, there was a re-emergence of Eurasian geopolitics because huge investments were made by the Dragon in the region as part of its BRI Initiative. The term 'Eurasia' refers to the combined landmass of the two continents of Europe and Asia and covers Central Asia, Eastern Europe, and European Russia. The region acts as a link between the two continents and has an abundance of resources which makes it attractive for other powers. The region acts as a crucial link between the two continents due to its geopolitical positioning as well as naturally rich energy resources. Its importance was mentioned by Sir Helford Mackinder in his theory of Heartland for the first time in 1904. As per the theory, Heartland refers to the Eurasian region and "whosoever rules the East ... commands the World Island", which indicates that if one aspires to become a dominant power in the region, it is important to control the vast Eurasian landmass; and the region could only be ruled by an industrially well-developed land-based power, which also possesses a superior sea power capacity.[3]

Discerning from the rise and fall of great powers, the British Empire once dominated the world system due to its maritime access and superiority; however, the emergence of railroads turned the tables soon afterwards. The railways facilitated travel of the military and traders and made it easier and quicker for them to access resources. The evolution of geopolitical games was also altered by the change in technologies; the land-based powers soon replaced the sea powers because they were now immune from maritime blockades which used to be their greatest weakness earlier. In fact, control over the pivot areas, viz., Central Asia and Eastern Europe, was historically important if any potential land-based power wanted to dominate, specially due to the vast amount of natural resources that would lead to prosperity and also immunity from sea powers for the latter, and it continues to be so even today. It would be easier for any Eurasian power to dominate the world, one that could challenge the British hegemony and establish its rule in the region. However, Mackinder was paid heed to by the German geopoliticians and leaders, who later went on to build an alliance with the Soviet Union with the agenda to access and control Eurasian resources. Logically, the Cold War also witnessed considerable competition between the US and the USSR (e.g. the Afghan war, 1979).

The common elements in conflict each time were the jostling for Eurasian resources, external power influence, and internal instability. Russia's dominance and its identity being considered as synonymous with Eurasia is now long over. China seeks to portray itself as the dominant actor in the region to replace Russia. Has the BRI provided China with one such opportunity to integrate its economy with the Eurasian landmass? The BRI is now portrayed as a continuation of the Silk Roads, which had roots in China's imperial history, and is directly linked to its own identity and approach to global governance. The timing of Chinese emergence on the global stage is important as Washington D.C. is struggling to overcome its Trump syndrome, followed by the Covid-19 crisis. On the other hand, through the BRI, China is also trying to project an 'old Russian- centric notion' of global dominance to challenge the American order. The legacy of Silk Roads relates to China's imperial history of power and accomplishment; hence, it is viewed as an opportunity to revive its glorious past. Chinese engagement in Eurasia can also be viewed as a means to counter dominance and interference from external powers, as well as to maintain its legacy. The collapse of the Soviet Union and the opening up of Central Asian countries to the world provided an opportunity to China for economic growth and reshaping the regional order. Europe in general and the EU in particular have been facing new challenges of the global order in the 21st century, viz., terrorism, organised crimes, regional conflicts, refugee issues, Eurozone crisis, and rise of populism, lately followed by the Covid- 19 pandemic, with the internal dichotomies and external environment providing substantial room for manoeuvre by the Dragon and its BRI.

Searching for a New European Identity

The BRI project certainly provides copious opportunities for trade, economic upliftment and growth; however, some actors involved are also sceptical about the bigger challenges that it poses to their national and regional interests. Europe is one such region, which, on the one hand, enjoys huge investment and trade opportunities being flaunted by the BRI, but on the other hand, also sees a growing risk to its interest by the rise of China's 'BRI rule-based international order'.

The initiative is in its seventh year of existence; however, it has not yet beckoned a unified approach from the whole of Europe or even the European Union (EU) for that matter. In fact, after the assessment and realisation of potential challenges, the EU has recently come up with a strategy for connecting Europe with Asia. This strategy seeks to make improvements in various sectors including energy, digital economy, infrastructure, and many more. At the same time, it also aims at observing carefully and creating a balance between its engagement with China and setting the limits thereof. However, it is not clear how the European Union will turn its strategy into a success. It is important to consider, in this context, how to bring all the member states on board to form a comprehensive approach in case of negative implications. How to allocate resources and coordinate with other important actors in case of a Chinese backout is also a significant concern.

However, before making any assumptions about the European continent and its contradictory approach towards the BRI, let us have a look at the European Union, its formation, history, and the set of challenges faced over time. It is a political and economic union of 27 European countries, which are subject to the privileges and obligations of membership. Out of 27 countries, 19 have the Euro as their national currency. The EU has constantly been surrounded by old and recurrent crises since the post-Cold War period, viz., regional conflicts, migration, eurozone crisis, Brexit, and a threat to democracy as the core of the EU's shared values, which have kept it occupied in the last decade.

The idea of a unified and peaceful Europe began with the formation of the European Coal and Steel Community in 1950 to integrate the war industries and to overcome the ghost of the World Wars quickly. In subsequent years, the European Economic Committee, Common Agricultural Policy, and Single European Act were able to generate commonness among the members. The fall of the Berlin Wall (1989) and signing of the Maastricht Treaty (1992) further enhanced cooperation, commitment, and commonness among the Western Europeans. The Treaty of Amsterdam (1997), Treaty of Nice (2003), and Lisbon Treaty (2009) managed to transform the Union not only into a regional organisation but also set global standards in norms-making, conflict management and peace-building. Today, the EU stands out from other international organisations due to the extent of its supranational political authority and legal and economic integration.

However, these goals of peace and harmony could not be properly achieved by the European Union because of an external unstable neighbourhood—the

Arab Spring, Ukraine Crisis, Syrian Crisis, and declining faith in multilateral institutions followed by the pandemic, which brought both challenges and opportunities. Besides these, the internal dichotomies—multiple voices to address the refugee issues, homegrown terrorism, the upsurge of populist leaders, the reinvention of anti-establishment, and rise in the influence of technocrats vis-à-vis the search for new leaders—have rendered unwanted trials in the EU's policy basket to be dealt with. Moreover, Europe tirelessly attempted to hold on to its old glory, but this attempt faded gradually.

From the Schengen agreement to the Dublin agreement, the EU witnessed a period of massive shift among its member states and their approach to open and free movement of people, goods, services, and capital. The shift has affected both medium-rung economies, like Germany and France, and erstwhile members, like the UK and Austria, to geographically larger countries like Italy, Poland, and Greece. The implications could gradually be seen as culminating into Brexit. The disintegration of the Union, while catastrophic, gave a reason to the EU to think about its internal and external role and its engagement with external powers like China and beyond.

Why China, is it the BRI?

During the last decade, America was more focused on its Asian strategy. Europe and Russia never treated or considered the US as a friend in need, but China demonstrated a vision for a liberal order and made inroads into Europe by creating 'one Euro shops and Chinese cultural centres'. When the BRI was introduced, the European powers were a bit sceptical about it, but considering the fact that Europe needed more opportunities[4] and economic benefits, the Union embraced the idea. Moreover, the fact that the BRI is an economic initiative rather than a political or military instrument added to its acceptability as it sought to create a flexible economic network with shared opportunity. Hence, China made its way into Europe through its economically troubled Southern (Greece, Portugal, Italy) and Central and Eastern (Baltic nations) states. In addition, the BRI has rewritten China's multilateral mechanics between the CEE countries and among troubled European nations (Balkans), namely, 16+1. This has also enticed others like Ukraine, Moldova, and Belarus to have a finger in the BRI pie.

Figure 8.1: Map of Europe

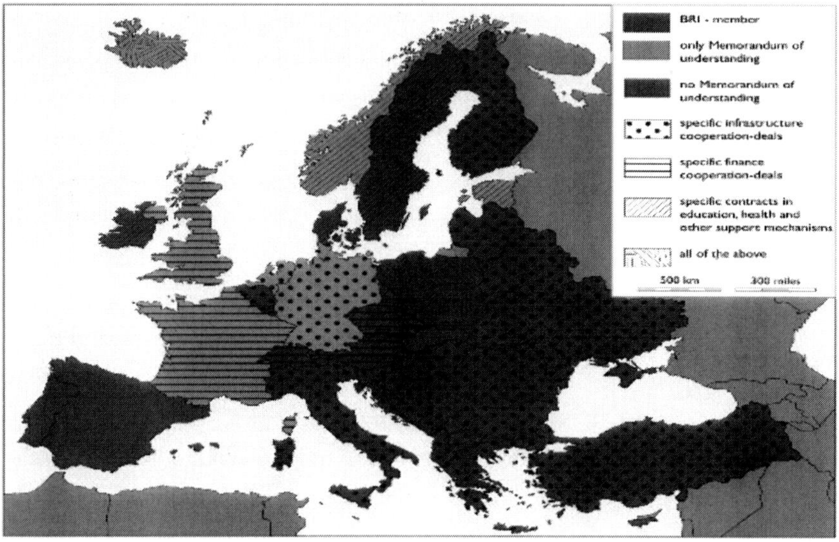

Source: Sielker& Kaufmann (2020) .

The heart of the concern is that Germany and France are neither harshly opposed nor quite positive about it and the UK is now out of the EU (post-Brexit) but sceptical about China and its technology. The Balkans or the Baltics are quite exposed to the BRI (16+1) because it opens an economic and infrastructure window of opportunities to rebuild and regrow at par with the Western European nations. Moreover, Italy being a member of G7[5], the EU is the first to kickstart talks with China. The above figure indicates the diverse impact of the BRI in Europe/the EU.

Over the last few years, both the strategic partners have been engaging in one way or other to enhance economic infrastructure and communication lanes. This was evident from 'EU-China 2020', 'Strategic Agenda for Cooperation–2013', 'EU-China Connectivity Platform–2015', and 'Connecting Europe and Asia Strategy–2018' (Donato 2020). Apart from these policy frameworks, both the parties have similar kinds of projects in place under the Trans-European Transport Network (TEN-T) and the BRI. In fact, experts are quite hopeful about the possible synergies between these two. The "China-EU Co-Investment Fund was established, jointly backed by the European Investment Fund and the Silk Road Fund … from the EU perspective, the fund was established to create synergies between China's BRI and the Investment Plan for Europe (the so-called Juncker Plan), showing its willingness to rebalance a narrative mainly centered on the Chinese "invasion" of the EU market through a fast-growing acquisition of overseas assets" (Yu, 2018; Donato, 2020). The EU initiatives primarily focused on establishing a rules- based international order for connectivity projects. However, much has changed since the initial bonhomie. From 2018 onwards, European scepticism reached its peak as the EU's diplomatic community blamed China for its 'economic nationalism and favouritism'. China has become infamous for its practices of 'debt-trap diplomacy'.

While most countries are convinced that the BRI is everything that China is projecting, and few are actually even accepting it the same way as offered, yet there are some who are asking the bigger questions about how the Chinese need to bring more clarity, transparency, and sustainability to the initiative. The EU fears that the BRI will create a further divide between the richer West European countries and the not so well-off Central and Eastern European countries and will lead to political involvement of China in this area. This might be further complicated with the presence of Russia. The EU is gradually coming out of the losses suffered during the pandemic by bolstering its economy with the help of the Berlin-Paris proposed plans for all its member states. It is significant to note that the ambitious EU-China Comprehensive Agreement on Investment is moving slowly due to political hurdles like disagreements on the Uyghur and Hong Kong issues. The leadership crisis in some of its countries and lack of common national interests are putting the EU into a vulnerable situation at the decision- making table.

The Dragon's Great Infrastructure Projects Game

At the outset, it is evident that Chinese investment packages, especially in Central Asia and Eastern Europe, have the potential to transform the infrastructure gap in the region and also uplift the debt-ridden economy. One of the prime focuses of the BRI is to enhance the railways connectivity to access energy trade markets. Eurasian geopolitics would see a new great game soon as the initiative is gaining success. This would further help in reducing Chinese dependency on troubled waters, such as the South China Sea and the Indo-Pacific, in which it faces choke points and global powers remain active in many adversarial contexts. However, recently, there have been several deviations, with the hype about the Sino-US trade war and global outrage against Chinese 5G and technology, which are making China a bit cynical about keeping the Eurasian agenda at the top of its priorities.

Can terrorism, organised crime, economic crises, ethnicity- driven wars, and rising insecurities be solved only by the market economy that will come along with the BRI? Will the BRI come with a package(s) of freedom and prosperity, which had been a distant dream for a long time for many of these countries? Discerning from European crises like refugee issues, terrorism, declining faith in multilateralism, and the melting pot syndrome in Western Europe, it seems the Easterners are looking at the EU as a milch cow. All these vulnerabilities are giving China scope to encash and dominate the region. The 16+1 or the 17+1[6] (Kavalski, 2019) platform truly helped China to use 'deceive and rule' to fulfil its old dream to become the leader of the Comintern, which is linked with the plan to bring the 16 post-communist states under Chinese influence. The 16+1 has been, in recent years, transformed to 17+1, as an additional member, Greece, is now part of this initiative. This is important for the BRI as Western scholars have always criticised the project as being a strategic move by China to gain access to land and resources of the countries, but if more and more countries are willing to cooperate, it shows the openness and transparency of these initiatives. Gradually, it will create win-win scenarios for China and the other regions.

Under the guidelines of the initiative, one link will enable Europe to connect through Russia's Trans-Siberian Railway and another one will connect Europe to Central Asia with Kazakhstan and finally, China. Besides these, the Chinese railways will be interlinked to ports, which will be very cost-effective. China, in this way, has scaled up its railways for competition at an international level. The state-owned China Railway Construction Corporation is the biggest actor in developing these corridors. For instance, the Warsa-Suzou and Lodz-Chengdu lines have reduced the time of transportation by more than 50 per cent, enhancing the profits of Chinese industries. The railways that pass through Russia are not open for negotiation with China, but in other corridors, the autonomy over the freight passages will be shared with higher stakes under China. To overcome Russian control over passages in the Eurasian region, Beijing is connecting Xinjiang province to Uzbekistan, Turkmenistan, Kyrgyzstan, and others. In this great game of geopolitics, China is slowly and steadily rising to displace Russia as the dominant power in the post-Soviet Central Asian (Eurasian) region. In other words, Putin's Russia is being considered equivalent to the US in the Latin American countries. This is also favouring China's rise in the region. Besides this, China is also trying to make inroads in the core European countries, and the port of Piraeus is extremely important in this regard. Historically, the port was of extreme importance from the ancient silk route perspective because it has always been the "gateway to Europe". It is a direct route to core European countries. During the Hu Jintao era, China cracked a deal with Greece to use and develop the port. Post- BRI rollout, the state-owned China Ocean Shipping Company has acquired majority shares of the port. Although the local people fear loss of livelihood, yet Chinese investment has been welcomed with an eye for development.

The BRI project has been instrumental in bringing the EU countries together on infrastructure development projects. Of the 16 (17) countries that are part of BRI infrastructure projects, 11 are EU members. A school of scholars argue that China is investing beyond its limits. For example, China has plans to develop a 350-kilometre high-speed rail network from Budapest to Belgrade connecting Central and Eastern Europe. Once completed, it will reduce travel time between the two capitals from eight to three hours. Moreover, the project is being financed and monitored by Chinese state-owned companies, which also have a hands-on approach to work, where work would be carried out by mostly Chinese workers with their own raw materials and technology. This is unprecedented and very unlike the EU's approach. Lesser involvement of EU nationals will definitely raise questions on the EU's policies on employment and European involvement internally. If China (un)intentionally deviates from the EU standards, it could create trouble for both sides.

Of late, the debate on "China finds itself firmly in the oasis of prosperity" (Pesek, 2021) is gaining momentum. Joe Biden's ascendance to the White House brought more faith in multilateralism among its believers. Now the challenge for China is to keep building on its domestic economy while trying to proliferate its Silk Route vision. At the very beginning, the EU was convinced about the win-win scenarios and the two-dimensional transactional relationship. Now, in case it benefits only China, then these interactions will backfire at any moment. As a dominant actor, the EU is also looking for new partners in Asia, as the Indo-Pacific is becoming the cynosure of global politics.

Even though the pandemic and the 5G backlash is not going in favour of China, it did not let the opportunity pass by and rather used the occasion to create a favourable atmosphere by furthering its 'mask diplomacy' (Bachulska, 2021) and improving its benign image in Europe and the rest of the world. Yet, if the EU doesn't come up with a comprehensive approach to the BRI, the Dragon will unfold the new great game. The EU leaders have already been talking about 'decoupling' and 'derisking' measures against China in the face of increasing trade deficit and worries about economic stability. The pandemic has been slowing down various infrastructure projects and development in various regions of the world due to lockdown that interrupted the supply chain. However, post-pandemic, the world will be seeing much faster economic growth as well as a rise in Chinese investment in the Eurasian region.

Recently, the Chinese president visited Europe for the first time in 5 years, visiting France, Serbia, and Hungary. During this visit, he signed several agreements with each country, including almost 29 with Serbia. He also held a trilateral meeting in Paris in which French President Macron and European Commission President Ursula von der Leyen participated.[7] There was a tacit political message underlined in this agreement with Serbia, that is, China considers Kosovo as part of Serbia and Belgrade views Taiwan as part of China. Serbia also became the first country from Central and Eastern Europe to sign a free trade agreement with China. The nation has garnered substantial Chinese investment through initiatives like the E763 highway, the Zemun-Borca bridge, and the acquisition of the Smederevo Steel Mill by HBIS Group.[8] The visit aimed to stabilise diplomatic relations with Europe by strengthening ties with friendly countries and capitalising on differences among European nations.

The Way Forward

Is the BRI trying to create the Ship of Theseus by linking both territorial and maritime silk routes and hoping to create a sphere of influence in the heartland? Is the Chinese dream too big to achieve? Are others also voyaging on the same boat? Is it possible to win the geopolitical battle without fighting it—through peaceful means? The speculations on the New Cold War between

China and the US or in a triangular shape between the US, Russia, and China have a lot to tell about the future of that dream—the BRI. America is least concerned about Central Asian geopolitics, Russia is neither welcomed nor far away from the region, but China's inroads in this region are going to create a new version of the great game. On the other hand, China is not a pawn in the grand chessboard, rather a dominant actor and very clear about its intention at this moment. The time will come when it would be imperative for all the countries involved in the BRI to protect it due to their shared resources and invested concerns. First, the BRI entials a fundamental change in the economic practices globally. The tendency to resort to protectionism amongst nations will gradually reduce. Second, the world is undergoing a 'complexly networked' process and there is no stop to this interconnectedness. Last but not the least, the way China is adding elements to the BRI ambitions one by one and looking at the 'wired world order', the new social contract between the nation-states would give them no other option but to protect the BRI that would ultimately lead to the success of the dream.

The Brexit, Covid-19, rise of populist leaders, Germany (the EU/Europe) without Angela Merkel, and rising unpopularity of Macron in France would generate a bigger setback for the Franco-German motto in the foreseeable future. This will further intensify the EU's leadership crisis both at the regional and the global level. If the EU wants to have a 'Ship of Theseus' after the success of the BRI, there are only two ways to do so—be a part of the dream; and revamp existing initiatives and create a rule-based connectivity order for the Eurasian countries. Else, there are higher chances that China would win the new great game in the region. It is imperative to find a substitute in Asia to counter China or drive the Indo-Pacific agenda if China is to be contained, otherwise a bigger chunk of the world would be under the Dragon's influence.

Notes

1. Since the outbreak of Covid-19, this particular agenda has suffered a lot.
2. Sun, Yun. (2013, January 31). March West: China's Response to the US rebalancing. *Brookings,* https://www.brookings.edu/blog/up-front/2013/01/31/march-west-chinas-resonse-to-the-u-s-rebalancing/ (March West policy by Wang Jisi focuses on China's comprehensive policy of development to the west of China).

3. Heartland theory talked about the importance of land power, sea power elements added here after looking at the new realities of the 21st century and China.
4. It may create a peaceful atmosphere in the neighborhood.
5. Italy is the first G7 country that joins the BRI
6. Kavalski Emilian, (2019, March 29), China's "16+1" is dead? Long live the "17+1." *The Diplomat.* Retrieved from http://thediplomat.com/2019/03/chinas-161-is-dead-long-live-the-171/ (The 16+1 is a cooperating platform of China with the other Central and Eastern European (CEE) states of which 11 are EU member states, it turns to 17+1 with the addition of another EU member state, Greece.)
7. Gulshan Sachdeva, Xi Jinping is Stabilising ties amidst global shifts, 10 May 2024, Deccan Herald, https://www-deccanherald-com.cdn.ampproject.org/c/s/www.deccanherald.com/amp/story/opinionper cent2Fxi-jinping-is-stabilising-ties-amidst-global-shifts-3016841
8. Ibid.

References

Pike, J. (2020), Deng Xiaoping's "24-Character Strategy". [online] Globalsecurity.org, https://www.globalsecurity.org/military/world/china/24-character.htm. Accessed on October 21, 2020.

The Centre's Reports – Eurasian Development Bank. [online] Eabr.org, https://eabr.org/en/analytics/integration-research/cii-reports/. Accessed on October 21, 2020.

Chin, Stephen (July 14, 2018), "Trans-Asian Railway chugs closer to becoming a reality", *The Asean Post*, https://theaseanpost.com/article/trans-asian-railway-chugs-closer-becming-reality.

Belt and Road News (November 12, 2019), "Piraeus Port the Head of the Dragon: President Xi", https://www.beltandroad.news/2019/11/12/china-greece-agree-with-coscos-piraeus-port-investment/.

Center For Strategic & International Studies, (March 6, 2018), "The Rise of China-Europe Railways", https://www.csis.org/analysis/rise-china-europe-railways.

Shakhanova, G. & Garlick. J.A. (2020), "The Belt and Road Initiative and the Eurasian Economic Union: Exploring the "Greater Eurasian Partnership"", *Journal of Current Chinese Affairs* 00(0), pp. 2-18, DOI: 10. 1177/1868 1026 20911666

Harper, T. (2019), "China's Eurasia: The Belt and Road Initiative and the Creation of a New Eurasian Power", *The Chinese Journal of Global Governance 5 (2019)*, pp. 99–121, DOI:10.1163/23525207-12340039

Mackinder, H.J, "The Geographical Pivot of History", *The Geographical Journal*, 23.4, April 1904, p. 421.

Macaes, Bruno, "The Dawn of Eurasia: On the Trail of the New World Order", 2018, p. 32.

Thomas Zimmerman, "The New Silk Roads: China, the US and the Future of Central Asia", Centre on International Cooperation, October 2015, p. 6, https://cic.nyu.edu/publications/new-silk-roads-china-us-and-future-central-asia. Accessed on September 29, 2020.

Wang, Y. (2016), "Offensive for Defensive: The Belt and Road Initiative and China's New Grand Strategy", *The Pacific Review*, vol. 29, no 3, pp. 455–463.

Habova, A., "Silk Road Economic Belt: China's Marshall Plan, Pivot to Eurasia or China's Way of Foreign Policy", *KSI Transactions on Knowledge Society*, 8.1, 2015, p. 68.

Li, X. and Wang, W., "The Silk Road Economic Belt and the China Dream Relationship: A Strategy or Tactics?", *Sociology Study*, 5:3, March 2015, p. 169.

Macaes, B., "Belt and Road: A Chinese World Order" (C. Hurst & Co. Ltd, 2018) p. 120.

Rolland, N. (2019), "A China–Russia Condominium over Eurasia", *Survival,* 61:1, pp. 7-22, DOI: 10.1080/00396338.2019.1568043

Svetlicinii, A. (2018), "China's Belt and Road Initiative and the Eurasian Economic Union: "Integrating the Integrations"". *Public Administration Issues*, Special Issue (electronic edition), pp. 7–20 (in English); DOI: 10.17323/1999-5431-2018-0-5-7-20.

Brattberg, E. & Soula, E. (October 19, 2018), "Europe's Emerging Approach to China's Belt and Road Initiative", https://carnegieendowment.org/2018/10/19/europe-s-emerging-approach-to-china-s-belt-and-road-initiative-pub-77536.

Pieper, M. (2018), "Mapping Eurasia: Contrasting the Public Diplomacies of Russia's 'Greater Eurasia' and China's 'Belt and Road' Initiative", Vol. 3, Issue 3 (*Public Diplomacy of Rising and Regional Powers*), pp. 217-237.

Tiezzi, Shannon (2013), "Xi Jinping: China's Hope and Change President?", *The Diplomat*, 19 November 2013, https://thediplomat.com/2013/11/xi-jinping-chinas-hope-and-change-president/.

Grammaticas, Damian (2013), "China's new President Xi Jinping: A man with a dream", *The BBC*, 14 March 2013, https://www.bbc.com/news/world-asia-china-21790384.

Franziska Sielker & Elisabeth Kaufmann (2020), "The influence of the Belt and Road Initiative in Europe", *Regional Studies, Regional Science*, 7:1, pp. 288-291.

Donato, Giulia Di (2020), "China's Approach to the Belt and Road Initiative and Europe's Response", Istituto per gliStudi di PoliticaInternazionale, 8 March 2020, https://www.ispionline.it/it/pubblicazione/chinas-approach-belt-and-road-initiative-and-europes-response-25980.

Pesek, William (2021), "China Is Not Out Of The Woods As Bubble Risks Abound", *Forbes*, 12 February 2021, https://www.forbes.com/sites/

williampesek/2021/02/12/china-is-not-out-of-the-woods-as-bubble-risks-abound/?sh=2ccd3db26692.

Chatzky, A. & McBride, J. (January 28, 2020), "China's Massive Belt and Road Initiative", https://www.cfr.org/backgrounder/chinas-massive-belt-and-road-initiative.

Menon (2016), "What China's Rise Means for the World", *The Wire*, 2 January 2016, https://thewire.in/external-affairs/what-chinas-rise-means-for-the-world.

Nurgozhayeva, R. (July 09, 2020), "How Is China's Belt and Road Changing Central Asia?", https://thediplomat.com/2020/07/how-is-chinas-belt-and-road-changing-central-asia/

Sullivan, A. (August 27, 2019), "Debt and doom loops: The eurozone's Italian nightmare", https://www.dw.com/en/debt-and-doom-loops-the-eurozones-italian-nightmare/a-50019077.

Ewing, J. (January 31, 2020), "European Economic Growth Slows Almost to Zero", https://www.nytimes.com/2020/01/31/business/economy/european-union-eurozone-economy.html

Szczepanski, M. (2019), "A Decade On From The Crisis: Main Responses And Remaining Challenges". European Parliamentary Research Service, https://www.europarl.europa.eu/RegData/etudes/BRIE/2019/642253/EPRS_BRI(2019)642253_EN.pdf

Nurgozhayeva, R. (July 09, 2020), "How Is China's Belt and Road Changing Central Asia?", https://thediplomat.com/2020/07/how-is-chinas-belt-and-road-changing-central-asia/

9

The BRI and South Asia: Tracing the Variations in Chinese Engagements

Cyriac S. Pampackal

In January 2023, the world saw Pakistan plummet into an economic crisis as inflation put a severe stress on the population, signalling a trajectory, similar to that of Sri Lanka, in the near future. With a global economic crisis looming large, there seemed a very slim chance for these South Asian states to recover economically as their growth and fiscal situation remained in a precarious state. While both these South Asian states faced severe economic distress and political turmoil, the factors that were responsible for this situation are worth scrutinising. At this juncture, the Chinese connection that both the states have in common can be discerned particularly because of the 'debt trap' accusations on Chinese financial investments. Both the states have huge Chinese- funded infrastructure development projects, which otherwise would have never materialised with their own resources at hand. However, these projects are often accused of being uneconomical and lack efficacy in generating monetary returns, making them huge liabilities to the host countries. Since the Chinese have investment-oriented relationships with most of the South Asian countries, such sort of inquiry towards the projects associated with the Belt and Road Initiative is inevitable. Moreover, it is important to track how these countries respond to the BRI projects and towards the Chinese foreign policy at large.

The BRI and China's Engagements with South Asia

South Asia is a region that lies within close proximity of the People's Republic of China (PRC). South Asia can be called as a gateway for the PRC towards the Indian Ocean where most of its shipping lanes pass through. Moreover, South Asia is too crucial for Chinese foreign policy, considering its need to enhance influence in the region and to restrain the Indian influence in the region (Miller, 2022). In the wake of the BRI, the PRC was in dire need for partnerships with regional actors, especially those with troubled relations with India. This led to the development of promising relations between the PRC and Pakistan, as Pakistan remains India's biggest rival in the region. India is the only country which shares borders with more than two South Asian states. Interestingly, the PRC is another country that shares borders with more than two South Asian states. All continental South Asian states, except Bangladesh, share a boundary with the PRC. Moreover, the exponential rise of the PRC's global image and influence, along with Sino-Indian rivalry across the Himalayas has caused the South Asian states to be caught between mutually contradicting interests of both these powers. However, each South Asian country's response towards the increasing Chinese influence in the region is different as they are subject to the varying dynamics of the region. Even though most of these countries share a common pool of ethnic identities, religion, history etc, the differences between them largely drive their relations within them. Moreover, these differences and bilateral dissents drive and dictate their responses to their foreign stakeholders, especially the ones such as the PRC, which are geographically proximate. For instance, the India-Pakistan rivalry is the major reason that drives Pakistan towards the Chinese sphere of influence and similarly, the state of relations with India influences most of these countries' response and association with the PRC and its diplomatic advances. Furthermore, a country's domestic politics plays a crucial role in dictating its relations with foreign stakeholders. For instance, the regime changes in Bangladesh and the Maldives have led to their relations being in a constant state of flux with the PRC. Along with these factors, the heterogeneity of the spectrum of the ethno-linguistic profile of South Asian countries further influences or steers their relations with foreign stakeholders. In addition to these, economic interests always pave the way for new partnerships in the international realm.

India and the BRI: A Partnership Stalled by Hostility

Since the BRI's unveiling, India has been one of the loudest opponents of this project. India's main worry with the BRI is that it may undermine India's power in the area. India sees China's BRI as an effort to surround and extend China's influence in South Asia. In addition, India has expressed worries about the BRI projects' lack of transparency and the potential financial load it may place on the participating nations. Most of these criticisms are propelled by the ensuing geopolitical issues that both the countries are engaged in. The long-standing rivalry and a jostle for regional supremacy have defined India and China's relationship. Many factors, including geographical conflicts, strategic distrust, economic competitiveness, and ideological disagreements, have created this rivalry. Territorial conflicts are one of the main causes of the competition between China and India. Territorial conflicts between India and China exist over a number of areas, including the Doklam plateau, Arunachal Pradesh, and the Aksai Chin region. Due to its strategic importance to both nations, the conflict over the Aksai Chin area, which is now governed by China, is highly critical. As Arunachal Pradesh is close to the borders of India, China, and Bhutan, the conflict over this region, which is part of India, is also detrimental to their closer relationship. Strategic distrust is a crucial additional aspect fuelling India-China competition. The long-standing enmity between India and China is a result of their rivalry in geopolitics and contrasting ideologies. Because of China's escalating military and economic might as well as its aggressive regional actions, India views China as a strategic danger. On the other side, China views India as a potential competitor and a threat to its supremacy in the area. The rivalry between China and India is also fuelled by economic reasons. China and India are two of the world's fastest expanding economies, both of which are competing for supremacy in the region. While China has been pursuing an aggressive economic agenda to increase its influence in the region and worldwide, India has been concentrating on internal growth and economic reforms to entice foreign investment. The two nations have experienced difficulties and disputes as a result of this economic competitiveness, notably in the fields of trade and investment. Last but not the least, the competition between China and India is also fuelled by ideological differences. China and India have quite distinct political structures and ideologies. China is a communist nation with a centralised, authoritarian political system, while India is a democratic nation with a diversified and pluralistic culture. Conflicts over subjects like human rights, freedom of expression, and religion have resulted from these ideological disagreements.

These problems, notably the ongoing territorial disputes, strategic distrust, and economic rivalry, have often resulted in border clashes, military standoffs, and diplomatic tensions between the two nations. The conflict in the Galwan Valley in 2020 and the stalemate in Doklam in 2017 serve as instances of how high the level of tension between India and China is (Rajagopalan, 2022). These episodes have also caused the two nations' commercial ties to worsen, with India placing limits on Chinese imports and investments. Significant consequences for the area, notably in terms of security and economic stability, result from India-China competition. Concerns about the likelihood of armed conflict and instability in the area have been expressed as a result of the continuous territorial disputes and military standoffs between China and India. The rivalry has also sparked a scenario of strategic competition, forcing nations in the area to take a side against either China or India or to remain neutral. The regional power structure has changed as a result, and rivalry for resources and influence has grown.

Notwithstanding their competition, India and China have the ability to work together and jointly pursue goals of interest, especially when it comes to regional security and economic growth. Both nations have an interest in the stability and economic expansion of the area, thus collaboration might be advantageous to both. A step in the right direction towards lowering tensions and enhancing the bilateral relationship is India and China's recent border disengagement and de-escalation. However, the Sino-Indian bilateral commercial trade is one sector where the animosity and scepticism haven't had much of an impact. Throughout the last several decades, there has been a tremendous increase in the amount of commerce between the two nations, to the mutual advantage of both. The early 1990s saw the introduction of economic liberalisation measures by India, while China had already introduced reforms in the late 1970s, which sparked a surge in commercial contacts.

China is now India's biggest commercial partner, with bilateral trade rising from USD 338 million in 1992 to USD 125 billion in 2021 (Krishnan, 2022). From 2001 to 2020, India's exports to China rose from USD 0.3 billion to USD 25 billion, while its imports from China rose from USD 1.1 billion to USD 97.5 billion (Krishnan, 2022). One of the major mismatches in trade right now is between China and India. The trade gap between India and China increased from USD 1.1 billion in 2001 to USD 72.5 billion in 2021 (Krishnan, 2022). China is India's greatest importer, making up 14.5 per cent of all imports from India but only making up 3 per cent of all imports from China. Iron ore, cotton, and copper are among the primary raw materials that India sends to China, while electronics, equipment, and medicines are among the primary finished commodities that China exports to India. India has been working towards closing its trade gap with China by boosting exports to that country and raising import taxes. Unfortunately, the trade imbalance has not yet decreased, as expected from these actions.

Apart from the economic deficit that it had with China and the general perception of rivalry, India has worrying issues directly linked with the BRI. The CPEC would traverse Pakistan-occupied Kashmir under this project (PoK). Building infrastructure in this area is seen as a breach of India's sovereignty since Pakistan-Occupied Kashmir is seen as a vital component of this country. Moreover, India has strategic concerns over the BRI as it views it as a Chinese effort to outweigh the Indian influence in South Asia. India has developed its own infrastructure projects in South Asia in response to the BRI. India introduced the "Neighbourhood First" strategy in 2015, with the goal of improving relations with its neighbours. India has launched various infrastructure projects in South Asia as part of this programme, including the India-Myanmar-Thailand Trilateral Highway and the International North-South Transport Corridor (INSTC) (Pattanaik, 2022). To combat the BRI, India has also forged alliances with other nations. The Asia-Africa Growth Corridor (AAGC) project, which seeks to promote economic growth and development in Asia and Africa, was established in 2017 by India, Japan, and the US. The AAGC, which intends to provide an alternative to the Chinese-led infrastructure projects in the area, is also being considered as a counter-response to the BRI.

The CPEC and Sino-Pakistan Partnership

The USD 62 billion worth China-Pakistan Economic Corridor is one of the flagship projects under the ambitious Belt and Road Initiative and it remains one of the explicit manifestations of the strength of Sino-Pakistan relations. Founded on the common counter-India sentiment and fostered by the estrangement of ties between the US and Pakistan, the Sino-Pakistan relations have cultured over a long array of cooperation verticals. These areas of cooperation include cooperation in the defence sector, technology transfer, large scale development projects etc. The CPEC remains as the biggest among this array of cooperation verticals. The CPEC is the largest/mega-infrastructure project under the BRI and is a crucial investment in upgrading and improving Pakistan's poor infrastructure, especially on the connectivity front. Collectively, the CPEC includes four different initiatives, including the construction of large-scale connectivity projects, such as highways, railways, tunnels, airports etc., along with the establishment of large energy projects, such as coal plants, gas and oil pipelines, and other renewable power projects based on wind, solar, and hydro power (Ali, 2018). In addition to these two, the CPEC includes nine economic zones, which are specially dedicated to these projects. The CPEC also includes the development of the Gwadar port, which will serve as the most vital part of the CPEC and also to the BRI itself. The development of the Gwadar port would enable the PRC to fulfil its energy needs through the Gulf of Oman, which will provide the PRC a better position, both economically and geostrategic ally. Through this, the PRC can by-pass its Malacca Dilemma and can economically benefit by saving 5,164 nautical miles of journey for its cargo vessels from the region.

Pakistan benefitted on multiple fronts through this multi-layered initiative, which originally contained 51 agreements and memorandums signed between the then Pakistani Prime Minister, Nawaz Sharif, and the Chinese President, Xi Jinping, on April 20, 2015 (Sayed, 2021). The biggest benefit for Pakistan from the CPEC is strategic rather than economical. The CPEC, being the largest of its kind of investments, automatically guarantees diplomatic support from Beijing to Islamabad. Moreover, the CPEC itself contributes heavily to the strategic objectives of the BRI, but it is stalled by Pakistan's geopolitical problems that now affect the largest Chinese investment and pose a problem to the Chinese ambition to eliminate its trickiest geopolitical dilemma on the

Malacca Strait. Furthermore, the CPEC passes through Pakistan-Occupied Kashmir, making it a direct stakeholder in the Kashmir issue and related problems.

In addition to these geostrategic aspects, the BRI projects are expected to boost Pakistan's economy and support its infrastructure network on a huge scale. Estimates for these projects suggest that these changes will be imbibed over a five-year period, and that the10 to 20 billion dollars that have been allocated are modest in comparison to China's present aspirations in relation to Pakistan. Notwithstanding its initial projection that focused solely on connectivity projects, the development purview of the project has expanded and the economic portfolio of the project has tripled over time. The expected expenses in Pakistan have increased to USD 46 billion as the focus has turned to electricity production (Sayed, 2021). The planned timescale for execution has also been subsequently expanded under the "Long Term Plan" by the two administrations, commencing in 2017 and expected to end in 2030. The estimated price rose to USD 62 billion, and Pakistani authorities have recently cited much larger figures (Mardell, 2020). Originally, the construction of such massive projects was designed to create job opportunities for the local populations and was projected to bring a huge economic surplus to the local economy. However, Pakistan's eco-political scenario remained inconducive and the progression of the development of BRI projects met with several hurdles. The economic burden that the CPEC brings upon Pakistan is huge as the total cost of the project equates to one-fifth of Pakistan's total GDP. The concerns are high about how the already economically struggling Pakistan would repay these loans.

In addition to the CPEC, Pakistan is also engaged in multiple projects with Chinese funding. A USD 7 billion upgrade to the Peshawar to Karachi railway, two hydroelectric power plants in the contentious Kashmir region, a metro system in Lahore, the creation of numerous special economic zones (SEZs), and Huawei fiber-optic cables connecting China to Pakistan are some of the other notable projects (Ali, 2022). Still, Pakistan's eco-political ability to complete these projects is under doubt as many of these projects have reached a standstill, and allegations of corruption and terrorist assaults also beset the CPEC. Furthermore, the overcharging by Chinese contractors has also raised concerns; a Pakistani government committee has found that USD 3 billion were overcharged for the construction of two power plants (Sacks, 2021). The speculated ineffectiveness and projected uneconomical nature has led to the slimming down of the CPEC budget. Coupled with Islamabad's previous economic struggle, the CPEC has transformed into a big burden to Pakistan's economy. Along with this, the Covid-19 pandemic has forced the Pakistani economy to contract by several measures in 2020, leading it to request a three-year, USD 6.3 billion bail- out to resolve the balance of payment crunch (Mardell, 2020). Despite these worries and failure projections with regards to BRI projects, Islamabad and Beijing are still on good diplomatic terms with each other, as Islamabad needs Beijing as a 'Big Brother' to balance the Indian threat and the Chinese hope to use the economic leverage over Islamabad to keep it under their influence to counter the Indian dominance in South Asia and the Arabian Sea.

Hambantota: A Reminder

In 2013, the Chinese and the Sri Lankan government signed a Memorandum of Understanding (MoU) under the BRI, officially announcing Sri Lanka as a partner. The Agreement included a number of initiatives, including the Matara-Kataragama railway, Hambantota Port, and Colombo Port City. One of the key infrastructural developments delivered to Sri Lanka by the BRI was the Colombo Port City. This project, which involved extensive land reclaiming, intended to develop a new satellite city near Colombo. This project was anticipated to provide Sri Lanka with major economic advantages, including expanding employability and accelerating economic development. The BRI, in Sri Lanka, has primarily focused on several such initiatives, especially on the connectivity front. Despite promising projections in the initial phases, most of the BRI projects in Sri Lanka remain quite a failure; some of them even failed to take off. The Hambantota Port is portrayed as the classic textbook example of the debt trap proliferated by the PRC. High interest loans amounting to USD 1.4 billion, financed by the Chinese- led institutions, have strangled the economic feasibility of the Hambantota port (Jones, 2020). It was considered infeasible in the first place, as Hambantota is not geographically well- positioned to be a major facilitator of global trade. This rendered Hambantota to be an under-utilised asset of Sri Lanka and also failed to generate the expected revenue, which resulted in failure of repayment of the Chinese loans. This resulted in a 99-year-long lease agreement to be instigated with respect to the Hambantota port with the Chinese, which was a serious blow to the sovereignty of Sri Lanka (Ondaatjie, 2019).

However, the economic crisis and political instability that followed in Sri Lanka cannot be attributed to the BRI-induced debt crisis alone. The Sri Lankan economy was already in a perilous situation, as by 2016, 61 per cent of the budget deficit of the Sri Lankan government was due to reliance on foreign institutions, and the total government debt had increased over USD 64.5 billion (Jones, 2020). It is worth noting that even though accusations on the Chinese debt trap policy remained strong, Chinese share in Sri Lanka's external debt constituted only 9 per cent. However, the unfair part of the deal was that Beijing forced Colombo into an equity swap over Hambantota, thereby forcing it to cede its ownership to China under a lease agreement through a Chinese SOE. In 2022, the PLA Navy docked one of its naval vessels in Hambantota, validating foreign accusations on China's security ambitions and designs over the Hambantota port.

Nepal: A Timely Bailout

Due to their shared border, linguistic heritage, and cultural traditions, Nepal and China have enjoyed strong ties over several years. These relations have become even stronger in recent years as China has expanded its political and economic influence in Nepal. In 2017, Nepal was inducted into the BRI network through an MoU signed in May 2017 by the then Nepalese Prime Minister, Pushpa Kamal Dahal (Welle, 2022). In this partnership, the Belt and Road Initiative plays a significant role, and Nepal has been constantly working to gain from it. In 2019, Nepal proposed a framework for Nepal's BRI chapter, which included nine project proposals (Pradhan, 2022). In order to increase connectivity within Nepal and with its neighbours, the PRC has committed several BRI projects for constructing new roads, railroads, and ports there. The projected Kathmandu-Kerung railway line, which would link Nepal's capital city with the Tibetan town of Kerung, is anticipated to increase the level of commerce and tourism between the two states (Pradhan, 2022). The Pokhara Regional International Airport is another significant BRI project in Nepal that is being developed with Chinese aid. This western Nepalese airport is anticipated to serve as a significant entry point to the nation's burgeoning tourist sector, which is a vital economic engine. The Chinese government has also offered support for Nepal's hydropower plant building, which would help in alleviating the nation's ongoing power shortages and minimise its reliance on imported energy. However, even after 5 years of the signing of the MoUs, none of these proposals have come to fruition (IANS 2022).

The delay in the materialisation of these projects has been primarily based on the ambiguity related to the financing methods of these projects. The Chinese only provide commercial loans rather than soft loans and grants, especially through the Chinese- led Asian Infrastructure Investment Bank and through the Silk Road Fund (Bureau 2022). Unlike the loans and economic aid provided by traditional western- led economic institutions, such as the World Bank, the Chinese assistance through the above institutions have higher interest rates and a shorter repayment schedule. Moreover, Nepal has also been worried about the feasibility and economic productivity of the proposed projects, especially in the context of the Humbantotta port in Sri Lanka, which was funded through such commercial loans at an interest rate of six per cent per annum. Coupled with these issues, the economic slowdown created by the Covid-19 pandemic has slowed down the progress of the BRI projects. Furthermore, on February 27, 2022, the long- pending pact between the Millennium Challenge Corporation (MCC) and the Government of Nepal was ratified by the Nepal Parliament, which involved the formal acceptance of USD 500 million (ANI, 2022). This pact focuses on energy transmission lines and the upgradation of the road networks across the country. Later, the US extended its economic aid with an additional sum of USD 659 million in support to the Nepalese economy, to the already committed 500 million, which stands as the largest amount of foreign aid that Nepal has ever received (Munjal, 2022). This initiative serves as a partial alternative to the stalled BRI projects, which have been delayed due to the ambiguous financial modalities and fears of debt trap (Bhattarai, 2020).

Maldives: A Swing State

Over the years, the Maldives' relations with India and China have kept fluctuating in accordance with its changing regimes. Traditionally, the Maldives and India had stable relations, especially after India helped in defeating the coup d'état in 1988 (Mishra, 2018). However, a serious level of estrangement of Indo-Maldivian relations happened during the presidency of Abdulla Yameen. Simultaneously, Sino-Maldivian relations saw a promising phase. The Maldivian acquaintance with the BRI started in 2014 when the Abdulla Yameen administration signed a free trade agreement with the PRC. Since then, the Maldivian regime showed an inclination towards the Chinese and got absorbed into their sphere of influence, and eventually, both the countries signed a MoU for BRI projects. This MoU secured several loans and grants for the Maldives to develop large- scale infrastructure projects with particular emphasis on transportation and telecommunications. The most significant among these projects is the initiation of new transportation infrastructure, as it is crucial for the 1192- island chain country where inter-island travel is primarily ferry- based. One such project is the Sinamalé Bridge, which connects the islands of Malé, Hulhulé, and Hulhumalé. This bridge was originally called the China-Maldives Friendship Bridge because China financed it. It was funded with a grant of USD 7.5 million to connect the capital island to the airport at Hulhulé. In addition to this grant, China has extended a USD 373 million loan to modernise and upgrade the airport (Samarathunga, 2022). This was intended to bring a huge boost for the Maldivian tourism sector and economy. Furthermore, the Maldivian energy sector also received a loan of USD 126 million to construct a solar power plant in the island of Addu (Samarathunga, 2022). This power project was expected to produce 5 megawatts of energy, significantly downsizing the Maldivian dependence on fossil fuels. Besides, the telecommunication sector of the Maldives also benefitted from a USD 85 million loan to build an underwater cable network connecting the Maldives to Sri Lanka to provide high speed internet connectivity, which gave the Maldivian economy a huge boost as it propelled the digital sector and e-commerce (Mitra, 2022). Improvement in the infrastructure network and connectivity and the development in telecommunications have boosted the country's tourism sector. Consequently, the Maldivian GDP marked a growth of 6.7 per cent in 2019 (IANS 2020).

However, the subsequent Maldivian regime, led by President Mohammed Solih, was sceptical about the growing Chinese investments and re-established ties with India, which were rapidly deteriorating during the previous regime. This stalled the Chinese influence in the Maldives and prevented the Maldives from following the course of Sri Lanka. By 2020, the debt sustainability of the Maldives had declined considerably, where the debt to GDP ratio rose to 87 per cent (IANS 2020). Moreover, the developmental projects that China funded caused severe environmental damage. The construction of the Friendship Bridge has caused severe damage to the marine environment and coral reefs. As these issues eclipsed the merits of BRI projects, the Indo-Maldivian relations took a turn towards the positive, which involved an economic aid of USD1.4 billion to the Maldives, financing the alternatives of the BRI projects. During Covid-19, India extended its support to the Maldives, which has significantly increased the trust factor in Indo-Maldivian relations. In 2021, India provided economic aid worth USD 100 million for various infrastructure projects, including the construction of water supply plants, leading the Maldives closer to fresh water self-sufficiency (Sharma, 2021). The positive growth in the Indo-Maldivian relations has caused a rift between the Maldives and the PRC, as, once a vital cog in the PRC's Indian Ocean strategy, the Maldives has now come back to the Indian fold.

Bangladesh: A Ticking Disaster

The Bangladesh chapter of the BRI is relatively different from that of its other South Asian counterparts. The developmental projects that the BRI has committed include those concerning the areas of energy, transportation, and communication. These projects include the construction of bridges, power plants, railway systems, roadways, and tunnels etc. The Padma Bridge is one such infrastructure project, which connects the southern part of Bangladesh with its capital, Dhaka. The 6.15 km- long bridge, which is the largest of its kind in Bangladesh, cost around USD 3.6 billion. The construction of the Padma Bridge has created around 30,000 job opportunities, which has boosted the country's economy (Hasan, 2021). Due to improved communication between this area and the rest of the nation, the project has also prompted economic development in the southern region of the country. The Payra Power Plant is another project that has been completed under the BRI funding. This power plant has a capacity of 1320 MW and has increased Bangladesh's capacity for energy production by 10 per cent (Muniruzzaman, 2019). This has considerably boosted the country's energy sector and contributed significantly towards the country's economic production. The BRI projects in Bangladesh also include the Dhaka Metro Rail and the Karnaphuli Tunnel, which are under construction. The Dhaka Metro Rail is built in the capital city (Dhaka has a 20 km- metro rail system with 16 stations) (Khokon, 2022). This project is expected to reduce the traffic congestion in Dhaka and will increase the international rating of the city. The Karnaphuli Tunnel, which is expected to be finished in 2023, will be a huge boost to the country's trade activities as it is built under the Karnaphuli river in Chittagong, connecting the city with the southern part of the country. Both these projects would facilitate a huge amount of trade and commerce and are expected to generate high margins of profits for the economic sector.

Even though the Bangladesh chapter of the BRI has met with initial success, delivering the promised growth to its economy, concerns still abound. The biggest concern is the monetary reciprocity of these projects, as many of the other South Asian countries have failed to deliver the promises entailed in the BRI (Rahman, 2021). In addition to this, all these flagship projects are financed by the same China EXIM Bank, which funded the infamous Hambantota Project. Many experts have also expressed concerns over the higher interest rates of the commercial loans that Bangladesh has been offered and the country's debt to GDP ratio, which has increased significantly in recent years.

Afghanistan: Uncharted Horizons

The Taliban administration of Afghanistan has stated that China is a main partner of Afghanistan (Fisher, 2021). This is primarily emphasised on the probable induction of Afghanistan into the framework of the BRI. Yet, there are significant uncertainties over Afghanistan's inclusion in the Belt and Road Initiative. The capacity of China to engage in Afghanistan will be hampered most visibly by the security situation there. Despite the Taliban's official declaration that they will not meddle in China's investment affairs in Afghanistan, there is still significant doubt about the Taliban's capacity and inclination to rein in Islamic forces hostile to China and other neighbouring countries. At the same time, China will perhaps be advised to exercise even more caution due to resistance to the Taliban rule, which takes the shape of both public demonstrations and military operations by the National Resistance Front under the leadership of Ahmad Masood (Marsden, 2021). Chinese soldiers have recently been attacked by a number of organisations in Pakistan;

if similar instances occurred in Afghanistan, China's cautious relationship with the Taliban would be disturbed and come under much more scrutiny by international organisations. There is a far more difficult and unpredictable reality than the diplomatic depiction of the BRI's easy flow of Chinese investment into Afghanistan. In years to come, policymakers will need to deal with a number of concerns, including political instability, the persistence of militant Islamic groups seeking transnational goals, and the relative frailty of pre-existing social links and bonds of trust between the two nations.

Conclusion

South Asia's response to the Chinese call for a development-oriented friendship is spread across a large spectrum of mutual interactions. Traditional partners of the PRC in South Asia, such as Pakistan, adhered to the project proposals under the BRI complacently, while the regional competitors of the PRC, like India, took a cautious stance regarding these projects. Some countries, like the Maldives, responded to the Chinese engagements in the region fundamentally driven by their domestic politics and the incumbent regime's mandate. Most of the South Asian states are still wary about the debt unsustainability associated with the BRI as Sri Lanka remains as a classic example of how gigantic uneconomical projects can transform into economic disasters. Many of the partnering countries in the region do not possess strong economies productive enough to monetise these large-scale investments into profits, and this often contributes significantly towards their foreign debt.

As a substantial development endeavour, the Belt and Road Initiative has the potential to change South Asia's economic and social environment. It may assist in solving the lack of infrastructure in the area, improve energy security, foster regional collaboration, and open up new growth and development prospects. Indeed, the developmental potential of the BRI cannot be ignored. Nevertheless, tackling the risks and obstacles connected with the endeavour, such as debt sustainability, environmental concerns, governance problems, and geopolitical conflicts, will be essential to its success. The BRI can contribute to South Asia's long-term prosperity and sustainable development by fostering sustainable development, social inclusion, and environmental protection while cooperating with all regional players. The Belt and Road Initiative may also assist in reducing certain geopolitical tensions in South Asia by fostering regional collaboration and economic integration. The project has the potential to increase economic interdependence between China and South Asian nations, easing tensions and fostering regional stability.

Undoubtedly, certain nations in the region, especially India, have voiced alarm about China's expanding influence in South Asia. India has declined to take part in the BRI, citing reservations about China's geopolitical objectives and debt diplomacy. From the Indian point of view, as long as the PRC employs the BRI as a draconian economic tool to expand its sphere of influence and as a counter strategy for India, the BRI will remain under a shadow and will not be able to realise its full potential.

References

Ali, I. (2022), "Importance of CPEC a crown jewel of belt and road initiative (BRI) for China and Pakistan", *Pakistan Journal of Social Research* 04(02), pp. 552–558.

Ali, M. (2018), "The China-Pakistan economic corridor: Tapping potential to achieve the 2030 agenda in Pakistan", *China Quarterly of International Strategic Studies* 04(02), pp. 301–325.

ANI (2022), "Nepal ratifies $500 mn grant assistance with 'interpretative declaration'", Business Standard News, *Business Standard*, https://www.business-standard.com/article/international/nepal-parliament-approves-500-mn-usd-grant-aid-with-explanative-declaration-122022800027_1.html. Accessed on February 20, 2023.

Bhattarai, K.D. (2020), "The Indo-Pacific vs. the Belt and Road: Nepal's great MCC Debate", *The Diplomat*, https://thediplomat.com/2020/01/the-indo-pacific-vs-the-belt-and-road-nepals-great-mcc-debate/. Accessed on February 20, 2023.

Bureau ET (2022), "BRI projects in Nepal suffer amid funding challenges", *The Economic Times*, https://economictimes.indiatimes.com/news/international/world-news/bri-projects-in-nepal-suffer-amid-funding-challenges/articleshow/90578344.cms. Accessed on February 20, 2023.

Fisher, L. and Squires, N. (2021), "Taliban declare China their closest ally", *The Telegraph*, Telegraph Media Group, https://www.telegraph.co.uk/politics/2021/09/02/taliban-calls-china-principal-partner-international-community/. Accessed on February 20, 2023.

Hasan, P. (2021), "BRI provides benefits for Bangladesh", *China Daily*, https://global.chinadaily.com.cn/a/202110/11/WS6163e762a310cdd39bc6e219.html. Accessed on February 20, 2023.

IANS (2020), "China's BRI promised prosperity, gave debt trap to countries like Pakistan, Sri Lanka, Maldives", *South Asia Monitor*, https://www.

southasiamonitor.org/china-watch/chinas-bri-promised-prosperity-gave-debt-trap-countries-pakistan-sri-lanka-maldives. Accessed on February 20, 2023.

IANS (2022), "China nudges Nepal to expedite BRI projects as Prachanda becomes new PM", Business Standard News, *Business Standard*, https://www.business-standard.com/article/international/china-nudges-nepal-to-expedite-bri-projects-as-prachanda-becomes-new-pm-122122700742_1.html. Accessed on February 20, 2023.

Jones, L. and Hameiri, S. (2020), "Debunking the Myth of 'Debt-trap Diplomacy'", *Chatham House – International Affairs Think Tank*, Chatham House, https://www.chathamhouse.org/2020/08/debunking-myth-debt-trap-diplomacy/4-sri-lanka-and-bri. Accessed on February 19, 2023.

Khokon, Sahidul Hasan (2022), "Bangladesh rolls out First Metro Rail to ease Dhaka traffic woes", *India Today*, https://www.indiatoday.in/world/story/bangladesh-rolls-out-first-metro-rail-ease-dhaka-traffic-woes-2314673. 28 December 2022. Accessed on February 20, 2023.

Krishnan, A. (2022), "India's trade with China crosses $125 billion, imports near $100 billion", *The Hindu*, https://www.thehindu.com/business/Economy/indias-trade-with-china-crosses-125-billion-imports-near-100-billion/article38272914.ece. Accessed on February 19, 2023.

Mardell, J. (2020), "The BRI in Pakistan: China's flagship Economic Corridor", *Merics*, https://merics.org/en/analysis/bri-pakistan-chinas-flagship-economic-corridor. Accessed on February 19, 2023.

Marsden, M. (2021), "China, Afghanistan, and the Belt and Road Initiative: Diplomacy and Reality", *The Diplomat*, https://thediplomat.com/2021/09/china-afghanistan-and-the-belt-and-road-initiative-diplomacy-and-reality/. Accessed on February 20, 2023.

Mishra, V. (2018), *Indian Foreign Affairs Journal*, 13(3), pp. 209-219.

Mitra, R. (2022), "The China-India Cold War in Maldives", *The Diplomat*, https://thediplomat.com/2022/01/the-china-india-cold-war-in-maldives/. Accessed on February 20, 2023.

Muniruzzaman, A.N.M. (2019), "Belt and Road Initiative: Perspective from Bangladesh", *The Daily Star*, https://www.thedailystar.net/round-tables/news/belt-and-road-initiative-perspective-bangladesh-1782928. Accessed on February 20, 2023.

Munjal, D. (2022), "Explained: What is the $500 million US grant to Nepal and the controversy around it?", *The Hindu*, https://www.thehindu.com/news/international/the-controversy-around-the-500-million-mcc-grant-to-nepal/article65090534.ece. Accessed on February 20, 2023.

Nair, A. (2017), "To counter OBOR, India and Japan propose Asia-Africa Sea Corridor", *The Indian Express*, https://indianexpress.com/article/explained/

to-counter-obor-india-and-japan-propose-asia-africa-sea-corridor-4681749/. Accessed on February 19, 2023.

Ondaatjie, A. and Sirimanne, A. (2019), "Sri Lanka leased Hambantota Port to China for 99 yrs. now it wants it back", Business Standard News, *Business Standard*, https://www.business-standard.com/article/international/sri-lanka-leased-hambantota-port-to-china-for-99-yrs-now-it-wants-it-back-119112900206_1.html. Accessed on February 19, 2023.

Pattanaik, S.S. (2022), "India's 'Neighbourhood First' Policy", *Parliament Library*, MP-IDSA, https://parliamentlibraryindia.nic.in/. Accessed on February 19, 2023.

Pradhan, S.D. (2022), "Nepalese population opposes Chinese BRI projects", *The Times of India*, Times Group, https://timesofindia.indiatimes.com/blogs/ChanakyaCode/nepalese-population-opposes-chinese-bri-projects/?source=app&frmapp=yes. Accessed on February 19, 2023.

Rahman, S.A. (2021), "The BRI in Bangladesh: 'win-win' or a 'debt trap'?" *The Diplomat*, https://thediplomat.com/2021/11/the-bri-in-bangladesh-win-win-or-a-debt-trap/. Accessed on February 20, 2023.

Rajagopalan, R.P. (2022), "China-India relations: 2 years after Galwan Clash", *The Diplomat*, https://thediplomat.com/2022/06/china-india-relations-2-years-after-galwan-clash/. Accessed on February 20, 2023.

Sacks, D. (2021), "The China-Pakistan Economic Corridor - hard reality greets BRI's signature initiative", *Council on Foreign Relations*, https://www.cfr.org/blog/china-pakistan-economic-corridor-hard-reality-greets-bris-signature-initiative. Accessed on February 19, 2023.

Samarathunga, W.H. (2022), "Chinese belt and road investments in South Asia under the influence of multiple social crises and natural disasters", *Sri Lanka Journal of Economic Research* 9(2).

Sayed, M. (2021), "China- Pakistan Economic Corridor: A voyage to shared destiny", *Journal of Pakistan-China Studies (JPCS)* 2(1), pp. 46–63.

Sharma, A. (2021), "India puts roadblocks before China's BRI in Maldives with another defense deal", *Eurasian Times*, https://eurasiantimes.com/india-roadblocks-before-chinas-bri-in-maldives-defense-line-of-credit/. Accessed on February 20, 2023.

Welle, D. (2022), "Nepal: What happened to China's 'Belt and road' projects?" *Frontline*, https://frontline.thehindu.com/dispatches/nepal-what-happened-to-chinas-belt-and-road-projects/article65466849.ece. Accessed on February 20, 2023.

10

Mahan's Theory of Sea Power and Chinese Politics in the Indo-Pacific

Anuraag Khaund

Introduction

The area known as the Indo-Pacific, which encompasses the oceanic realms of the Indian Ocean and the Pacific Ocean and stretches from the eastern coast of Africa to the Western Pacific islands or the US Pacific coast, depending on several perceptions, has emerged as the new centre point and hotbed of geopolitical, geostrategic, and geoeconomic rivalry. The region, which encompasses vital and strategic Sea Lanes of Communication (SLOC), such as the Strait of Hormuz in the Persian Gulf, Strait of Malacca near the Andaman and Nicobar Islands, and other SLOCs, such as Lombok, Sunda, and the Bab el-Mandeb, accounts for around one-half of the world's container ships, one-third of bulk cargo trade, and two-third of the world's energy shipments, thereby increasing its strategic value in the eyes of major regional powers like India, China, Japan, and Australia, as well as the US.[1] Primarily, a strategic competition has been spelled out between the US and China given the latter's vital interests in the Indo-Pacific SLOCs, like the Strait of Malacca, which is the passageway for around 80 per cent of Beijing's energy imports required to stimulate its huge economic rise, as well as due to vested interests of both the powers in the inclusion of the South China Sea (SCS), which is currently a major area of Chinese strategic interest.[2] Hence, in the current era, since the ascension of President Xi Jinping in 2012, China has started paying a lot of attention to its naval capabilities and enhancing its presence in the Indo-Pacific in order to secure its interests as well as counter the traditional presence of the US.

The significance of the Chinese actions in the Indo-Pacific is reminiscent of the ideas of the 19th century US naval officer and historian, Alfred Thayer Mahan, whose work, *The Influence of Sea Power Upon History 1660-1783,* continues to dominate the study of geopolitics, especially with relation to oceans and the importance for great powers to develop strong naval capabilities for not only defence but also mostly to project their power and reach overseas. His work was deemed as influential in his contemporary times, which can be gleaned from the fact that a copy of his work was kept by German Emperor Kaiser Wilhelm II and the Japanese imperial government[3] to guide their naval strategies 'in the pre-1945 period. Regarding the developments that are unravelling in the Indo-Pacific today, Mahan's ideas of sea power are perceptible as manifesting in the actions of all the major powers, especially China. The present paper is an attempt to trace the manifestations of Mahan's ideas in the Chinese strategy in the Indo-Pacific. It begins by briefly exploring the main ideas put forward by Mahan and the following section tries to trace the imprints of Mahan's ideas in Chinese politics, especially in the maritime sphere.

Mahan's Theory of Sea Power

The defining spirit of Mahan's work, *The Influence of Sea Power Upon History,* is summed up in the lines – "*Whoever rules the waves, rules the world.*"[4] In other words, the status of any country or nation as a great power will be. determined by the extent, strength, and capabilities of its naval power. As per Mahan, there were many factors that determined and shaped the naval power of any country. These include geographical position, physical conformation, extent of territory, number of populations, character of the people, and the government.[5] The geographic position of any country or landmass, according to Mahan, determined the latter's attitude and interest towards the sea or maritime domain. In case the country in question is situated in such a position whereby it faces no external invasion from land or has no need for continental expansion, naturally, the main threats to it would emanate from the sea, thereby leading it to focus all its interest there. Mahan highlights this point by referring to the example of England, whose need for a continental army was less as compared to its rival, France, and hence, London was able to devote its resources to the development of sea power.[6] At the same time, the most advantageous geographical position was one in which a country not only had easy access to the sea but also lay in close proximity to passageways of cargo and traffic. This was again underscored with the example of England where the oceanic trade from Sweden, Holland, Russia, and others destined for Germany had to pass through the English Channel, while the loss of the Strait of Gibraltar by Spain not only affected its revenue from the oceanic trade but also removed the easy junction between the Spanish navies of the Atlantic and the Mediterranean.[7] However, the most important lesson that was drawn from geography by Mahan is the advice given to the US to obtain overseas stations 'fit for contingent or secondary bases of operations; which by their natural advantages, susceptibility of defense, and nearness to the central strategic issue, will enable its fleets to remain as near to the scene as any opponent'.[8] Such bases, according to him, were to be obtained in the Caribbean or Central American region for protecting the US interests in the oceanic realm—a point that will be further discussed.

The second major factor of sea power is the physical adherence of the country in question, or in other words, whether the geographic features, even if facing the sea, allow the country to utilise them as a springboard for its maritime dominance. Even if the country is blessed with a long seaboard, in the absence of deep ports and harbours, it would be difficult to build a base from which to project its power in the maritime domain. Hence, the presence of deep ports and harbours can be a source of strength and wealth, if situated at the outlet of navigable streams. At the same time, it can also be a source of weakness, allowing enemy ships easy access, which could threaten the capital if not properly defended. Hence, the Dutch, in 1667, found little difficulty in sailing up the Thames River and destroying a major portion of the English fleet, while the combined navies of France and England were unable to land in Holland because of the difficult defences of the Dutch coast.[9] Another major aspect discussed is the nature of land upon which the country was situated that determined its will to develop its naval power. Mahan elaborates this by citing the example of France, whose disinterest in naval power was due to the fertile conditions of the French soil and its pleasant climate—aspects that left it satisfied with the present conditions, instilling no interest to expand in the ocean. On the other hand, England's lack of resources forced it to look towards the seas and expand its military power.[10] In addition, Mahan also said that in case the geographical condition of a country is such that it is separated by the sea into two or more parts, it becomes imperative for it to develop interest in a strong navy, as is the case with Italy.[11]

The third factor is the extent of territory, or in other words, the length of the coastline possessed by the country. In case the country has a coastline spanning long distances which cannot be covered by its human resources, this would impede the development of an effective sea power. Here, Mahan illustrates this point by citing the example of the Civil War of 1860-64, where the Southern Confederate states were defeated despite the presence of a long coastline because of the lack of adequate manpower and ships to defend it.[12]

The next factor is the population within a country. This determines the amount of reserve, both military as well as civilian, which could be called upon in times of war in order to man the ships as well as provide technical and logistical assistance—a fact that was realised and exploited by Britain despite its lesser population as compared to France. This was primarily because while England invested in the development of its population and reserves of sailors, France did not. In fact, despite having a larger populace, France did not pay much attention to it.[13]

The next factor relates to the character of the population of the country. This means that the presence of an adventurous and mercantilist spirit in the populace of a country leads to the development of its sea power. Here again, Mahan cites the example of the English population, whose instincts as traders and shopkeepers engaged in maritime commerce helped build a more vibrant naval community, and their skills in manufacturing in the home country attracted customers and buyers from faraway lands. Even France stimulated the interest of its population in maritime domain and created conditions for the development of its naval power.[14] Another major factor behind the British dominance in terms of naval power was the success of its overseas colonies, which lay in the character of the British colonists, who would accept the new settlement as their own and work towards improving it without any active guidance from the mother country. In this case, the British colonialists, driven by their inherent maritime outlook, took upon themselves the necessary steps to establish ports and harbours to be used by British ships in the colonies as well as their own colonial navies.[15]

Finally, the last crucial factor cited by Mahan is the character of the government or its institutions, which determined the level of naval strength of the country. According to him, while the maritime traits of a population are inherent in the beginning of an individual's career, the role of the government or its institutions in furthering and supporting the maritime instincts of the populace is akin to the exercise of willpower, which leads to progress or decline in the power of a nation or career respectively. Here again, Mahan mentions the role of the monarchy and government of Britain in actively supporting its maritime populace and entities, such as the East India Company and commercial merchandise, for whose protection, the Crown also invested in building strong naval capabilities.[16] The above-mentioned factors, outlined by Mahan, in the development of sea power can be gauged to some extent in the Chinese attitude towards the Indian Ocean, as will be shown in the next section.

Mahan and Chinese Politics in the Indo-Pacific

As mentioned in the introduction, China has developed an increasing interest in the Indo- Pacific region, especially the South China Sea (SCS) and the Indian Ocean, for strategic as well as security interests. This has also led to increased attention in China's naval capabilities, which was apparent in the 19th Congress of the Communist Party of China (CPC), where Xi Jinping called for deployment of 'world-class' armed forces, including a blue water navy. Moreover, the People's Liberation Army Navy (PLAN) has been receiving increasing attention since the 1990s, which saw the launch of Beijing's first anti- aircraft carrier in 2012.[17] In addition, the apparent rivalry and challenge posed by the US, as seen in its actions such as the 2011 Rebalancing to Asia strategy of the Obama administration or the 2017 Trump administration and later, the Biden administration's focus on the Indo-Pacific with China as a 'strategic rival'[18], has only led to an upsurge in efforts to increase China's naval presence and outreach in the region. These attempts as well as Chinese maritime history conform to the ideas of Mahan, as mentioned above.

Traditionally, China's coastal regions, such as Guangzhou and Quanzhou, evolved as centres of maritime trade as well as cosmopolitan towns, which harboured diverse populations of merchants hailing from the Arab world, Southeast Asia, and South Asia.[19] Along with the overland trade routes of the Silk Road passing through current Central Asia, the maritime routes brought revenue to the Southern Song dynasty that had shifted its capital to Hangzhou, which was nearer to the eastern Chinese seaboard and hence, focused on maritime trade.[20] While throughout its history, the Chinese dynasties were mostly occupied with their land borders given the ever-present threat of invasions by nomadic communities, such as the Mongols, yet there were instances when China did undertake an active role in maritime domain. This was especially the case with the Zheng He voyages of 1405-1433 during the Ming dynasty, which, starting from Nanjing and covering Southeast Asia, extended till South Asia and the African kingdom of Mogadishu.[21] As per Geoff Wade, these Ming voyages were a kind of proto or 'maritime colonialism', which saw the Ming fleet, through display of its superior naval power as well as gifts and treasures, induce or coerce maritime polities, such as Palembang, Malacca, Cochin, Kotte kingdom in Sri Lanka, and Samudera, to accept Ming overlordship while allowing China to control trade routes and strategic ports in these kingdoms, including through the provision of a Ming garrison in Palembang and Malacca to secure Ming interests.[22] At this point, one can say that while Mahan's idea of geography, as illustrated in the case of England, does not apply completely in the case of China, which was mostly limited to being a continent power since its history, yet the aspect regarding securing of overseas bases can be seen to some extent in Zheng He's stationing of Ming military garrisons in the territories of the port cities from which they monitored trade routes as well as kept the other kingdoms in check.

The desire for control over strategic locations and ports has come to be manifested again significantly under the BRI, a 1.3 trillion connectivity and infrastructure project joining Asia with Africa and Europe. The 21st century Maritime Silk Road (MSR) of the BRI, involving the development of port and infrastructure in a string of countries across the Indian Ocean[23], has been interpreted by some scholars as China's attempt at building or acquiring bases in strategic locations, such as Djibouti, which became the first Chinese overseas base in 2017. The Djibouti overseas base, along with ports which are being developed with Chinese assistance under the BRI such as Gwadar in Pakistan, Hambantota and Colombo in Sri Lanka, Chittagong in Bangladesh, and Kyaukpyu in Myanmar, have been dubbed as the 'String of Pearls', with the twin objectives of overcoming the Malacca dilemma as well as possibly encircling India who is Beijing's regional rival in the Indian Ocean.[24] In the case of Kyaukpyu, the port is located near pipelines carrying oil and gas from the Myanmar coastline to the Chinese province of Yunnan,[25] while the overland China- Pakistan Economic Corridor (CPEC), connecting the province of Xinjiang with Gwadar in the Pakistani coastline, would allow energy supplies coming from the Middle East to be transported overland to China;[26] in both cases, it would allow China to overcome the Malacca dilemma by acquiring bases in strategic locations. At the same time, the Djibouti overseas base, although established with an aim to combat piracy, allows China to target the US base of Diego Garcia as well as those in the Middle East,[27] thereby giving China an edge over its strategic rivals in the maritime realm.

The second element of physical conformity can be discerned in the sense that although Chinese attention was mostly focused on its continental base, yet the eastern Chinese coastline as well as Quanzhou and Guangzhou allowed Chinese kingdoms, such as Southern Song, to derive benefits from maritime commerce. In addition, the Zheng He voyages were facilitated by the connection between the shipbuilding yards of Nanjing with the Yangzte River, allowing the ships to easily set sail in the sea.[28] The link between Nanjing and the Yangzte highlights the point regarding the importance of ports situated at the outlet of navigable streams, allowing countries to use them as the springboard of maritime operations. At the same time, it has been said that the Chinese sense of its 'self-sufficiency', given its fertile lands and the trade established through tributary relations,[29] did not induce the Chinese dynasties to invest much in naval outreach, with exceptions such as the Zheng He voyages. This could be compared with Mahan's point on France's disinterest in enhancing its naval capabilities. However, the years after the Opium Wars (1840-42 & 1856-58) as well as the discovery of energy resources in the South China Sea and the East China Sea and the resulting disputes forced China to develop its naval outreach.[30] Besides, the Taiwanese question and the Chinese aim of 'reunification', either peacefully or through military means, has led to increased naval deployments in the Taiwan Straits.[31]

This is also aimed at the development of the PLAN's strength to counter the US. This naval deployment near Taiwan fits into Mahan's idea of maritime separation of a country's landmass necessitating the development of sea power.

The next two factors of the country's ability to protect the extent of its coastline as well as its population can be observed in the way China is bolstering its naval capabilities to the extent that it has emerged as the largest navy in the world in terms of number of ships deployed with approximately 355 ships and submarines, including 145 major surface combatants, as per the US Defence Department report of 2021[32]—a force which is capable of protecting not only the Chinese coastline, which includes the Chinese sea board, but also its overseas bases. In addition, the vast human resources of China as well as Chinese uptick in acquiring and increasing the scale of its naval construction activity[33] further highlight the manpower advantage enjoyed by China, which is another prerequisite according to Mahan.

Regarding the character of the country's population, Chinese merchants engaged in commerce during the Southern Song dynasty with the kingdoms of South, Southeast and West Asia. Similarly, the Zheng He voyages were also facilitated by Chinese merchants, some of whom held high positions, like Shi Jin-qing, who was appointed as the Superintendent of Palembang port and region. This led to the establishment of a diasporic Chinese merchant community, which, in turn, facilitated trade between these regions and China.[34] However, the attitude towards merchants was not positive in Chinese history as they were accorded the lowest status in the Confucian hierarchy.[35] Although since the 1990s, China begun developing an interest in naval capacities not just for defence purposes but also for power projection, yet the traditional Confucian disdain for military service[36], which has continued in part till today, has resulted in reduced enthusiasm to join the PLAN. At the same time, reports have also emerged regarding the inefficiency of PLAN cadres due to low morale fostered by conditions, such as long appointments in the same unit, less chances of promotion, no provision for married personnel to stay with family when not sailing, and most importantly, the earlier 'one-child policy'. Hence, some scholars believe that given the low morale of personnel, China is trying to rely instead more on 'non-manned modes of warfare relying more on artificial intelligence and information warfare not involving physical combat'.[37] Compared to the nature of traditional colonists, while China does not possess any overseas colonies like those of the British Empire, yet the support (either willingly or through coercion) given to Chinese projects such as Hambantota and Gwadar by the governments of Sri Lanka and China demonstrate a similar tinge. However, what has come to light regarding the investments as part of the BRI is that most are focused on the home provinces of the recipient countries' leaders, such as in the case of the now ousted Rajapaksha family of Sri Lanka,, which is termed by Dreher as 'home province favouritism'—a trend observed in African countries as well.[38] The Gwadar port within the CPEC was envisioned as a 'game changer' for Pakistan's economy as well as those of Central Asia, which had led to Islamabad's support for the project. Now, reeling under external debts of which a major portion is owed to China, Pakistan has no option but to accede to Beijing's demands on Gwadar in return for loans and aids.[39] Given the Chinese dominance through economic projects and aid endowments in these countries, Pakistan and Sri Lanka can be dubbed as sort of Chinese 'colonies or dependencies', whose governments, similar to the British colonists, supported the actions of the Chinese.

The last characteristic or factor concerning the character of the government or institutional support has varied throughout Chinese history. While dynasties such as the Tang and the Southern Song encouraged overland and maritime trade,[40] yet not much emphasis was laid on the development of any significant navy. While the Zheng He voyages during the Ming era did exhibit Chinese interest in developing a strong military navy, yet post the voyages, Ming China scrapped these maritime expeditions during the reign of Emperor Xuande and returned to the policy of isolation of the first emperor, Hongwu—that of prohibition of as well as limited maritime commerce.[41] However, the experience of the Opium Wars and the superior maritime strength of Britain and France had led China to invest more and more in developing its naval capabilities in the post-1949 period, whose scope was extended to include development of a blue water navy in 1990. Since the ascension of President Xi Jinping, China has witnessed large investments in military capabilities, especially the navy. This process had originally begun with the reorganisation of the earlier regional commands into integrated theatre commands, which has reduced the earlier dominance of the land forces within the military structure.[42] This has been followed by rapid developments in the Chinese naval sector, with the rise of the Chinese Coast Guard (CCG) and the People's Armed Forces Maritime

Militia (PAFMM) as the largest among their peers in other countries. Together with the PLAN, both the CCG and the PAFMM have been increasingly used to assert Chinese claims in the SCS.[43] The launch of China's third aircraft carrier Type 003 'Fujian', powered by the latest Electro Magnetic Launch System (EMALS), under the leadership of Xi Jinping only highlights Beijing's deepening interest towards the maritime realm.[44] Moreover, the BRI, which also included the Maritime Silk Road (MSR), envisaged connectivity through development of port facilities in the Indo-Pacific region from Djibouti and the Indian Ocean. In addition, the invocation of the legacy of Zheng He's voyages in the inauguration speech of the BRI[45] also highlights the Chinese motives of not only economic but also simultaneous strategic engagements.

Along with the enhancement of its naval strength and capabilities as well as through projects such as the BRI, China is well set to realise the 'first' and 'second' chains of its maritime 'three- island chain strategy' first enunciated in 1988. While the first chain of the PLAN's presence in 'Japan-Taiwan-Philippines' seems to have been partially fulfilled, especially in the SCS, Beijing has also taken steps to realise the 'second island chain' by entering into a security pact with the Solomon Islands in 2020 to develop a port infrastructure in the Western Pacific, given that this chain also encompasses the strategically important Strait of Malacca. At the same time, a Chinese base or presence in the Solomon Islands also gives Beijing proximity, in terms of firing range, to the US base of Guam[46], thereby offering a strategic advantage. All these have been achieved with active support from the Xi Jinping regime currently in power, which believes in the aim of 'China Dream' or 'Great Rejuvenation of the Chinese People'[47]—symbolising Beijing's global power ambitions, both in the continental as well as maritime stretch. Here, one can easily argue that the current Chinese government is treading upon the path set by the British Crown in its promotion of naval strength and outreach for both commercial as well as strategic reasons.

Conclusion

The factors of sea power, as mentioned by Mahan—geographical features, extent of territory, the number and character of population as well as that of the governing institutions—can be traced, in one way or the other, in the Chinese naval presence in the Indo-Pacific region today. The maxim of Mahan,

'Whoever rules the waves, rules the world', is true as far as the basic two important factors of the six mentioned earlier are concerned, that is, acquisition of bases and control over routes of maritime commerce and the active support from governmental institutions. Through projects such as the BRI, China has begun developing strategic ports, such as Hambantota, Kyaukpyu, Gwadar, and Chittagong, as well as acquiring overseas bases in Djibouti and recently, the Solomon Islands. Through the 'String of Pearls' as well as its 'three- island chain' strategies, China seeks to enhance its presence in strategic locations, such as the South China Sea, as well as the vital SLOCs, such as the Strait of Malacca and Hormuz. At the same time, the current naval outreach of China has progressed well due to the increased attention and investment given by the Xi Jinping regime, which manifested in the launch of the Type 003 Fujian class aircraft carrier in June 2022. At the same time, other factors outlined by Mahan, such as a large population capable of defending the coastline and the sea- going character of people and colonists, are also met with some challenges in the sense that, while China possesses a large population, yet the morale of its cadres is low and the naval command is marked by a degree of inefficiency while a traditional disdain for a merchant and military career have not led to much enthusiasm for joining the PLAN. However, the role of the colonists is a corollary to that of the governments of countries under the BRI, like Pakistan and Sri Lanka which have willingly or under 'debt trap' acquiesced to Chinese presence in their ports. Despite these shortcomings, China has emerged as a power to reckon with in the Indo-Pacific.

Such a situation should be a wake-up call for other countries like the US and especially, regional powers like India. While the US has maintained significant naval assets in the Pacific region since 1945, yet India has of late neglected and not paid much attention to its naval capabilities. While under policies, such as the Act East 2015, and through groupings, such as the Quadrilateral Security Dialogue (QUAD), India has tried to strike strategic naval partnerships with other regional powers like Australia, Japan, the US, and the ASEAN countries, yet it has a long way to go to match its naval capabilities with China, contending with the handicaps that the Indian Navy faces. For example, it still continues to get the lowest amount of funds for its defence expenditure.[48] Perhaps revisiting the lessons of Mahan would help not just India but all the other regional powers who are worried about the rise of an assertive and aggressive China in the Indo-Pacific.

Notes

1. Muhammad Saeed, 'From the Asia- Pacific to the Indo- Pacific- Expanding Sino- US strategic competition', *China Quarterly of International Strategic Studies,* vol. 3, no. 4, 2017, pp. 499-512, see pp. 503-504.
2. Saeed, 'From the Asia- Pacific to the Indo- Pacific- Expanding Sino- US strategic competition', p. 504.
3. Alfred Thayer Mahan, *The Influence of Sea Power Upon History 1660-1783,* Dodo Press, 1890, pp. 1-2.
4. Mahan, *The Influence of Sea Power Upon History 1660-1783*, p. 1.
5. Ibid., p. 4.
6. Ibid., p. 4.
7. Ibid., pp. 6-7.
8. Ibid., p. 8.
9. Ibid., p. 9.
10. Ibid., p.10.
11. Ibid., p.13.
12. Ibid., pp. 15-16.
13. Ibid., pp. 17-19.
14. Ibid., p. 23.
15. Ibid., pp. 25-26.
16. Ibid., pp. 28-29.
17. Shyam Saran, *How China Sees India and the World- The Authoritative Account of the India- China Relationship,* New Delhi: Juggernaut Books, 2022, p. 213.
18. Saeed, 'From the Asia- Pacific to the Indo- Pacific- Expanding Sino- US strategic competition', pp. 501-502.
19. Saran, *How China Sees India and the World- The Authoritative Account of the India- China Relationship*, p. 88.
20. Ibid., p. 83.
21. Ibid., p. 99.
22. Geoff Wade, 'The Zheng He Voyages: A Reassessment', *Journal of the Malaysian Branch of the Royal Asiatic Society,* vol. 78, no. 1 (288), 2005, pp. 37-58, see p. 51.
23. Saeed, 'From the Asia- Pacific to the Indo- Pacific- Expanding Sino- US strategic competition', p. 505.
24. Bertil Lintner, *The Costliest Pear- China's Struggle for Indian Ocean,* London: C. Hurst & Co (Publishers) Ltd, 2019, p. 4.
25. Lintner, *The Costliest Pear- China's Struggle for Indian Ocean,* p. 2.

26. Saeed, 'From the Asia- Pacific to the Indo- Pacific- Expanding Sino- US strategic competition', p. 506.
27. Lintner, *The Costliest Pearl- China's Struggle for Indian Ocean,* p. 4.
28. Louise Levathes, *When China Ruled the Seas,* New York: Simon & Schuster, 1994, p. 77.
29. Henry Kissinger, *On China,* London: Penguin Group, 2011, 2012, p. 31.
30. Balaji Chandramohan, 'China's maritime strategy', *New Zealand International Review,* vol.39, no.3, May/June 2014, pp. 22-24, see p. 23.
31. 'China Warships Detected Near Taiwan After US Navy's Strait Transit', *Newsweek,* 3 May, 2022.
32. Snehesh Alex Philip, 'Chinese navy is planning ahead. India's approach doesn't match up, above sea or below', *The Print,* 26 November, 2021.
33. Philip, 'Chinese navy is planning ahead. India's approach doesn't match up, above sea or below'.
34. Wade, 'The Zheng He Voyages: A Reassessment', p. 47.
35. Kissinger, *On China,* London: Penguin Group, 2011, 2012, p. 15.
36. Ibid., p. 94.
37. Snehesh Alex Philip, 'Chinese Navy is the largest in the world, but not the best. Don't underestimate it though', *The Print,* 22 April, 2022.
38. Pia Krishnankutty, 'Lanka to Africa, Chinese funding follows a pattern: Home base of leaders gets more fund, book says', *The Print,* 8 June, 2022.
39. Husain Haqqani & Aparna Pande, 'Sri Lanka to Pakistan, South Asian nations are tying fortune to China's infra projects and failing', *The Print,* 9 July, 2022.
40. Saran, *How China Sees India and the World- The Authoritative Account of the India- China Relationship*, p. 87.
41. Ibid., p. 105.
42. Ibid., p. 219.
43. 'A powerful Chinese navy is ready to flex its muscles', *ANI,* 3 January, 2022.
44. Parth Satam, 'Dominate or Navigate? China's 3rd Aircraft Carrier, the 'Biggest' Outside Us, to boost its Protectionist, Non-Interventionist Policy', *The EurAsian Times,* 18 June, 2022.
45. Full text of President Xi's speech at opening of Belt and Road forum, *Belt and Road Forum for International Cooperation,* 14 May, 2017.
46. Aadil Brar, 'China- Solomon Islands deal marks a power shift. US paying for reluctance in Asia- Pacific', *The Print,* 27 April, 2022.
47. Saran, *How China Sees India and the World—The Authoritative Account of the India- China Relationship*, p. 211.
48. Philip, 'Chinese navy is planning ahead. India's approach doesn't match up, above sea or below'.

References

"A powerful Chinese navy is ready to flex its muscles", *ANI,* January 3, 2022, https://www.aninews.in/news/world/asia/a-powerful-chinese-navy-is-ready-to-flex-its-muscles20220103115541/.

Alex Philip, Snehesh, "Chinese navy is planning ahead. India's approach doesn't match up, above sea or below", *The Print,* November 26, 2021, https://theprint.in/opinion/brahmastra/chinese-navy-planning-ahead-india-doesnt-match-up-above-sea-or-below/772059/.

Alex Philip, "Chinese Navy is the largest in the world, but not the best. Don't underestimate it though", *The Print,* April 22, 2022, https://theprint.in/opinion/brahmastra/chinese-navy-is-largest-but-not-the-best-dont-underestimate-it-though/926042/.

Aadil, Brar, "China- Solomon Islands deal marks a power shift. US paying for reluctance in Asia- Pacific", *The Print,* April 27, 2022, https://theprint.in/opinion/eye-on-china/china-solomon-islands-deal-marks-a-power-shift-us-paying-for-reluctance-in-asia-pacific/931885/.

Chandramohan, Balaji, "China's maritime strategy", *New Zealand International Review,* vol. 39, no. 3, May/June 2014, pp. 22-24.

"China Warships Detected Near Taiwan After US Navy's Strait Transit", *Newsweek,* May 3, 2022, https://www.newsweek.com/china-warships-detected-near-taiwan-after-us-navy-strait-transit-1684439.

Full text of President Xi's speech at opening of Belt and Road Forum, *Belt and Road Forum for International Cooperation,* May 14, 2017, http://2017.beltandroadforum.org/english/n100/2018/0306/c25-1038.html.

Haqqani, Husain & Pande, Aparna, "Sri Lanka to Pakistan, South Asian nations are tying fortune to China's infra projects and failing", *The Print,* 9 July, 2022, https://theprint.in/opinion/sri-lanka-to-pakistan-south-asian-nations-are-tying-fortune-to-chinas-infra-projects-failing/1031731/.

Kissinger, Henry, *On China,* London: Penguin Group, 2011, 2012.

Krishnankutty, Pia, "Lanka to Africa, Chinese funding follows a pattern: Home base of leaders gets more fund, book says", *The Print,* June 8, 2022, https://theprint.in/diplomacy/lanka-to-africa-china-funding-follows-a-pattern-home-base-of-leaders-gets-more-funds-book-says/986369/.

Levathes, Louise, *When China Ruled the Seas,* New York: Simon & Schuster, 1994.

Lintner, Bertil, *The Costliest Pear- China's Struggle for Indian Ocean,* London: C. Hurst & Co (Publishers) Ltd, 2019.

Saeed, Muhammad, "From the Asia- Pacific to the Indo- Pacific- Expanding Sino-US strategic competition", *China Quarterly of International Strategic Studies,* vol. 3, no. 4, 2017, pp. 499-512.

Saran, Shyam, *How China Sees India and the World- The Authoritative Account of the India- China Relationship,* New Delhi: Juggernaut Books, 2022.

Satam, Parth, "Dominate or Navigate? China's 3rd Aircraft Carrier, the 'Biggest' Outside US, to boost its Protectionist, Non-Interventionist Policy", *The EurAsian Times,* June 18, 2022, https://eurasiantimes.com/dominate-or-navigate-chinas-3rd-aircraft-carrier-the-biggest/.

Thayer Mahan, Alfred, *The Influence of Sea Power Upon History 1660-1783,* Dodo Press, 1890.

Wade, Geoff, "The Zheng He Voyages: A Reassessment", *Journal of the Malaysian Branch of the Royal Asiatic Society,* vol. 78, no. 1 (288), 2005, pp. 37-58.

Editor and Contributors

Editor

Dr. Bhavna Singh is currently a Senior Research Fellow (2023-2025) at the Centre for Chinese Language, Culture and Historical Studies, Shaanxi Normal University, Xi'an, China, under the CSC Government scholarship, where she is working on 'Tang Dynasty Merchants and Trade'. She previously worked as a Consultant with the New Delhi-based MEA think tank—Center for Contemporary China Studies (CCCS) from 2021-2023. Her Chinese language proficiency is HSK Level 4 and she has cleared HSK-K. She worked as an Associate Fellow at the Centre for Air Power Studies (CAPS), New Delhi (2018-2020) and was awarded her PhD in Chinese Nationalism from the Centre for East Asian Studies, Jawaharlal Nehru University, New Delhi, in 2021. She worked as a Senior Research Officer with the Institute of Peace and Conflict Studies (IPCS) from 2010-2013 and remained attached with the V-Dem project based at Gothenburg University, Sweden, as a Country Expert on Hong Kong and Fiji (2013-2020). She was briefly an editor with Akos MD (2020-2021). Her work focuses on nationalism, sub-nationalism, and China's foreign policy. She is the author of the book, *China's Discursive Nationalism: Contending in Softer Realms* (Pentagon Press; New Delhi, 2012), and co-editor for *India, China and sub-regional connectivities in South Asia* (SAGE; 2015).

She worked on a project on 'China Dream' at CAPS and 'Xi's Policies'. She has also written for several esteemed journals like the *Liberal Studies Journal, the Economic and Political Weekly, Mainstream Weekly, World Focus, Epilogue,* and *China Daily*, and web-portals like ISN-ETH Zurich, NIICE. She was a part of India's Youth Exchange Delegation to China in the year 2008. She was nominated to the 'Taiwan Study Camp for Future Leaders of South Asia' in 2010 and participated in several international conferences, such as the One Belt One Road Summit organised by the Shaanxi University in September 2016. She can be reached at bhavna.singh984@gmail.com

Contributors

Eshita Rudra is currently engaged as Assistant Professor of Chinese Language in Gujarat University, Ahmedabad. She has taught at Mumbai University and Doon University. She did her M.Phil from the Centre for East Asian Studies, School of International Studies, Jawaharlal Nehru University. She is currently pursuing her PhD from the same centre. She has worked as a Research Associate with the National Maritime Foundation and has published a number of articles in well known journals. She can be reached at eshiru.rudra@gmail.com

Dr Md. Yasin teaches at the Aligarh Muslim University and has completed his PhD from the Centre for East Asian Studies, Jawaharlal Nehru University (JNU), New Delhi. He received the Harvard Yenching Institute of Chinese Studies Multi-year Fellowship (2018-2022). Yasin, a fluent speaker of Mandarin, focuses on China's participation in the United Nations. Following his B.A. and M.A. in Chinese Language, Literature and Culture from JNU, he qualified for UGC-NET with a Junior Research Fellowship (JRF). He completed his post-graduate diploma at Beijing Language and Culture University on a joint scholarship from the Ministry of Human Resource Development (MHRD), India, and the China Scholarship Council. In 2017, Fudan University sponsored him to attend the BRICS Program in Shanghai. He previously taught at Indian universities, such as Apeejay Stya University and Doon University. He was a visiting Fellow at Central China Normal University (2018-19), Peking University (2019-20), and Harvard University (2021-22). His recent publications have appeared in the *Indian Journal of*

Politics and the websites of the Institute of Chinese Studies (ICS), Nepal Institute for International Cooperation and Engagement (NIICE), *The Quint* and *China Daily*. He can be reached at langman.mdyjnu@gmail.com

Dr Gunjan Singh is an Associate Professor at the OP Jindal Global University. She was a Research Fellow at the Indian Council of World Affairs till January 2020. Before that, she was Research Associate at the Institute for Chinese Studies (ICS) and Research Assistant at the Institute for Defence Studies and Analyses (IDSA). She was awarded Doctor of Philosophy at the School of International Studies, JNU, in 2018. Her research interests are in the fields of Chinese foreign policy, China-South Asia relations, domestic politics in China, Chinese media, Mainland-Taiwan relations, and space security. She has written extensively on these subjects in academic and media publications. She is the co-editor of *Space Security and Global Cooperation*. She has contributed to journals like *Journal for Asian Security and International Affairs, India Quarterly, Strategic Analysis, International Affairs Review, Harvard Asia Quarterly, World Affairs: A Journal of International Issues,* and *The Book Review*. She can be reached at gunjsingh@gmail.com

Vishal Rajput is the Intelligence Manager (Asia-Pacific) at MAX Security, headquartered in Tel Aviv, Israel. Previously, he worked on the Ministry of Defence's Border History Project at the Prime Ministers' Museum and Library in Delhi. He holds a postgraduate degree in International Relations and Area Studies from Jamia Millia Islamia, Delhi. His professional experience includes associations with the National Security Council, Government of India, and the United Service Institution of India. Vishal has co-edited *Decade of Power Politics*, published by Knowledge World (KW) Publishers, and authored. numerous research articles and commentaries featured in *Pakistan Reader, The Quint, South Asia Monitor, Indonesian Quarterly*, Australian Institute of International Affairs, Jindal Centre for Global South, Centre for Security Analysis and Prevention (Prague), and Centre for Strategic Studies and Simulation at the United Service Institution of India. Vishal's research focuses on international/global order discourses, non-Western theories of international relations, Chinese foreign policy, and the role of BRICS in global politics. He can be reached at vishalrajput.alg@gmail.com

Anuraag Khaund is pursuing a PhD in International Studies (IP), Department of International Politics (DIP), School of International Studies (SIS), Central University of Gujarat. He has published opinion pieces in *The Diplomat, The Kashmir Observer, Modern Diplomacy* and *Deccan Herald*. In addition, he has also penned his thoughts on international geopolitical affairs under the column, "Yours Geopolitically, Khaund", in the *Global Strategic and Defence News* (GSDN). His areas of interest include East Asia, West Asia, South Asia, and the Indo-Pacific and the linkage between civilisational history and international politics of countries. He can be reached at khaundanuraag@gmail.com

Dr Raymond Kwun-Sun Lau is an Assistant Professor at the Department of Political Science and Sociology, North-South University, Bangladesh, and was formerly a Lecturer in History at Hong Kong Baptist University. His research interests include international relations, geopolitics in the Indo-Pacific Global South (Africa and South Asia), Chinese foreign policy, and Hong Kong politics. Dr Lau is the author of *Responding to Mass Atrocities in Africa: Protection First and Justice Later* (London and New York: Routledge, 2022). He can be reached at dr.raymondlau@gmail.com

Dr Jayadev Parida is an Assistant Professor at the School of Liberal Studies, University of Petroleum and Energy Studies in Dehradun, Uttarakhand. He specialises in cyber security and governance, data protection, emerging technologies & international security, non-traditional security threats, and Indian defence and foreign policy. He completed his PhD in European Studies at Jawaharlal Nehru University (JNU). His thesis focused on the comparative study of the EU and US approaches to cyber security. Dr Parida has held fellowships from the Konrad Adenauer Stiftung and DAAD-UGC at Freie University, Berlin, Germany. He has also worked as a Research Assistant at the ORF, Foundation for National Security Research and as an Analyst at Wikistrat's Cyber Security Desk. His publications include articles on cyber security and data protection in journals like *Liberal Studies Journal* and *World Focus*. He has presented papers at various national and international conferences, showcasing his active role in academia and research. He can be reached at jayadevaparida2009pir@gmail.com

Cyriac S. Pampackal is currently a research scholar at the School of International Relations and Politics, Mahatma Gandhi University, Kottayam, Kerala. He is a former Assistant Professor of Political Science on contract at Mar Athnasius College (Autonomous), Kothamangalam, Kerala. He is a former intern at the Centre for Air Power Studies, New Delhi. He completed his M.Phil and Masters in Politics and International Relations from the School of International Relations and Politics, Mahatma Gandhi University, Kottayam, Kerala. He has presented several papers at various international conferences and national seminars. He has published articles in several journals and has written several book chapters. He is currently engaged with research on India's maritime policy in the Indo-Pacific region from 2014-2024. His other areas of interest include South Asian geopolitics, national security and counter-terrorism, environmental security, India's foreign policy, and International Relations Theory. He can be reached at cyriacpampackal@gmail.com

Index

Abe, Shinzo 22, 151
  advocacy of Asia's democratic security diamond 153
Afghanistan (Taliban administration) and China's BRI 211–212
Aksai Chin region 201
Andaman and Nicobar Islands 107–108
Arunachal Pradesh 201
Asia-Africa Growth Corridor (AAGC) project 203
Asian Development Bank 36
Asian Infrastructure Investment Bank (AIIB) 4, 39, 63
Asia-Pacific Economic Cooperation (APEC) 132
Association of Southeast Asian Nations (ASEAN) 22–24, 95, 117, 147
  ASEAN Regional Forum 151
Atmar, Haneef 51

Bangladesh and BRI projects 210–211
Bangladesh-Bhutan-India-Nepal (BBIN) 52
Bangladesh-China-India-Myanmar Economic Corridor (BCIM-EC) 52, 101, 181
Belt and Road Initiative (BRI) 1, 25, 46, 61–62, 72–73, 93, 100, 133, 147, 156, 181
  advantages of 144–146
  and Afghanistan 7
  and Africa 13–14
  aims and objectives of 36–38, 60, 78–80
  and ASEAN 16–19
  and Bangladesh 8
  and Central Asian countries 9–10
  China-Nepal BRI cooperation 6–7
  China's advocacy for Free and Open Indo-Pacific Strategy 133
  corridors of dominance 182–185
  decision-making 64–66
  defined 62
  domestic dynamics 66–69
  economic affairs 63
  economic challenges 80

and European countries 11–13, 187–189
focus to enhance railways connectivity and infrastructure projects 191–194
impact on China's GDP 3–6
investment packages and infrastructure projects in Central Asia and Eastern Europe 191–194
and Latin America 14–16
launch of 141–144
multilateral mechanics between CEE countries and China 189–191
and Myanmar 8–9
origin of 78–80
and Pakistan 7
parts of 76
proposed routes 101
Ship of Theseus 194–195
Silk Road Economic Belt (SREB) 61–63
and Sri Lanka 7–8
strategic economy 64
strategic military 64
value of projects 77
Biden, Joe 193
blue economic passage of China-Oceania-South Pacific 101
Brazil Russia India China South Africa Bank (BRICS Bank) 4
Brexit 195
BRICS countries 154
Build Back Better World (B3W) 1

Changjiang Survey, Planning, Design and Research Co., Ltd (CISPDR) 14
China
economic reform 36
exports to Pakistan 38
great power status 100–106
impact of economic diplomacy on economic policies 47
imports and exports of goods 36
main trading partner of Bangladesh 38–39
manufacturing consensus 2
new outlook of global governance 61
opening-up policies 36
PLAN (People's Liberation Army Navy) 103, 105
strategy of String of Pearls 104
transformation to dragon 179–182
China-Africa Development Fund (CADFund) 14
China-Central Asia-West Asia Economic Corridor (CCAWEC) 10–11, 181
China Civil Engineering Construction Corporation (CCECC) 14
China Development Bank (CDB) 4, 14
China ENFI Engineering Corporation 14
China Gezhouba Group Overseas Investments Co. Ltd 14
China-Indian Ocean-Africa-Mediterranean Sea Blue Economic Passage 101
China-Indochina Peninsula Economic Corridor (CICPEC) 181
China Investment Corporation 4
China-Mongolia-Russia Economic Corridor (CMREC) 181
China-Myanmar Economic Corridor (CMEC) 8–9
China Overseas Infrastructure Development and Investment Corporation (COIDIC) 13–14
China-Pakistan Economic Corridor (CPEC) 3, 7, 20, 46, 52, 101, 103, 128, 181, 185, 203–206
China Telecom Global Limited 14
Chinese Marshall Plan 183
Clinton, Hillary 147
corruption charges in BRI functioning and projects 85–86
COVID-19 pandemic 2, 27, 51, 77, 93, 134, 145, 157, 187, 195, 210

impact on BRI projects 20–22, 83–85
Cross-border Interbank Payment System (CIPS) 12–13

Dahal, Pushpa Kamal 207
debt trap and BRI 81–83, 199
Deng Xiaoping 37, 135, 181
24-Character Strategy 180
Digital Silk Road (DSR) 19–20
Doklam crisis/standoff in 2017 6, 46, 110, 202

economic liberalisation in India 202
Eurasia
BRI in 187, 195
conflict for resources 186–187
defined 186
re-emergence of geopolitics 185–186
Export-Import Bank of China 4

foreign policy of China
domestic political legitimacy 138
and role of assertive nationalism 138–139
wolf-warrior diplomacy 134, 139–141

G7 countries 1
Galwan Valley conflict in 2020 202
Global Civilization Initiative (GCI) 25
Global Development Initiative (GDI) 25, 87–88
global financial crisis of 2008 64, 141
global or regional dominance 92–93
global politics 2
Global Security Initiative (GSI) 25
Green credit Guidelines 21–22

Hambantota port project in Sri Lanka 7–8, 46, 81–82, 105, 128, 206–207
Health Silk Road 157
Hu Jintao 146, 181, 183, 193

Ice Silk Road (also known as Polar Silk Road) 19
India
bilateral trade with China 203
Neighbourhood First strategy in 2015 203
opposition to BRI 2–3, 201–203
India-Myanmar-Thailand Trilateral Highway 203
Indian Naval symposium (IONS) 107
Indian Ocean region (IOR) 153
China's presence in 38, 53, 96–97
India's strategic and economic interests 106–110
Maritime Silk Route (MSR) initiative 35
quality infrastructure shortage 36
strategic geopolitical landscape 95
Indo-Pacific region 22–28, 217
Chinese navy presence in 97–99, 110–112
comprises Indian Ocean and Pacific Ocean 94
conflict between US and China 96
economic development plan 132–133
Free and Open Indo-Pacific Strategy 154
power play in 95
seaborne trade 95–96
strategic importance 95
US policy during Trump administration 147–150
US propaganda to isolate China 93
Indo-Pacific Regional Dialogue (IPRD) 23
Indo-Sri Lanka Free Trade Agreement (ISFTA) 39
International Monetary Fund (IMF) 46
International North-South Transport Corridor (INSTC) 203
international politics 92

Jaishankar, S. 51
Japan's Free and Open Indo-Pacific 22
Jiabao, Wen 151

Khan, Imran 51

Li Keqiang 52

Mahan, Alfred Thayer
 and China's politics in Indo-Pacific region 220–225
 control of sea power 225–227
 theory of sea power 217–220
Malabar Exercise 23
Malacca Dilemma 21, 65, 100–106, 146, 204
Maldives
 geographical location 40
 and India, bilateral relations 41, 51–53, 208–210
 pearl in Indian Ocean 40
 political turmoil 41
 population 40
 tourism 40
Maldives and China, bilateral relations 43–44, 208–210
 China's financial assistance and investment 34–35, 42–43
 debt trap and tension in New Delhi 49
 employment to Chinese nationals 45–46
 internal problems and MSRI 47–48
Mao Zedong 184
March Westward policy 184
Maritime Silk Route (MSR) 19, 35, 37, 40
 Fujian Province as central position of 69–71
Merkel, Angela 195
Modi, Narendra 22, 46–47, 51, 108–110

National Maritime Foundation (NMF) 107
Nehru, Jawaharlal 106
Nepal economic crisis, China's bailout package for 207–208
New Cold War between China and US 117, 194–195
New Eurasian Land bridge Corridor (NELB) 181

Obama, Barack 96, 147
offensive realism 93–94

Pakistan economic crisis 199
Pakistan-occupied Kashmir (PoK) 203, 205
Patel, Sardar 106
Project Mausam 109

Quadrilateral Security Dialogue (QUAD) 22–24, 95, 134, 151–154, 157, 226

Rajapaksa, Mahinda 8, 46

SAARC 39
SAGAR (security and growth for all in the region) 23, 108
SAGARMALA initiative 23
Sea Lanes of Communication (SLOC) 216
Shangri La Dialogue 22
Sharif, Nawaz 204
Silk Road Fund 4
Solih, Mohammed 209
South Asian Association of Regional Cooperation Preferential Free Trade Agreement (SACPTA) 50
South Asian Free Trade Agreement (SAFTA) 50–51
South Asian region and investment by China 36–40, 212–213
 BRI projects challenges 45
 and its impact on India 49–51
 PRC gateway towards Indian Ocean 200–201

South China Sea (SCS) 216, 220
Soviet Union 93
Spykman, Nicholas
    Rimland Theory 94
Sri Lanka economic crisis 199

tariff barriers 39
Thucydides Trap 184
trade protectionism 39
Trans-Pacific Partnership (TPP) 147
Trump, Donald 83, 187
    Indo-Pacific dream 132, 147–150

Ukraine-Russia war and BRI 86–87
Unipolar World Order 93
United Nation Convention on Laws of Seas (UNCLOS) 106
US
    Free and Open Indo-Pacific Strategy 154–155
    -led Humanitarian Assistance and Disaster Relief (HADR) 151
    pivot to Asia policy 147
    strategic distrust of China 155
US Indo-Pacific Command (USINDOPACOM) 152
US Pacific Command to the US Indo-Pacific Command (INDOPACOM) 150
US Strategic Framework for the Indo-Pacific 110, 134

Western civilization 2
Westphalian world order 92

Xi Jinping 2, 7, 16, 46, 60–61, 72, 76–77, 87, 100, 117, 127, 134, 156, 181, 184–185, 204, 217, 220, 226
    21st century Maritime Silk Road ('One Belt One Road') 1, 34, 36–37, 40, 221
    advocacy for Asia-Pacific Century 27, 154–156
    China model of development 144–145
    China's Dream 135, 141
    four confidences doctrine 136–138, 156–157
    major country diplomacy 3
    pledge 35
    Silk Road Economic Belt 1–2
    visit to Maldives 34
    Xiconomics 3–6

Yameen, Abdulla 34, 41–42, 53

Zheng He voyages 117–118, 126–128
    maritime consolidation 120–126
    Ming expansion 118–120